SATURDAY NIGHT WIDOWS

SATURDAY NIGHT WIDOWS

The Adventures of Six Friends
Remaking Their Lives

BECKY AIKMAN

CROWN PUBLISHERS
New York

The story of the Saturday Night Widows was drawn from tape recordings and notes of interviews and meetings. Otherwise, I relied on memory for episodes from my own past. For a few people who might have crossed our paths briefly or unwittingly, I altered names and some identifying characteristics. And I have condensed some conversations and incidents slightly to provide greater clarity for readers.

Copyright © 2013 by Becky Aikman

All rights reserved.
Published in the United States by Crown Publishers,
an imprint of the Crown Publishing Group,
a division of Random House, Inc., New York.
www.crownpublishing.com

CROWN and the Crown colophon are registered
trademarks of Random House, Inc.

Portions of this book appeared previously in MORE and gourmet.com.

Library of Congress Cataloging-in-Publication Data

Aikman, Becky.
Saturday night widows : the adventures of six friends remaking their lives /
Becky Aikman. — 1st ed.
p. cm.
1. Aikman, Becky. 2. Widows. 3. Widowhood. 4. Self-help groups. I. Title.
HQ1058.A55 2013
306.88'3—dc23
2012021057

ISBN 978-0-307-59043-5
eISBN 978-0-307-59045-9

PRINTED IN THE UNITED STATES OF AMERICA

Book design by Jaclyn Reyes
Jacket design by Jaya Miceli

1   3   5   7   9   10   8   6   4   2

First Edition

For Bob

SATURDAY NIGHT WIDOWS

preface

i got kicked out of my widows' support group. I would say that things had gone from bad to worse, except the worst, no question, had already happened. When your husband has died while you're still in your forties, seriously, anything less and you have to laugh.

The hallway at the Y was fairly jumping the night of the first meeting as I dashed past signs for options more likely to perk a person up: *Beginning Ceramics. Make Your Own Collage. Wine and Cheese for Singles.* Once, my involvement with any of these exercises in self-improvement would have seemed as unlikely as it got, but for sheer strangeness, nothing could top my actual destination. *Support Group for Widows and Widowers,* said the notice on the door. End of the corridor, end of the line.

Inside, the room was ridiculously mournful. There were torturous-looking folding chairs arranged in an oval and industrial carpeting the color of worn asphalt. Fluorescent bulbs cast a pickled glare over the whole affair, granting it the ambiance of a drug rehab center, or maybe a parole board. I couldn't help wondering—how long 'til I got sprung?

Most of the other widows were already in place. Pretty much everyone, I could tell, was a couple of decades older than me. No surprise there. Widows don't have a lot of company in my usual demographic. Still, I was gasping for a connection, any connection, with women like me, uncoupled in what now seemed like a world of couples. I was eager to meet them and start sharing positive, inspiring, even practical ideas about Moving Forward After Loss, as promised in the brochure.

There were props. A small box of tissues rested on one of the last empty seats. God, was it going to be one of those? I inched in, sat down warily, and balanced the tissues on my lap. There was nowhere else to put them. No tables, no cushions on those metal chairs, no amenities, strictly economy class. Unlike those starry-eyed singles down the hall, we widows weren't offered refreshments. *Whine without cheese*, I thought, swallowing a crooked smile.

The other widows and I cut each other glances, but no one spoke a word. There were eleven—no, twelve of us, most wearing basic black. This was New York—we all had the wardrobe. So did I, of course. But tonight I had thought carefully about what to wear. It was the opposite, I hoped, of widow drab—a pale green linen skirt and skinny-ribbed tank top, with silver flats that I'd bought for dancing at a wedding when my husband was still alive. I intended this ensemble to send a signal: that I might be a widow, but I was a widow on the move, ready to march forward in stylish yet relatively comfortable shoes. Forward, whatever had happened up to now.

Or perhaps I was sending a subconscious plea: *I don't belong here. I can't belong here. This is a cosmic mistake that will surely be corrected once somebody up there notices that I should be down the hall, rocking the macramé studio.*

Aside from the women, I now saw, there was one dapper, pixie-sized gentleman, even older, giving us all the eye. Wearing elastic-waist slacks and clunky grandpa shoes, he engaged the room with sprightly curiosity. The others had the closed, raven-eyed look of a jury, keeping their sentiments to themselves. A jury of my peers? Everyone seemed somehow jumpy and dispirited at the same time, and suddenly, in that shuffling silence, so was I.

I was having one of those out-of-body moments, one of too many in the last few crazy years—at the oncologist's office, the intensive care unit, the funeral home. Now here. What was the point of squirming in unforgiving chairs, illuminated by ghastly greenish light, with these strangers, no Chardonnay or Gouda to break the ice? I wasn't looking for help with the grieving part of widowhood. I already had that one down. The five a.m. weeping; the stony, vacant stare. No, it was all the rest of it that I needed to tackle now. The part about what to do next. The part about who to *become* next.

I'd never faced such a predicament before. Everything had always been simple: I was a brisk, modern, independent woman, and I worked at a brisk, modern, independent job, as a newspaper reporter in midtown Manhattan. But I had also been half of a whole, and now, without that other half, I wasn't certain what was left. During twenty years of marriage, my husband and I had been partners and collaborators, personally and professionally. Not a day passed, sometimes not an hour, when I didn't call Bernie, a writer and teacher, from my office and ask, "What's a better word for *unctuous*?" Or when he'd want to know, "When will you be home?" Tonight, it didn't matter. I was a widow. No one waited for me now.

Widow . . . I could barely get the word out of my mouth . . . *widow.* I didn't seem to fit anyone's definition of a proper widow, least of all my own—you know, the Ingmar Bergman version, gloomy, pathetic, an all-around, ongoing downer. Surely, I thought, sneaking another look, these other widows wanted to bust out of the stereotype as much as I did. We'd be in this together, *compañeras.* It had been one year and three months now since Bernie's death, and I knew I needed to leave behind the nightmares, the heartache, the perpetual yearning for what I couldn't have. I needed to function again, and fast. It was time to—what was that called again?—Move Forward After Loss.

———————————

ANOTHER MAN ENTERED the room, closer to my age, holding a clipboard and a sheaf of papers the size of the federal budget.

"My name is Jonathan," he said with studied solemnity. "I'm the social worker who will be leading the group." Jonathan was a man of average height, nice enough features, and a putty-colored pallor that was shadowed with uncertainty. "First, let me say that I am sorry for your loss." He employed the commiserative tone and hangdog look that I recognized from every encounter I'd had with everybody since the funeral.

I expected him to turn the floor over to the widows, but instead he contorted himself into one of the chairs and passed around some photocopied pages. *The Stages Of Grief,* said the title, *by Elisabeth Kübler-Ross.* Not these again—the Holy Grail of Pathos! Ever since Bernie died, these five stages of grief had been pushed on me by my landlady, a clerk in human resources, the cashier in a taco truck. It seemed that the whole world had heard of these famous stages and was expecting me to follow them on some sort of widowcentric timetable. In the last year, I kept checking my calendar, waiting for them to show up.

Jonathan read aloud from the handout like a tech support worker in Mumbai. There were the usual five stages, in the usual order: denial, anger, bargaining, depression, and acceptance. These stages, every time I heard them, made as much sense to me as computer code. Anyway, it seemed that I should have left them in the dust by now if I were adhering to a schedule. I wasn't following any sorts of stages at all. Instead, I swung back and forth, sometimes wallowing in early-morning weeping, sometimes laughing my ass off like a normal person. Then I'd turn to share the joke with Bernie, and . . . back to the weeping again.

I was failing the stages of grief. I didn't even understand them. I was a misfit widow.

I glanced around the circle again, seeking eye contact, a fellow misfit perhaps, but the widows were following their handouts through an assortment of reading glasses, hiding their thoughts behind invisible veils. When Jonathan finished, he passed us another tract. We were supposed to check off boxes next to symptoms like Insomnia, Crying Spells, and Difficulty Making Decisions. These were typical signs of grief and nothing to be alarmed about, he said in his mechanical voice, and I had to agree that they were a nice summation of the new, more depressing me on my worst days. He added that we were probably clinically depressed if we checked Psychomotor Retardation, Prolonged and Marked Functional Impairment, and something called, simply, Worthless.

More reading material followed, this time on Low Self-Esteem.

An hour had passed, and Jonathan said we'd have to rush through the last twenty minutes to introduce ourselves and explain how our spouses had died. I knew this was what I'd signed up for, but now my self-esteem plummeted at the thought of it. The first woman to speak launched into a graphic account of her husband's long final illness, which involved a lot of bedpans and disputes with insurance companies. With billowing frustration, she complained that her neighbor had stopped asking how she was doing three weeks after the funeral. "I'm here because my friends don't get it," she concluded.

From there, others followed her lead, and the meeting devolved into a Who's Most Pitiful contest. The widows, one by one, vented their bitterness toward friends who didn't sympathize enough, family members who interfered too much, doctors who failed to do enough, and husbands—yes, husbands—who left too soon. Everyone's spouse seemed to have died within the last couple of months, and I remembered my own morbid absorption in the negative at that time, but did I want to dredge it up all over again? I shuffled the stack of psycho-literature on my lap. This wasn't at all what I'd had in mind. I'd come to brainstorm with new confidantes about what to do now. Like, what should I do with Bernie's old jazz records? And should I try to meet another man, and if I did, where would I find one? This grim gathering was magnifying everyone's sorrow, not assuaging it. We were cramming our personalities into the boxes on Jonathan's checklists. Anger, check. Depression, check.

I noticed an expectant silence and looked up to see the circle of faces trained on me.

"Um, well . . . my husband died just over a year ago from a rare cancer," I began, trying to convey the basic facts. "He managed to live for four and a half years with all kinds of chemos and surgeries and . . . everything else. The last couple years, the cancer spread to his brain, so that was . . . hard."

I sputtered and stopped. *Quick*, I thought, *try something else.*

"What I want now," I blundered ahead, "what I want to say is . . . well, I want to cheer up! Something awful happened to him, and to me, but I don't want to live in some kind of purgatory for the rest of my days because of it." I managed what I hoped was an optimistic smile. "I want to be happy again, don't you?"

I looked from face to face, but the veils were back in place. There was a perfunctory silence, and the woman up next gave me a squinty look. "You notice there's only one man here," she addressed the group. "That's because all the men are out there already, dating other women."

"Yeah," said the woman on my other side, jerking her thumb in my direction. "A younger one."

Was I paranoid, or were these ladies ganging up on me?

I hoped for a break in the mournful tone when a widow directly across from me captured my attention with a dignified manner of speaking.

"I'm seventy-five years old," she said in a measured voice. "My husband and I had fifty wonderful years together." The rest of us nodded in respect to that achievement. "Now, I feel like my life is over." She broke off to collect her thoughts. "But that young woman over there"—she fixed me with a murderous stare and thrust her finger straight at me across the ring of folding chairs—"she has it all! Her whole life is ahead of her! And I . . . I have nothing." She lunged for a tissue box.

Whoa! Hold on, babe, I wanted to say. *Fifty wonderful years might have been nice!* Instead, I froze, stupefied. The rest of the group intervened, speaking out of turn for the first time, directing sympathetic murmurings at Mrs. Fifty Wonderful Years and slinging accusing looks at me.

Jonathan announced that time was up. Reaching for her bag, the widow beside me, the one with the squinty eyes, glanced my way. I recognized those eyes, so much like my own, unmoored but searching. Of course our circumstances were different, but here, face to face, just the two of us, I had the strongest urge to say, *Hey, let's cut the bullshit. What's this widow business like for you?* Had we met somewhere else, outside this totalitarian format, I felt sure, we could have found our way to common ground, or at least a civil conversation.

"I'll see you next time," she said, her features softening with a suggestion of kindness, perhaps even of apology.

The room cleared, but I stayed fixed for a moment, alone, numb in my hard little chair.

THE BAD JUJU of the support group haunted me through the night in my profoundly empty apartment. Was this the role I was expected to play? Jonathan had said we could call him with questions or concerns, so in the morning, I dialed a number he'd scrawled on his stack of papers.

"I was a little uncomfortable," I said. "Did you notice anything strange about the meeting?"

"Yeah," he said. "They really went after you."

"There seemed to be a lot of hostility in the room."

"That happens all the time," he assured me, his voice complacent. "Especially if one of the women is younger."

"I could have used some empathy," I said. "I was hoping we could all share some constructive advice. Like, what *do* you do with your husband's old jazz records?"

"With what?" He continued frostily, "Anger is one of the stages. People need to get it out."

"Really? I mean, couldn't you have said something? Like, maybe, we all have problems, but let's try to understand and support each other, too?"

Jonathan started to sound more than a little uneasy. "It's your group. I can't interfere with what anyone wants to say."

"But you spoke for more than an hour! You talked about all that depression stuff, how worthless we must feel, how inconsolable we must be. Don't you think we *know* that? If we weren't depressed before, we sure are now. Couldn't you have said something about not attacking each other, too? You're not a potted plant."

Congratulations, I thought. *You've finally achieved the anger stage!*

Jonathan, it seemed, was getting there, too. "You seem really upset about this," he said with growing resentment. "If you don't like what the others are saying, you need to stand up for yourself. You need to put up a fight."

"I didn't go there to fight! I felt sorry for them! 'My life is over,' she said—it doesn't get worse than that. Why would I want to pile on top of that?"

The line went quiet while we both considered our positions.

"You seem unhappy with the group," Jonathan said at last, regaining his even tone. "Maybe you just don't fit in. Maybe you shouldn't come back."

"What? I shouldn't come back?"

"I don't think you should," he said. "It's disruptive to the group to have someone be so critical." He repeated, slowly, as if he doubted my ability to comprehend: "I don't think you should come back."

A white blaze of confusion silenced me. I hung up and shredded Jonathan's dismal paperwork in my shaking hands, straining to make sense of the whole loony episode. What had just happened here? Something both weirdly sad and weirdly funny. I had been kicked out of my widows' support group. I didn't fit in—Jonathan had said so. I was a wife without a husband, and now I was a widow without a widows' support group. I wasn't like myself anymore, I wasn't like my friends anymore, but if I wasn't like these widows either, who was I now?

Screw Jonathan, I thought. I even said it out loud—who was to hear? "Screw Jonathan." I wasn't about to let this depressing guy or Elisabeth Kübler-Ross or that my-life-is-over lady tell me what I could or could not do. An idea began to form through my grief-muddled agitation. I would start my *own* group of widows. A renegade group! That was it—Outlaw Widows! I couldn't help but laugh. There would be no tissue boxes. No folding chairs. No mental health checklists. We would simply live and explore and share, together and apart, out there in the world, whatever that world might hold.

I didn't know how I'd find them, but I knew this: If I wanted to Move Forward After Loss, I'd have to round them up on my own. A support group of renegade widows—how bad could it be? The worst, you see, had already happened.

chapter

ONE

i plopped a sad glob of guacamole into an exquisite black Art Deco bowl, and I knew. The guacamole would not be right.

In fact, now I was sure, none of the food would be right. Potluck indeed. Too insecure about my cooking to prepare the dinner myself, I had asked everyone to tramp through the January cold with a dish. Now I didn't know what would turn up—sodden casseroles, gluey bean dip, goopy guacamole. Oh, right, the goopy guacamole was mine, the same guacamole that once came in last in a family guacamole-making contest. And my family originated in Scotland. Worse, I had run out of time and left out the jalapeño, and I had forgotten the cilantro completely. And possibly the lime. So the guacamole, at least, would not be right. This party would be lost.

The room would not be right, either. I could see that now, as I placed the bowl on a side table next to the couch and straightened up to scope out the scene. Denise had offered to host in her Upper West Side apartment, one of those classic 1920s buildings with

French doors and endless bookshelves and rooms the size of Stockholm. It was the most convenient location for all of us. But now, after arriving early and waiting around for everyone else, I was sure that the living room would not be right for our purpose, the layout a nightmare, too spaced out for any real intimacy. There was a couch, backed up against the wall on one side, facing one lonely armchair along the other. I could picture it now, five of them, sitting shoulder-to-shoulder along that couch, like patients in a waiting room, waiting for bad news, and me in that chair, like Jonathan without his five stages of grief to fall back on, wondering whatever had possessed me to plan this evening.

The people wouldn't be right, either. They were strangers, a real grab bag. I was the only unifying factor. Me. They'd each met me, just once. Some of them twice. I'd collected them haphazardly by asking around, consulting friends and friends of friends. Only now, as Denise was dressing in the bedroom and I plunked down on that couch, sinking, sinking, it began to hit me: These women had practically nothing in common. The youngest was thirty-nine, the oldest fifty-seven. One was a blunt, scary-successful lawyer, one a chatty homemaker, and every postfeminist option in between. Some lived in the city, some in the suburbs. Some had children, some did not.

I reviewed their names in my head, hoping not to botch the introductions: Denise, Dawn, Marcia, Lesley, and Tara. Why had I invited them? There was only one thing they had in common, and that was not the sort of thing guaranteed to light a fire under a party: Every one of them had become a widow in the last couple of years. And that was definitely not right. That was not right at all.

What was I thinking? Why had I tried to orchestrate what

would surely be a social debacle on the scale of ... well, getting kicked out of my widows' support group? I tried to remind myself that this evening had grown out of an idea that hadn't seemed so misguided until a few minutes ago, an idea that grew out of my own confusion and pain and rebuilding when I too became a widow, and what I had learned from all that. What I still hoped to learn.

The idea was pretty straightforward. I would invite these five women, five young widows, to join me once a month for a year. We would meet on Saturday night, the most treacherous shoal for new widows, where untold spirits have sunk into gloom. We would do something together that we enjoyed, starting small—this dinner would certainly qualify—and ending big, maybe a faraway trip. By the end, we would test my theory that together we might find a way to triumph over loss, take off in unexpected directions, and have some fun along the way. There would be setbacks and pain, I supposed. And tears, certainly there would be some tears. But there would be kidding and silliness, too. There would be progress. There would be hugs. No one would be asked to leave.

If nothing else, these women would provide each other with traveling companions past the milestones of this common but profound transition—the first holidays without a mate, the first time taking off the ring, the first time daring to flirt. We would converge at this most vulnerable, weak, and awkward turning point and pledge to each other that this was not an end, it was a beginning.

I also reminded myself that I was basing this project on some actual research. A fair amount of time had passed since I escaped the defeatist vibe at that widows' support group, perhaps a low point in the annals of social services for the bereaved. Four years, in fact. Throughout that interval, I hadn't been able to let go of the conviction that there must be a better way to help people move past heartbreak. I consulted scientists who were beginning to conduct serious research into our natural ability to recover after loss and learned that they were challenging the conventional wisdom. They were finding, to my relief, that the famous five stages were a bunch of hooey. Many of the researchers said that happy experiences with real people can be more helpful than wallowing in old-fashioned support groups based on outdated theories. Jonathan's widows' support group, I had learned, wasn't only bad juju, it was bad science. This new group, I hoped, would be informed by the principles of what most helps those who have become uncoupled: friendship, practical help, openness to new experiences, and laughter.

I was acting on my own intuition, too, gleaned from all the changes I had undergone in those four years. I had kept at it, plotting to start my own widows' group even as my own life evolved in extraordinary ways. It was a long list, but an abridged version might include the following: I met a divorced dad, a writer who lived in another state, and married him a year and a half before this meeting. Quite unexpectedly, I now found myself with a new man, a new home, a new teenage stepdaughter, a new job, and a very old dog with one eye. I had learned that one life doesn't have to end because another one does. Mine continued to offer up surprises, many of them happy ones.

But it's also fair to say that new relationships at this stage of life come wrapped in complications. Wounded as I was by grief, I was still full of doubts, still seeking guidance, still wondering whether I had what it took to work through all the complications—new man, new home, new stepdaughter, new job, and old dog come to mind— that arise from creating a new life when the old one is broken.

So I would be the sixth member of the group that was gathering tonight. More as an observer—at least that was what I thought at the time. Whatever happened, the other widows and I would agree, we'd share it in this book.

We would share our stories, and we would share one story. We couldn't know where it would lead, but I resolved that ours would not be a story of sorrow. No, it would be an adventure story. Not that we'd be paddling through the deepest reaches of the Amazon or scaling the jagged walls of Annapurna, but an adventure story nonetheless. An exploration of life, of new opportunities, of new-found desires—dangerous territory indeed. The story of six women, remaking themselves. Six women seeking new discoveries and new purpose. Six women heading into the unknown, navigating life in extremis.

———————————

THAT WAS THE THEORY. This was the reality: These women were strangers. They were widows. They were supposed to be sad. They wouldn't like the guacamole.

"Are you nervous?" Denise already knew the answer when she joined me in the living room.

"No. No. Not at all," I lied. "I'm completely confident it's going to be great." When what I really meant was, *Would you mind if I step out . . . for the next few hours?*

Denise looked at me as if I were a mutt that she wished she could adopt. "I've had other parties here," she said, taking in my dubious expression. "It always works out. People sit on the floor. I'll have my shoes off by the end of the night."

If I was trying to calm myself down, Denise was the person to see. Her allure lay as much in her imperturbable composure as in the well-proportioned harmony of her face and body. Only thirty-nine years old, she managed to conceal the grief she was feeling behind a serene mask. Denise was one of those people who practice yoga with the kind of discipline an honors student brings to final exams, and it gave her the grace of a gladiola, tall and true. Even her apartment was hushed, Zen, filled with books. Denise, in fact, was an editor of books, and I could tell that she had applied the measured care of her profession to organizing her library shelves, interspersing classics and current titles with black-and-white photographs taken by her husband. Now that Denise and I were sharing the room, I knew what had been throwing me off about it. This apartment was too spacious for one. Denise's husband was missing. Together, they had been restoring the place and adding furnishings from the 1920s, like reclaimed lamps with shades made of mica, casting soft amber light. I could see his taste. I could feel his absence.

I had shown up at this meeting dressed with no particular effort to impress, in jeans and a black turtleneck, and Denise had put me at ease when she met me at the door in her yoga clothes. Now, minutes later, she'd emerged from the bedroom, still casual, but in ballet flats and a bell-shaped black skirt with a boatneck sweater that showed off her waist. Her fine brown hair was slicked back, wet from a quick shower, her face free of makeup, the better to emphasize her eyes: the wide-set eyes of a sorceress, the pale, ghostly blue of a winter sky. Looking closer, I saw something beneath the surface of those eyes, a subtle expression that seemed to be saying, seemed to be whispering, *Help me.* It was the look of a tourist lost on an unfamiliar street but too timid to ask for directions. I recognized that look. I'd employed various masks to cover it myself.

On the surface, though, as we waited for the others, Denise radiated thoughtful stillness. Whereas I radiated a sort of toxic anxiety.

Would anybody show? Everyone had confided doubts about walking in on five unknowns with nothing but their stories to share. Who could blame them? Then the bell rang. Fortified by Denise's encouraging smile—a smile informed, no doubt, by all the wisdom of Eastern philosophies that I did not comprehend—I opened the door, and our Saturday night adventure began to unfold.

chapter

TWO

*t*wenty minutes later, one of our guests was still missing. Perhaps she'd lost her nerve. But the four who had turned up
so far were enough to keep me occupied. They made their
introductions while I struggled to find my voice and retreated to
the chair, nodding like a bobble-head doll. Denise nimbly folded
herself cross-legged onto the floor and beckoned Lesley to join her.
They seemed comfortable enough. Facing me on the couch, though,
legs crossed and hands folded on their knees, sat as unlikely a pairing as I could imagine, a Cabernet and a cupcake, Marcia and Dawn.
I winced as I realized that few people would have less in common.

Dawn was pure confection. Everything about her said, *This
widow situation is not going to slow me down.* In fact, she had told me
as much when I answered the door—she was planning to dash out
after dinner for a drink with a guy she had met the week before, and
she was dressed to thrill. Her slim sheath of a skirt, printed with a
pattern of black-and-white diamonds, had an I-dare-you silver zip-
per running up the side, and her black sweater featured a scoop

neck that dangled on the risky side of low. All of it showcased a Barbie-doll figure. Long crystal earrings sparkled in her blinding blond hair. Nothing about Dawn indicated that anything was amiss in her life. If this was a mask, she wore it with flair.

"Where do you live?" she asked Marcia.

"Upper East Side. And you?"

"New Jersey."

"Huh."

Dawn was forty-five, an Italian American from a working-class town near Newark. Now she lived farther out in the country, but clearly she was a Jersey girl through and through. Northern New Jersey—not quite the Shore and not quite New York, but one high heel planted in each, equal parts style and sizzle. Her voice was showy, too, musical and full of passion.

"Belleville was the wrong side of the tracks," Dawn explained. "The hometown of Frankie Valli and the Four Seasons. My parents took my name from the song."

Close your eyes and you could hear Frankie Valli's high tenor as Dawn worked to find common ground with Marcia: "*Dawn*, go away, I'm no *good* for *you!*"

I could only imagine her take on the woman planted next to her. Marcia was all business—serious, sensible business: rust-blond hair chopped in a sensible bob, sensible rimless glasses, and a sensible uniform of crewneck sweater and boxy jeans. It looked to me like the jeans had been ironed. Marcia's expression gave little away, and when she spoke, her words were terse, logical, precise, and, of course, sensible. I understood what Dawn must be feeling—Marcia had frightened me the first time I met her at a restaurant after work. She had worn a black suit then that called to mind a member of the

Politburo. At her office, she told me, she had been known to make underlings cry. I hoped there was more to Marcia than the brusque demeanor. It was only later that Lesley let me in on something she'd noticed about Marcia that night. Under that sensible getup, she was wearing a pair of kick-ass cowboy boots.

Marcia and Dawn gamely faced each other across a wide chasm in the arts of feminine presentation. Seeing them there, I realized, I should have given more thought to compatibility when I assembled this group. They reached a truce, talking about Marcia's favorite subject: work.

"I have a big job," she told Dawn, which was no exaggeration. At fifty-seven, she had risen to the top of her field as a corporate lawyer, making the kinds of deals you read about in *The Wall Street Journal*, working late into the night, every night. She lived alone and collected fine wines.

Dawn was more of a mojito girl. You might think by looking at her that those shiny eyes would glaze over at Marcia's talk about balance sheets and assets, but that would be a mistake. Over the years, Dawn had started a series of scrappy businesses. Now, she told Marcia, she ran a company that provided two-way radios to police departments, fire departments, and entertainment events like rock concerts and the Macy's parade. Before she had children, Dawn had traveled the world helping acts like the Rolling Stones and U2.

"Your kids must think that's cool," Marcia said without inflection.

"My kids aren't interested yet. They're eight and nine. They loved the Barney tour, though." I could see Marcia's mind flipping through her mental address book. Barney. Barney who? Dawn continued: "But everyone loves Barney, because—a guy in a dinosaur suit—no entourage, right? And if the talent acts up they just get another one." She laughed, a big, frothy laugh, as free as spun sugar.

"Huh," Marcia said again.

I looked toward Denise to settle myself. She and Lesley were keeping up a steady chatter, or at least Lesley was. Apparently, conversation would rarely stall with Lesley in the room. She spoke with the animation of a teenager at a sleepover, clearly determined to keep it light. But what in God's name would those two discuss? Denise, the editor, didn't have children, and she ran in a circle of writers and artists. Lesley had met her husband when she was seventeen and married him by the time she was twenty. Now forty-eight, she had raised three girls, forgoing both education and career to manage a home.

Miraculously, the two found a compatible wavelength. Denise listened with quiet attention as Lesley talked about a smaller house she was planning to buy near her old one in Connecticut now that the girls were grown.

"I'm looking forward to playing in a new sandbox," she said.

I laughed. There was something youthful and flirty about Lesley, dressed down in jeans and a loose-knit sweater. It was hard to tell what was going on underneath. Could anyone be that cheery to the core, or was she protecting herself? Too soon to know. Only five feet tall, she reminded me of a Russian nesting doll. Short brown hair framed her round face, which projected an expression of perpetual surprise—eyes large, eyebrows arched, and mouth puckered as if she were always exclaiming a startled *Oooh!* She spoke in a high, chirpy voice with a strong accent from South Africa, where, she explained, she had grown up.

"Everything sounds a lot sexier when you have a little accent," she confided with a wink. "Even after all this time, people have trouble understanding what I say."

"People have that problem when you come from Brooklyn, too," said Marcia, picking up on the conversation.

Tensions must be easing, I decided, if Marcia was starting to loosen up. Still, the women were drinking more water than wine. No one had touched the guacamole, no surprise, but they also shied away from a splashy platter of sushi that Marcia had brought. Soon, all that tuna and snapper would smell like the docks of Biloxi in July. I had known that such a gathering of strangers was bound to be stiff at first, and so it was. Denise, I noticed, still had her shoes on.

Half an hour passed, and no sign of our sixth invitee. Of all the women, Tara had been the most hesitant about joining this project. She worried, she had told me, that meeting other young widows would conjure up memories she'd sooner put to rest, that the others wouldn't understand the complicated nature of her grief, would draw out secrets she'd rather not share. Asked whether she'd ever considered joining a more official widows' support group, Tara had told me, "I'd rather jump off a cliff." Just when I'd decided she wouldn't make it, the bell rang again.

At the door, Tara handed over a gargantuan bowl of salad, but still she looked like someone carrying something heavy. We'd met before at her country club in a New York suburb. More in her element there, Tara, fifty-four years old, had been wearing black cashmere that day, her honey-colored hair in a luxe cut that swept dramatically off her face. She greeted friends with the innate sociability of a woman accustomed to playing hostess in a high-gloss world. Once, I knew, Tara had excelled in advertising, and later in philanthropy. Her two daughters had recently finished college. To-night, though, there was nothing but tension in her face. Worse than tension—dread.

"I'm sorry," she said slowly, with stagey pauses between each word. "I underestimated . . . how long it would take me . . . to drive." Tara's voice was her most distinctive feature. A slow, deliberate, and sexy alto, like Lauren Bacall's, it was filled with drama, command-ing attention even though she kept the volume purposely low. Con-versation stopped when she greeted the others and took the only chair. She wrapped a cashmere cardigan tighter around her. Lesley told me later, "I took one look at Tara and thought, such a broken woman."

I balanced on the armrest of the chair, wanting her to feel some-one close. Now the group formed a loose but wary circle, every-one protected by a different veneer. Denise was calm. Dawn was frothy. Marcia serious, Lesley chatty. My persona, I hoped, was confident. Tara was the only one who seemed to have shown up without a mask.

I could see how tricky this project was going to be. On the one hand, I wanted the group to find its own natural flow. I was deter-mined not to play the part of social worker—no lectures, no com-pulsory recitations of individual tragedies. But on the other, the one bond that we shared was lurking in the dark recesses of the room as conversation trod safely in the daylight domain of home, work, children, weather.

"Let's start with a toast," I suggested, and fetched champagne from the kitchen. That got tricky, too, as everyone stood and fumbled over which of us knew how to pop the cork. It went unspoken—that had been a job for the men. Denise did the honors smoothly enough, and I poured.

We raised our glasses, and everyone looked to me. Whatever was going to go wrong tonight, I thought with mounting unease, the fault would lie with me. I hid behind my confident mask, forcing myself to smile and speak. "None of us expected to find ourselves in this strange situation, having to reinvent ourselves when we least expected it. But as long as we're doing it, here's to doing it in style, and here's to doing it in good company."

"Cheers to that." Lesley took the first swig.

"Here's to a great new year," Dawn said brightly.

"For me," Tara said, "it couldn't be worse."

The room grew hopelessly still as her words hung in the air. Everyone sipped and looked down at her glass as if contemplating a rare object. I was ready to write off the entire evening, maybe even the entire year, when a low, commanding voice broke the silence, and the taboo.

"How long . . . has everyone been widowed?"

It was Tara. She'd said the word. Not *the* word, *widow*, but close enough. No one had dared go near it up to now.

The silence stretched, and we sat back down, deflated. I felt the full weight of the moment, knowing we'd arrived at the point that would decide what this party, what this group, might be about.

"It's been a year and a half." Marcia, sensible woman of few words, spoke first.

The rest of us answered, everyone except Tara. A year and a half for Dawn. Five and a half years for me. Just over two years for Lesley. Only five months for Denise, our youngest.

"Ooh, yours is so new," said Lesley, her eyes round, her voice tender.

"Yes."

"It's very different then," said Marcia.

Tara still hadn't spoken, holding her thoughts in reserve as the rest of us fell mute again.

"You know," Dawn turned her sparkly countenance toward Denise, who was perched again on the floor, "people are going to tell you that *time* makes all the difference." Her smile remained blistering bright. "And you just want to kill them."

A couple of us laughed. Denise smiled, tucking her knees under her skirt and arching her back in a fluid motion.

"No, they're not saying that," she said placidly. "They're saying, 'You seem fine.' That's what I get. They say, 'I'm glad you're fine.'"

"Are you telling everyone you're fine?" I asked.

"No, no, that's just what they want to say. That's what they want to believe. If I could tell people one thing, it would be, *just acknowledge* that this happened. Don't pretend it didn't happen." She took a hasty swallow of champagne.

"Are you getting 'You're so strong'?" Tara asked.

There were knowing nods all around. Of course we were strong—what choice did we have? "I get that, too," said Marcia. "But one of the things I've found is, even now, I get to where I feel strong, and then I go backwards."

I hadn't expected to hear that, the buttoned-up and—I'll be honest—strong-looking Marcia with a hole in her armor. In fact, I was surprised that all these women who hadn't known each other an hour ago were willing to share such thoughts.

"Yes," Lesley said intently. "I still have that sort of day. I'm buying this new house, and I want to, I really do, but I keep thinking I shouldn't be doing it by myself."

Tara listened to her with sidelong remove. Finally and abruptly, she offered some information. "My husband died last February . . . so it's coming up on a year." She stopped at that.

Dawn rescued us from another silence with a loopy non sequitur. "I find that the only cure for sadness is happiness." Everybody cracked up at the obviousness of the remark, but I couldn't help recognizing that she seemed to have hit on the hypothesis for this group. Perhaps the hypothesis was loopy, too.

"No, really," she said, trying to maintain some gravitas. "I figure out what will give me the most happiness, the most fun, and I go out, and I do it. I don't always feel like it. But I force myself. Really, really, *really* force myself."

"And you get lost in it," Marcia said abruptly. "And then you say, 'Gee, I had a good time.'"

Dawn and Marcia exchanged a brief jolt of recognition. Perhaps they had more in common than I thought.

"But back to my point," Dawn insisted, her voice swooping with operatic dexterity. "People said to me that time makes all the difference, and I just wanted to hit them. I'd be like, *Shut up!* But, I have to say, now, a year later, it *does* make a difference. I was in a blur six months after my husband died."

"A blur," several women chanted, nodding.

We were beginning to engage with each other now, taking a real interest, finding patterns of similarity. Once again, Tara cut in and stopped us cold. "Were your husbands . . . *ill* . . . for a period of time?"

I could see that she had braced herself against the inevitable—what she didn't want to hear, what she didn't want to say—but still, she had asked the tough question. Tara was probing for what had to be everyone's worst memory, the calamity that had set each of us off on an unfamiliar, lonely course, but I thought she was prodding herself as well, forcing herself to share what her instinct told her to conceal. I braced myself, too. I feared that her question would set off the same spiral of resentment I'd witnessed at my last support group washout.

No one seemed keen to follow where Tara was steering us, nor was I. But I had gotten everyone into this mess, I figured, so I took the lead. Okay—so go: the cancer, the four-plus years of caregiving—I didn't feel the need for much elaboration. This group would know what those years had done to my husband, and to me.

When I finished, Dawn spoke up with none of her usual flourishes. "My husband died in an accident," she said. "He went away for a weekend with his friends, riding all-terrain vehicles in West Virginia. He went over a cliff. That's it." She shrugged. "He went away for a weekend, and he didn't come back. Yeah. So." She looked from woman to woman, palms up, casting us a go-figure expression.

"How old was he, Dawn?" Lesley asked.

"Forty. Yeah."

"So young," said Lesley.

"He was . . . gorgeous."

And he'd left two young children behind, children for Dawn to raise alone. There was barely time for us to register the stark tragedy of it before Marcia succinctly outlined her own: "Mine had cancer. He wasn't sick for that long. Maybe five months. Not long. It was particularly difficult, though, because by the time he was diagnosed, it was stage four colon cancer. He opted for alternative treatment, so he never went through chemo. I don't know how it would have turned out if he had."

We waited, feeling the force of these revelations, to see who would go next.

"I still don't know how my husband died," Denise said after some hesitation. I'd been worried that these cumulative tales of loss might be too much for a widow of only five months, but she spoke with presence. "He went into the shower in the morning, and he came out and collapsed. I was with him. The last thing he said was, 'Help me.'"

He died in her arms. Five months later, she was still awaiting results from the autopsy.

"Mine was really...complicated," said a muted voice. This time, Tara didn't wait to go last. We leaned in toward her as she worked that silken instrument, slower and softer even than before, holding us captive as she curled her body forward in the chair, taking up as little space as possible. "Because...I lost my husband slowly...over stages." She stopped, and I thought that might be all she planned to say, but she went on. "He was an alcoholic." She gave a decisive nod, as if to confirm this to herself. "He was. So we watched him transform into something...entirely different from the man we knew."

"Is that what he actually died from?" asked Lesley.

"No, he died of heart failure. But, you know...it pickles all the organs. He was fifty-six when he died."

Without taking a beat, Lesley straightened herself from her spot on the floor and plunged like a swimmer into a cold lake, not allowing herself time to think. "My husband committed suicide," she said abruptly. Everyone registered the shock of it but managed to maintain a level gaze. "He was the most adventurous, hard-working...He loved life to the fullest, and he was only fifty. And much like your husband, Tara, dying of a disease like alcoholism, I think Kevin probably suffered from depression."

"And you didn't know?" Marcia asked.

"No," said Lesley. "Obviously, he had been thinking about it for a while, because he left all sorts of notes to help me through." Her eyebrows went up again, her coquettish eyes grew rounder, and her voice recovered some of its chatty tone. "I was a little bit precious, you know. He did everything for me. He left us a three-page letter, a beautiful letter, the girls and me."

"You have children?" Dawn asked.

"Yes. The youngest had just gone off to college two weeks before."

Next to me, I could feel Tara unfold as she realized that Lesley, so capable of cheer, had weathered such a trauma. It must have placed Tara's own ordeal in sharp relief. She sat up taller and looked at Lesley with new respect. We were all tempted to say it: "Lesley, you're so strong."

The stories were out at last, the rough outlines at least. They were almost too much to take in, let alone keep straight, the only common thread being in the telling, squarely, without embellishment, without self-pity. Perhaps that was why, rather than bringing everyone down, the disclosures seemed to open everyone up. Taut shoulders loosened, jaws relaxed. The rush of release that swept through the room was palpable. We couldn't seem to wait to release our most closely held thoughts.

Dawn told us with some embarrassment that she'd been unwilling to hear the details of her husband's accident. "I still don't even want to know," she said, her musical voice grainier but still emphatic. "The guys who were there would try to tell me, 'We tried to do this or that,' and I didn't even care, really. It was too painful for me. I'm like, it doesn't matter! As long as he's not lost or missing and I should *do* something about this, what the hell difference does it make? He's *dead*."

This set off a wave of what-ifs from the others. Lesley revealed that she had found her husband in their home after what he'd done to himself—she didn't say what. "I tried to save him, and for the longest time I thought, oh my gosh, he died because I didn't do something right."

"Yes," said Dawn. "I was in this crazy place for a while where I thought that if he died, it somehow had to have been my fault. Somehow *I* did it. *I* was bad. It's hard when your husband dies and it totally affects your whole life to think that it didn't have anything to do with you."

Widow's remorse and widow's guilt. The pangs seemed to be just under the surface, and everyone was mining them now. "It's hard not to go over all the scenarios," I said, in an effort at soothing. "To think, I could have done this differently or that differently."

"You must have felt that, too," said Lesley, turning to me.

"Me? Yes." I was caught off guard. I had expected to keep my distance in this conversation—I was the organizer, after all. But I could hardly avoid answering. "My husband's illness"—did I want to do this?—"was very long. We made hundreds of choices along the way. Do we do radiation? Do we do surgery? Do we do another chemo? It's hard not to beat yourself up. You don't know what would have happened if you'd done something differently. And he suffered so much, maybe we shouldn't have gone to such lengths."

I hadn't planned to volunteer this information, wasn't prepared to revisit it. Five years later, it still unnerved me.

"You *can* beat yourself up about things where you have some control," Dawn said gently. "But I don't think that life and death fit into that category."

"There's nothing you can do," Lesley agreed. "My husband was the best thing I ever had. When I lost him, my life changed in an instant. But this has made me totally fearless. Because the worst thing that could happen has already happened."

It was my turn to feel a jolt of recognition. That was my line! "Yes," I said. "Anything less and you have to let it go." I tried to steer the conversation toward the future. "That's why we're here. Now. Tonight. To let this go and head wherever we need to be next."

The eyes of the others brightened with possibility. "It's funny," Lesley said. "We've all just met, but we're already talking about things I don't dare say to anyone else."

We had polished off that bottle of champagne in less time than it took to pop the cork. I stepped into the kitchen to grab a new one from the fridge and held its cool weight for a moment against my overheated brain. A real rumpus was fulminating out there, the group jabbering away, talking all at once and laughing now, too. I was struck by the collective wallop of all that mortal experience assembled in one place, not sure whether what had happened so far was at all what I'd had in mind. I'd felt driven to convene this group to see if there was a better way, but I hadn't intended to immerse myself so deeply. Already, I was beginning to comprehend that detachment wouldn't be possible, that I'd be back in the soup. I'd be pressed to revive harrowing memories, to see them again in the light cast by the group.

Dawn's remark—what was it? "The only cure for sadness is happiness"—was more the model I'd had in mind. I wanted us to have fun. But, clearly, it wasn't possible to ignore the memories, dark or light. I weighed the option of bolting out the back door. The others were probably as leery as I was of letting dark genies out of the bottle. Maybe they'd go their separate ways in an hour or so and spare everyone, me included, from further revelations. On the other hand, who was I kidding? I wouldn't have set this in motion if I hadn't felt the tug to explore more myself. And it was too late to lose heart now. I felt no choice but to push forward, through the end of dinner at least.

I put my shoulder to the swinging door, back to the group. They were all standing now, forming a tight circle, a near-tribal connection around the appetizers, neglected up to now. Tara looked up and called to me across the room, that room that had seemed so wrong before they all came in. She looked like a different person from the one who had shown up an hour ago. The tension in her face was gone. I swear I couldn't have picked her out of a lineup. She had taken on some of Dawn's glow, Denise's poise, Marcia's certainty, Lesley's energy, maybe my confidence.

"Becky," Tara said, beaming now, "this guacamole is delicious."

chapter

THREE

"ou could try looking in the Yellow Pages under *Funeral*."
The nurse with the sugar-coated voice was back again.
Clearly, she wanted to move me along.

My sister fixed her with a withering look, perfected over
generations of bossy women in our family. "Do you *have* a copy of
the Yellow Pages?" she asked.

"No, but maybe you could check around the phone booths? In
the lobby?" The voice was taking on a synthetic edge, more Nutra-
Sweet than honey. It was a couple of hours into the evening shift at
the hospital. I had been a widow for only an hour or so, and already
it was going badly. Now it seemed I was expected to do something,
but my brain was scrambled, and I couldn't grasp what that something might be. Every ten minutes or so, somebody would pop into
the room, avoid looking at the bed, and kindly suggest that I go
home, go get something to eat, *go*. My inability to move was starting to make the entire staff of the hospital uncomfortable.

I'm sure the picture I presented to them was odd. I imagined a proper widow might have been weeping softly, tenderly clutching her husband's hand. But there was so much equipment at that end of the bed—oxygen paraphernalia, a pole with an IV drip, a bedside table that held a telephone and my husband's reading glasses, and all sorts of monitors that suddenly had stopped beeping—that there was no place for a chair. I was too drained to stand, so I'd planted myself near the bottom of the bed, dry-eyed, holding on to his foot.

Meanwhile, the nurses clearly wanted the room, the way waiters at Babbo want a table on a Saturday night. At first they assured me with big sympathetic eyes, "Take as much time as you want." But now a different nurse stopped by every few minutes to give me a nudge.

"If you call a funeral home, they will arrange to come pick up your husband," one of them offered.

Leave him here? To be picked up? Like the dry cleaning or the re-cyclables? I couldn't do that. "I don't know what to do," I answered.

My mother, my sister, and three or four friends had gathered in the hallway outside. Someone asked if the hospital had a social worker who could speak to me. The hospital employed such people for situations like this, situations when the family had Failed to Plan Ahead. I liked the idea. The social worker would know what to do. I could sit there surrounded by the all-too-familiar fluorescent lighting and waxy linoleum floors and inert machinery until one appeared, but it was Friday night, and no one was answering the page.

On some level, I grasped what they were all saying to me. I needed to leave. My husband was gone. I knew that. And yet I couldn't leave him just like that, without a plan in place, and my brain couldn't form a plan. Whatever anyone said to me—"I'm so sorry." "Would you like some hot tea?" Would you like to go home now?"—I could come up with only one response: "I don't know what to do."

It felt as if someone with a remote control were changing channels in my brain every few seconds, before any thought could reach a logical conclusion. The loop ran something like this:

"Bernie is gone. There is no point in staying here."

"I can't leave him here. He hates the hospital."

"Let's face it, Becky, he's not really in the hospital now."

"I should start planning a funeral. The nurses think I should be planning a funeral."

"I have no idea how to plan a funeral."

"Everybody is waiting for me. They must be hungry."

"I should eat, too. I need my strength."

"Wait—I don't need my strength anymore. I can finally sleep."

"I should have made plans for a funeral."

"What kind of person doesn't plan for a funeral when her husband has had cancer for four and a half years?"

"A person who has been Staying Positive. Wasn't that what I was supposed to do?"

"I don't know what to do."

"I need to talk to Bernie."

Ah, that was it. I needed to talk to Bernie. Somewhere in my head I knew that that could never happen again. Not even once. Not ever. My head was refusing to process that information. It was like a pinball machine that someone had bumped too hard, and it was going *Tilt! Tilt! Tilt!* I'm as independent as the next person, but I had talked to Bernie about everything, big or small, for twenty years. Everything from what article I should write to what sweater goes with what skirt. The idea that it wouldn't happen again was simply too big to grasp. My brain was shutting down rather than taking it in.

Still, somehow, the brief thought that I couldn't talk to Bernie gave me a wedge in, a way to start functioning, however feebly. No, I couldn't talk to him now. But I could try to put together what he would have said if he'd had a chance.

I thought back to the day, four and a half years ago, when we first learned that Bernie had cancer. And not just any cancer, but a softball-sized tumor so perilous that even the most hardened oncologists, armored with emotional defenses as secure as maximum-security prisons, patted us on our shoulders and looked at us with open pity. A cancer so rare—they called it thymic carcinoma—that no one knew a protocol for treating it, only a prognosis that, in essence, came down to this: There was no use making long-term plans. A cancer in a part of the chest so obscure (the thymus? I'd never even heard of it) that scarcely anyone had a clue what purpose it served, let alone what to do with a sick one.

My assignment as the supportive spouse got off to an undignified start. Somehow, the doctor who was supposed to break the news to us was under the impression that somebody else already had. We walked into an appointment that we thought was about a persistent but routine respiratory infection, and his first words were, "The tumor is very large. It has to come out."

"*What tumor?*" Bernie and I cried in unison, like the Two Stooges.

The doctor slapped some film onto a backlit board and pointed to what looked like a massive ink stain, blotting out everything that mattered in the middle of Bernie's chest.

Speechless, I dropped like a rock into the nearest chair. The room went momentarily black, and everyone from Bernie to a posse of interns rushed to my side to tend to me—me, the well one.

"Put your head between your legs," the doctor advised. I struggled to absorb the blow from this inelegant angle.

Bernie took my hand. "I'm so sorry, Beck," he said.

Afterward, I stood next to him outside the hospital, dizzy and devastated. I was forty-four years old, and I knew that whatever happened next, nothing would be the same. Bernie looked shaken, too, but he took my arm, and his demeanor took on an upbeat energy, common to him whenever he undertook a new project.

"Beck," he said with resolution, "we just have to put our heads down and go."

And so we did. Like the journalists we both were, we hopped into a cab, headed home to Brooklyn, and started doing research, reading anything we could about the disease, calling any expert we could find, working the story, the story of how to save his life, for as long as we could, anyway. We didn't think about the future. We didn't think about the larger implications. We didn't think about death. We applied ourselves to the concrete task at hand. We succeeded, I suppose, in that he lived far longer than anyone predicted. The approach became a model for us throughout his illness. Every time we got bad news—the tumor was growing, the chemo wasn't working, the surgery didn't remove the whole thing, it was spreading through the chest, it had spread to the brain—we put our heads down and figured out something to do about it, a new specialist to see, a new procedure to try.

Now in the hospital once again, Bernie's body inert beside me, I was dizzy, devastated, again. And once again, I realized, the only way to keep going was not to think too deeply right now, not that the channel clicker in my brain would let me anyway. I needed to figure out something to *do*. I couldn't think about loss. I couldn't think about how profoundly alone I would be, stretching years into the future. I couldn't think, except in the most practical way, about death. I suppose that's one of the handy realities about funerals. They provide the bereaved with a task that's tangible but not too profound—Danish or bagels afterward?—for the first day or so, holding the enormity of what has happened at bay, if only for a time. I'd have something to do for now.

It was shocking how ill-prepared I was to accomplish even that. Planning a funeral—*This is a job for grown-ups!* I told myself in disbelief, feeling like I was twelve. Nobody else in my circle seemed any better equipped. My mother had helped arrange funerals before, but she had come from out of town and didn't know the ropes in New York. My friends were all too young to have firsthand experience. And the nurses . . . well, the phone book idea was their go-to suggestion. One of my friends said to me a week later, "Gee, a cancer hospital—you'd think no one had ever died there before." The ultimate certainty in life may be mortality, but most of us, me most of all, are caught flat-footed when confronted with it for real. Even as it was overtaking Bernie and me like a tidal wave, we had refused to look out to sea, pushing all thoughts of death aside. For our generation, in our culture, in our lives, death was the one unmentionable.

We weren't alone. The doctors had started retreating already in the preceding week. As Bernie grew sicker and sicker, his vast team fell away, avoiding eye contact, standing on the far side of the examining room, leaving bedside visits to skittish interns. I couldn't blame any of them. Many had become fond of Bernie, and fond of me, too, I suppose. They had been proud of his unexpected perseverance. For his most devoted physicians, this would be a sad defeat. Our usual oncologist wasn't doing rounds that week, so one of the hospital's leading specialists had spent the last several days alternately avoiding me and patronizing me while Bernie lay unconscious in a haze of narcotics. Whenever I asked a question, this doctor would advance into my personal space, back me into a corner in some sort of alpha male display, and speak to me loudly and slowly, as if I were mentally challenged. "Your husband has sepsis. It's an infection in the bloodstream. Almost nobody survives sepsis, even healthy people, and your husband isn't healthy."

I *knew* that. Chemotherapy had left his immune system too weak to fight a common cold. When I'd rushed him to the hospital on Monday, shaking with fever, I knew we were in trouble, and over the next several days, he slipped deeper and deeper into a coma-like twilight. By Friday, he hadn't spoken in days, not since Tuesday when he woke up briefly to say what turned out to be his last words. "I love you," he wheezed, and then something else that started with the letter S—I'll never know—before he slipped back under.

Meanwhile, if I probed for any glint of hope, any suggestion of a solution, the doctor threw up his hands in exasperation and repeated, "Your husband has sepsis..." and then officiously hustled away. Just the day before, he had seen me approaching in the corridor and turned so hard on his heel that he lost his balance, throwing up his hands and waving his arms like pinwheels trying to right himself. My mom and I did a spit take as he did his best to restore his dignity. Deathwatch humor—you take what you can get.

Now I asked my friends in the hall to call some funeral homes for me while I stayed put on the end of the bed. I heard them as they whipped out their phones, eager to help, reaching the same few late-shift funeral home employees who would say, "Didn't somebody else call about the same guy a couple minutes ago?" Nobody knew quite what to ask, and everybody learned the same few things, which they reported back to me. Yes, someone would come to pick up the body, later that night or in the morning. Yes, they all would charge a ridiculous sum for this service. You'd think they were sending him to Tierra del Fuego and back. And they would all like to know what sort of funeral I was planning. I didn't know. I didn't know what to do.

It began to look as if the nurses might call security to give me the heave-ho, except someone finally showed up to break the stalemate. David Goldenberg was a psychiatrist who had managed a complicated cocktail of medications intended to keep Bernie's mind on track as the cancer wreaked havoc in his brain, causing memory loss, confusion, anxiety, and sleeplessness. It was a wretched existence, profoundly dispiriting to a man who prided himself on reading obscure books on public policy and knowing every sideman who ever played with Ben Webster. Most people with brain metastasis live for only a few months. Bernie had lasted more than two years in this state, and the drugs helped keep him on an even keel. Dr. Goldenberg turned up at the hospital that night for a visit, and I took an easier breath. He would know what to do.

"How are *you* doing?" he asked briskly as he strode into the room. He pulled up an ugly plastic chair and sat opposite me. If he found it strange to speak to a woman who was perched on her deceased husband's bed, her knees hugged to her chest, his face did nothing to betray it. I had drawn a sheet over Bernie by now to spare everyone from seeing him.

I told Dr. Goldenberg about the remote control running amok in my head.

"That's actually quite normal at a time like this," he said. I found that information comforting. I might have been a mess, but I was a *normal* mess.

I told him I didn't know what to do. "I feel guilty leaving Bernie in the hospital," I said. "He hated it when I'd leave him here. He kept fighting, no matter what horrible procedures got thrown at him, so we wouldn't be apart. I can't walk away from him now. It seems my end of it shouldn't be so easy."

"It's normal to feel guilty," Dr. Goldenberg said. "There's no avoiding it." Then he got down to practicalities. "You don't have to make any decisions right now," he said. "You're exhausted. Go home, get some rest, make some choices tomorrow. Your friends are all here. Let them help you. This isn't a time to insist on doing everything yourself."

Granted, it didn't take a medical degree to come up with this advice, but it had enough ring of authority to give me some backbone. Maybe a copy of the Yellow Pages would have accomplished the same thing.

After Dr. Goldenberg left, I took a crack at pulling myself together. I might have lost Bernie, my trusted guide, but I knew I couldn't remain frozen forever in this void between what my life had been and the scary territory that lay ahead. Immobility was the act of a coward. I also knew that I'd have to push back against the guilt I would feel walking out of there. For some time to come, I could see, I would have to contend with this guilt, this new unwanted companion of mine, whenever I did what was necessary to keep on living myself.

I stood up, stepped out the door, and informed my little group of supporters that I would go now. They told the nurses I would arrange for a funeral home to come for Bernie tomorrow. Back at the bedside, I said a few words to him, feeling the full absurdity of talking out loud for the first time in my life to someone who wasn't there. I gathered his things, his glasses and his keys and his clothes, no longer of any use, in a hospital laundry bag. Then I kissed him. His skin was smooth and cold. One more moment. "Good-bye, sweetie," I said, and turned away, hard.

I walked out into the hall. I didn't speak. I didn't look from side to side. I certainly didn't think. If I had, I might have had to acknowledge what I was leaving behind me: a twenty-year union, the most important of my life, with a man who could never be replaced. I took one step ahead, then another.

I couldn't know what awaited me beyond those steps, that it would take all my depleted strength, that it would be harder than anything I had known. My friends drew close. I could feel them encircling me like a ring around a dark penumbra. I summoned Bernie's words from the start of this nightmare: I put my head down, and I went.

chapter

FOUR

*i*t was too soon for me to form any coherent, conscious thought, but on some level, that was probably the beginning of my wish to find someone else like me. I had the first inkling that I might have found not one but five of them that January night of the first meeting of our group. On the surface, we weren't much alike—we weren't even at the same stage of widowhood. But there was something extraordinary about that meeting. It was heartrending but exhilarating, too. It filled a long-empty hole.

Let me put it this way. Have you ever been to a party where everybody shared their deepest feelings about everything closest to their hearts and then laughed until their insides hurt and then went home and stayed up all night as everything kept spinning in their heads—and they *weren't* stoned? Me neither. Until the night of that dinner at Denise's.

On the subway back home to Brooklyn I couldn't stop going over and over the evening in my mind. Oddly, I kept coming back to the movie *Thelma and Louise.* One catastrophe in the first reel and the characters were on the run, speeding toward an uncertain future, their identities up for grabs as they propelled themselves through one hair-raising scrape after another. Our gang at dinner wasn't exactly on the lam in an old Thunderbird, but the death of each husband had set in motion a world-changing series of unfamiliar predicaments. All the women, we learned, were in the process of remaking, reinventing, and rethinking who they were and how they lived and where they lived and what they did and who they cared about and who cared about them—all the issues that overwhelmed me at first when Bernie died.

As Louise said to Thelma—or was it Thelma to Louise?—"We seem to have some kind of snowball effect going on here."

But putting it all into words, telling anecdotes, framing it with humor, lightened it somehow, because, finally, we'd found women who knew exactly what we were talking about. Women who got the sorrow, women who got the jokes.

After that first hour, as Denise had said, there was no use pretending that what had happened hadn't happened. We were comfortable talking about death and its aftermath—these were our lives, after all. There were no tears. But getting through the hard stories about what had befallen our husbands freed everybody up to talk about the stuff nobody else wants to talk to widows about, the messy stuff everybody was working on right then.

The challenge for me was getting a word in edgewise. Over dinner, I had planned to explain the details of my utterly amateur widows' support scheme and ask the women whether they would be willing to risk it for a year. But faced with the formidable personalities assembled in front of me, I couldn't get up the nerve. Why would the independent Tara conform to anybody's schedule but her own? Wouldn't the busy Marcia find this a frivolous use of her time? And would all of them regard the idea of consorting with widows irredeemably glum? Dawn seemed to enjoy ample opportunities for dating. Maybe the others did, too, not to mention working, raising children, mastering the violin for all I knew. Every time I got closer to bringing up my idea, I backed off, and somebody steered the conversation further from my goal.

I lost my first chance when we moved into Denise's jewel box of a dining room, where the walls were painted a glossy shade of vermilion.

"I love this red room . . . it's so feng shui," Tara said. "And I love the door."

Denise was backing through it, carrying Tara's salad from the kitchen. "That's the reason we bought this apartment," she said. "My husband saw this door."

It was a swinging door, an original Art Deco beauty with a porthole in it, like the doors on classic ocean liners. Denise and her husband, Steve, had bought the apartment only two and a half years ago, a year before they married. The place was a wreck when they first saw it, and the door was lying on the floor with broken hinges, but Steve restored the door's original luster, along with everything else.

"Steve could fix anything," Denise said, pleased but wistful.

All that work had fashioned a room with informal charm, the unassuming product of the couple's personal touch. The door, the red walls, the golden light from a vintage chandelier, and a flea market table lacquered in shiny black enamel imparted a cozy glamour. Our gathering took on some of that personality as we sat down to dine.

Steve's death, we learned, had placed this home in jeopardy, because the mortgage was too steep for Denise to manage alone. Everyone she knew was urging her to move, but instead she was working like a demon to bring in more money, signing up new novels at her publishing house and loading up her nights and weekends with part-time jobs. Sleep would have to wait, not that she was sleeping anyway. She might need to rent out the second bedroom, too. A roommate at the age of thirty-nine—hardly anyone's dream scenario.

"People tell me I should take a year off to recover from the trauma," Denise said, "but I don't have a choice. I will do whatever I have to do."

Widowed after only a year of marriage, of course she would want to stay in this apartment, I thought. It was not only her home but a reminder of who her husband was, of who they were together. How could she let that go without a fight?

I considered my own home, an apartment in a Brooklyn brownstone full of period details I'd always found a bit grand for my humble modern life. Next to my grab bag of latter-day furnishings, the building's parquet floors, high ceilings, and majestic moldings felt borrowed from a more formal past. Often I was struck by the tension between past and present there. That home had sheltered me through my marriage to Bernie and beyond. It was the place where I most felt his absence, the place where I most felt his presence. Every time I returned to that empty apartment in the months after his death, I dropped my bags and walked to the mantel, where I still displayed his photograph, a little overexposed. The washed-out light gave it a haunting, spectral quality. I felt the familiar yearning for his company, the urge to tell him everything that had happened. We had shared everything, as happy couples do. I spoke aloud: "Hey, sweetie."

My home was full of light, and its familiarity had been a comfort during the worst times. Yes, it had been expensive maintaining the place on my own, but like Denise, I wasn't willing to give up something I loved because the person I loved was gone. Holding on there through so many momentous changes, I often wondered about the definition of home. Is it the place where you live, or is it the place where the people you love reside? And if the people you love are gone, where is home then?

Most of the women that night at Denise's were wrestling one way or another with the question of where they belonged. "Ever since this happened," said Dawn, "I feel like Dorothy in the *Wizard of Oz*, like a tornado has picked up my house and is spinning it around. I just want to know where it's going to land."

Where to land—it came up again and again as we squeezed tightly around the table, unveiling dishes and passing them family style, hand to hand. Lesley contributed chicken tartly perfumed with sliced lemons, rosemary, olives, and a South African chutney made with apricots. I had brought sinfully buttery mashed potatoes and sautéed brussels sprouts, a nice contrast, I hoped, with Tara's crisp salad. Dawn poured a late-vintage Malbec.

That would have been the moment for me to present my idea for the group, but I let the opportunity get away from me again. Marcia told us she was facing a dilemma about her home, too. Like many couples with all-consuming jobs, she and her husband had relied on each other to make the most of what little time they spared from work. He had been the gregarious one, hosting clamorous parties on weekends at a country house that they owned. During the week, with Marcia logging long hours at the office, they camped out in a basic city apartment that was more like a dorm room.

"After he died, it was too hard to manage the house," Marcia said. She sold it, but now she was holed up alone in that claustrophobic apartment, isolated, extending scant invitations to family or friends. It was where she lived, but it didn't sound like where she belonged. Between her corporate schedule and that spartan setup at home, I wondered whether she had any space or time for pleasure, any inducement to engage a wider world now that her partner was gone.

For Tara, the question of where to live was only one strand in a snarl of problems tangled up with her husband's alcoholism. First: work. She had quit her job under the strain of his final years, and now she was looking for something else. Next: social standing. She had filed for divorce after one of his failed attempts at rehab, but she hadn't followed through with it before he died, which made her role in society even more confused than it was for the rest of us.

"Divorced or widowed...I don't fit in anywhere," she said in her elegant, smoky voice. "That's the problem with labels. It doesn't mean that I didn't...love my husband. It doesn't mean that I wasn't...in shock when he died." But it did mean that she now felt like an oddity in her circle, where society revolved around couples.

That left the matter of home. "I love my house," Tara went on. "But I'd like to live...somewhere where there are a lot of single people...and whether you're divorced, widowed, whatever... you're still included."

Everyone nodded. "Moving would be good for you," said Dawn.

"Except I don't know where I'm moving." Tara toyed with some chicken on her plate. "I'd just like to be more...settled. I'd like to know where I'm going to live . . . what my life will be like." I was sure the others knew how she felt. I certainly did, even now. "But I'm also trying to embrace the openness of this situation. I don't think there's a timetable for everything . . . falling into place. I'm trying to come to appreciate the lack of knowing." She gave a skewed little chuckle at the absurdity of that quest.

The glamorous Dawn told us that she knew where she belonged—with her children, guiding them through their own course of grief—but that she also wished she could meet the right man and re-create a family like the one they'd lost.

She had tried dating a couple of times but was daunted by the complications with an eight-year-old girl and nine-year-old boy at home. None of the other women had dipped their toes in the intriguing waters of dating yet, except for Lesley, who was considering whether to leap to the next level.

"I have a revelation," she said in her flirtiest tone. "I met a man seven months ago, and when I move into my new house, I'm thinking of asking him to move in with me."

Dawn's eyes popped. "How did *this* happen?" We dropped our forks and leaned forward, ears cocked like directional antennas.

"The old-fashioned way, on Match.com." Lesley's voice was lighthearted and bright, but then she softened it. "I wasn't expecting this, you know. I was married for twenty-six years. I knew that I had been loved and that I had loved so deeply, so after he died, I felt like, that's fine, if that's all I'm going to have, then I've had it. Some people don't even have that."

"That's how I feel, too," Dawn said firmly. "Anything I get from here is a plus."

"But after I went through this for a couple years," Lesley

continued, "I thought, hell, I have so much to give away. To waste it, to never be in love again..."

I had to admire Lesley's nerve to even consider jumping into the deep end again after the shock of her husband's suicide. The anxiety was there on her face, but there was elation, too. "I'm telling you, girls, I was in the desert for a couple of years, and I'd forgotten how wonderful it was to have somebody hold my hand. The first time it happened I thought I was going to die! I thought, am I twelve?"

"Yes!" Tara said. "Twelve years old. I know what you mean. Some friends offered to fix me up with somebody. Nothing happened, but I was...sick...to...my...stomach."

Now that we had gravitated to the subject of men, I could see there was no hope of me bringing up anything else until dessert. I saw faces lighting up all around the table as everyone absorbed what Lesley was saying. It's okay to think this way. It's okay to *feel* this way. It's okay to want love again and to act on that desire. That it was Lesley, who had suffered such a brutal shock, who could find the nerve to invite a new man into her life made it seem tantalizingly possible. I felt pulses quicken around our tight little circle. Dating again—after many years of marriage followed by one or two more of grief-imposed celibacy—it had all the scary, forbidden thrill of that first kiss in adolescence. It occurred to me at that moment how much widowhood reminded me of adolescence: a time of uncertainty, of transformation, of trying on new identities, of wondering what it would be like if the cute boy in algebra class asked you out, or more.

Tara was on the same wavelength. "I have to say, honestly... I haven't been with another man...for thirty-two years. I was twenty-two when I met David."

"I promise you," Lesley said, eyebrows high. "It still works."

"But ... it has to be serendipitous," Tara said.

"I love that word—*serendipitous*," said Dawn.

"But you have to try," Lesley advised them sternly. "You have to get back on the bus no matter what."

"I'm happy to get on the bus. I just don't know if I want ..." Tara paused longer than usual, "a relationship."

"Then you just need to bonk and look for something later," said Lesley. "But bonk in the meantime. You haven't had it in a while."

"I'd be delighted to ... bonk," Tara said with exaggerated dignity. "But I would need to find ... a bonkee."

"Or a bonk-*er*," said Lesley.

"If it's good," said Dawn, "you'll switch positions after a while."

Marcia looked askance, but the rest of us shrieked with laughter. When Tara found an opening, she tamped down the frivolity by interjecting a thoughtful note.

"Talking to all of you, I realize," she said, "there is this interesting thing ... about our situation. We can be free to explore ... and relive our twenties again, but have the experience of being ... older."

Denise passed out cookies for dessert, padding around the table barefoot, as she had told me she would. Things had loosened up all right, far more than I could have predicted. I surely hadn't expected to find bonking on the agenda, in whatever position, within the first couple hours of our acquaintance. But sex, I recognized, was something widows couldn't talk about with anybody else, even though sex, companionship, love, lust—call them what you will— weren't frivolous concerns. They were some of the foremost features of a happy life, or had been up to now, anyway. Sooner or later, all these women were going to face a difficult series of choices. Do I get involved with someone else? Who should it be? How involved do I get? It was still largely hypothetical for most members of the group, and it was stressful to contemplate, but we had found a place to talk about it, a place with no judgments.

"We're having so much fun," Lesley said. "Who knew these poor, sad women could have such a ball?"

"I was so afraid," said Tara, "that this wouldn't be fun."

We'd been there nearly four hours, and I still hadn't asked my question. Dessert was on the table. It was now or never. Don't blow it.

"Now that we've all met, what would you think if we did this once a month?" I asked. "We could do things together, fun things, things we've never tried before, and not feel pressure to be sad. There's so much social pressure on widows that if they're not acting sad enough, they aren't proper widows."

"*That* is so true," Tara said.

"I would personally like to fail Widow 101," said Dawn.

"*Widow* is such a terrible word," Lesley said, to vigorous agreement all around.

"We should come up with another word," said Marcia.

"Let's eliminate it altogether," said Dawn, releasing her feelings with escalating brio. "And everything that goes with it. All the old ways of thinking about *what* you should be and *how* you should feel, and if you feel a certain way you should feel guilty, and if you *don't* feel a certain way you should feel guilty. It's crazy, the whole widow thing."

"To me, it means old," said Lesley.

"And sad," said Denise.

"And black and dark," Lesley went on.

"That you should die along with him," said Dawn, not one to hold back.

"I don't want people to feel sorry for me," Marcia said curtly.

"Exactly," said Lesley.

I seized an opening. "It shouldn't have these connotations," I said. "I came to realize this after a while. *I* became a widow, and I am not *any* of those things. That's how I came to embrace the word eventually. And that's why I'd like us to try this for a year. I don't want this to be a stodgy group following preconceived ideas. I want us to get out there, out of our comfort zones, because, let's face it, we're out there already."

They waited a good long beat while they pondered the proposal. I studied their faces, considered the almost comical mismatches in their personalities, temperaments, and manners of living.

"I think," said Lesley, relishing the suspense, "that this has the makings of a wild and raucous group."

Ideas started flying like fireworks. Six of us meeting once a month—the permutations were endless. Someone suggested we pamper ourselves at a spa, not exactly an extreme adventure, I thought, but sure—why not enjoy ourselves? Someone else proposed dancing lessons. "We need to get our hips busy again," Lesley said in her saucy way. We talked about volunteering or traveling, maybe to Peru, or Italy, or Southeast Asia. Tara, of all people, suggested we buy new lingerie together.

"I've been wearing what my daughters call . . . The Mummy, this spandex microfiber flesh-colored whatever," she said. "I need help."

"Does this mean you're all in?" I asked.

Four voices answered in sequence, like the Four Musketeers: "I'm in."

Tara, of course, with her flair for drama, couldn't say it flat out.

"You know what I decided, on my way here? If this is negative . . . if it's not feeding me . . . if it's not making me a better person . . . then I'm not interested. I'm bailing. I need to do everything that feels right . . . and good . . . for *me*, without apologies to anybody."

Dawn tried to cut her short. "You suggested the lingerie, girl, so that means you're in."

"I would have bailed," Tara persisted. "But the thing is . . . it didn't take two minutes for me to know. I'm not going to let this go. I've had to let so many things in my life go." The room was quiet now. "And my story, which is so fucked up on so many levels . . . I need to let that go, too. I need to take control of my story from now on."

She was in. We all were. It all seemed so right as we stood to clear the table. So many choices to face, so many paths to try, so many stories to tell, if not to control—as Dawn had said, *serendipity* was a good word, too. Whatever happened, at least we'd have this. We wouldn't be alone. There, in that bewitching red room, we made a pact, once a month on a Saturday night, to stand together, whatever had happened up to now, whatever would happen from now on.

Back home at four in the morning, hopelessly buzzed, I couldn't sleep. Hearing so many of my own once-solitary impressions echoing back at me had been a relief—I wasn't alone—but also disturbing. It reminded me of the nights the first year after Bernie died, nights when I stared at the high white ceiling of my bedroom, trying to give order to thoughts that resembled some garish rococo wallpaper. Back then, I was unable to see my way forward. Like these women tonight, I didn't know who I was; how I would get by on my own; who, if anyone, I might love in the future. I knew the questions well. The snowball effect gets most acute in the hours just before dawn. I flashed on *Thelma and Louise* again, the scene at the end when the women look at each other when they think they've run out of options and say, "Let's keep going." I hoped the women tonight saw that they still had choices, more choices than they knew, more choices than I knew I had when Bernie had just died.

Yes, I thought, *let's keep going.*

chapter

FIVE

*a*s far as I could tell, the only one having second thoughts was me. The laughing was great—the laughing and the possibilities. But spending a few hours in the company of women whose loneliness was still so new and raw reminded me of my earlier existence as a misfit widow at a time when I wanted to leave it behind.

Nothing about that existence was what I would have expected, assuming I had expected any of it, which I did not.

Before Bernie got sick, I had led one of those normal, happy lives straight out of *Archie* comics. I grew up the middle child of a normal, happy family in a normal, happy small town in normal Pennsylvania. The main street had all of three stoplights, and it seemed that the worst that could happen was a cloudy day at the swimming hole. Places like that still existed then, probably somewhere now, too. I spent dreamy afternoons at the town reservoir, sunning in a bikini on the coarsely mowed grass, playing Hearts with friends and wishing for something heartfelt to happen. Later, in New York,

I would meet people who claimed to be bigger hicks than me, but usually I'd win hands down on two points. For most of my childhood, there was no movie theater in my town. And I never tasted pizza until I went to college. Or Chinese food, for that matter.

There was a fair amount of sensory deprivation in such a backwater upbringing, and I was hungry for knowledge, experience, and maybe some spicy food. After college, I headed to graduate school in journalism in New York, seeking a stimulating existence in a stimulating place. Which is where I met Bernie, a writer who taught there as an adjunct professor.

The next two decades granted me all the sensory overload of my youthful daydreams. I signed on as a fast-breaking news reporter in the Manhattan office of *New York Newsday*, downing the city's potent highball of culture and business, covering food, fashion, media, and Wall Street. It was intoxicating, the most fun a person could have and still get paid. And my partnership with Bernie somehow rounded it all out. I wrote about the cultural overlords of the day, fielding whatever assignments the editors lobbed onto my desk, while Bernie was a genuine crusader for the underdog, a tenaciously independent journalist who took on only work that mattered to him. He wrote about homeless teenagers, youth unemployment, and his masterwork, a book about a sensational rape case that exposed the fissures of class, gender, and justice in a small town. It took him years to pull it off and had the kind of impact that fulfilled his passion for challenging the status quo.

Our marriage was symbiotic, a true collaboration, as we shared story ideas and edited each other's writing. I aired out my serious side through Bernie; he picked up the latest buzz through me. When I helped with one of his projects, I felt that I was contributing to the betterment of the world. When he made suggestions for my profile of a fashion designer or my take on an overhyped new restaurant, he got to exercise his ever-present sense of whimsy.

Our careers advanced, and our marriage followed the same fantasy script. You know the one I'm talking about: a fairy-tale romance, or reasonable modern facsimile, with elements of drama and comedy, part Frank Capra, part Judd Apatow. Sometimes Bernie's nervous energy set my more pokey sensibility on edge, but like me, he was an enthusiast, only scrappier. He had grown up in Brooklyn before it got all gentrified, and he was sixteen years older than I was, so our partnership gave the former bumpkin in me the confidence I needed. We weren't always lucky—we couldn't have children, for example, perhaps a forewarning that something inside Bernie was amiss. But he told people he felt as if he'd won the lottery when he found me. To me, the union felt like a happy ending, certain, complete. It safeguarded me with stability, security, and perhaps a protective set of blinders.

I was shocked when the script turned into something else altogether, full of sudden twists and alien words. Oncology. Chemotherapy. Metastasis. Resuscitate. This scenario played out over more than four years, nearly a quarter of our marriage. The news that mattered to us now was breaking in the hospital, a constant, harrowing tumult of test results and risky treatments.

I could scarcely believe the level of fear, or frustration, in the daily hand-to-hand combat against this monster that was trying to kill Bernie. Instinct told me to fight, but how? In primitive times, the hunter-gatherers who had the best shot at living needed the crazy strength to club a wildebeest or outrun a bear. But in the brave new world of technological medical interventions, it seemed that those who lived the longest were the ones who could restrain themselves long enough to remain polite on the telephone. Adrenaline only made it harder to tamp down the screaming meemies when some overburdened functionary would tell me, "The doctor's schedule is full for the next three months." Clubbing a wildebeest would have been a relief, almost as satisfying as clubbing a functionary. I kept plugging without rest for months on end, trying to perform my job while a nurse stayed with Bernie during the day. At night, it was my turn, as he wandered the dark apartment in a muddle of pain, needing oxycodone and comfort, constant comfort.

All of that had nearly been enough to break me, and then it ended with the added shock of finding myself, at an age when my friends were dealing with parent-teacher conferences, corporate promotions, and Pilates classes, *a widow*.

By the start of the memorial service three days after Bernie died, I could already tell that nothing about this role would match my admittedly ill-informed expectations, let alone those of most of the people who knew me. "This is going to be an ordeal," one of them said before the service began at a chapel on the Columbia campus. Suffocating in a long-sleeve dress in sudden, unseasonable heat, I girded myself to make it to the benediction without disintegrating completely. I'd invited anyone who felt like saying a few words to get up and speak, so anything could have happened. What did, however, surprised me. The reminiscences reintroduced me to the Bernie I'd forgotten during the illness, the *well* Bernie, the one who still lived in the stories of those who hadn't seen him when he was sick, stories about his generosity as a teacher, his mischievous wit. I came out less sad than I went in.

Afterward, I expected to collapse in exhaustion, but all that pent-up adrenaline wouldn't let me. The next day, I found myself frantically planting geraniums in the apartment's window boxes, flinging potting soil around with demented abandon, so tired was I of the ugliness of the hospital. I felt like a Looney Tunes character whose legs kept spinning in the air after she went off a cliff.

"Sit down. Rest," said my mother, who stayed on with me for a couple of days.

But sitting only made me more desperate to find a wildebeest to club. Entitled to a week off from work, I'd never felt so profoundly that there was nothing for me to do. I was strangely disappointed to find that the busy working friends of a younger widow didn't have time to drop off tuna noodle casseroles to break the sudden solitude. Instead they sent enough fruit baskets for me to open a produce stand, along with a few party platters of fancy nuts, cheeses, and olives for my nonexistent parties. I'd never been anywhere so quiet and eerie as the apartment in those first days with Bernie gone. And I'd never seen objects as poignantly useless as his wallet, his watch, and his wedding ring at rest on the bedside table.

Even more shocking—I missed cancer. "At least his suffering is over," visitors consoled me, and that was true. But cancer had provided me with such a pure, fierce, clarifying urgency for so long that I was lost without it. On any given day, deciding my priorities had been a snap. Should I get a haircut, pay the electric bill, or save Bernie's life? No contest! Now everything seemed equally irrelevant. How bad could my hair look? Did I really need electric lights?

During the day, I felt too anesthetized to speak. Condolence callers encouraged me to talk about my feelings, and I was vaguely aware of this directive myself. I needed to air out the pain, I thought, or it would fester and come back at me later, worse than ever. My job, it seemed, was to wallow, to let myself feel depressed. But—call me crazy—even then, at the depths, I still felt optimistic, hopeful that my life would become full and happy again. Yet nothing I'd ever read or heard about mourning spoke to that.

At night, spent as I was by Bernie's illness, I couldn't sleep to save my life. I stared at the ceiling as my mind came painfully alive with the need to—what? My task now, as I understood it, was to give in, to let myself screw things up for once, to feel the grief. Again, I didn't know what to expect, except maybe the Kübler-Ross five stages, which I couldn't even comprehend. I supposed I should be starting with the denial stage, but trust me, when somebody is gone, somebody who made your toast every morning and shared your bed every night, it's hard to pretend that he's still around. Bargaining also threw me. Was a better deal available, and what could I possibly offer as a trade? I'll give you a fruit basket if you give me back my husband?

When I did manage to doze for an hour or two, I was terrorized by nightmares. Usually, Bernie was in some ghastly peril and I tried and failed to save him. He would slip off a ledge, or fall into a river. One memorable night, a robot was performing surgery on him, but I saw that Bernie was awake. I tried to stop the mechanical surgeon, but it kept slashing him wildly, indiscriminately, faster and faster, with hands like razors, until I woke up clammy with horror.

Then there was the missing. The bottomless missing. Of course, I knew that I would miss Bernie, but what I didn't know until those hyperconscious nights was that grieving would be so much more than any missing I'd experienced up to now. Missing, the way I looked at it, was what you felt for someone who didn't happen to be around at the moment. Someone you'd see again in an hour or a week or a month, swooping in from the airport, spiral-eyed with jet lag. Someone off at Gorilla Coffee to buy Sumatra Roast, or away at an academic conference, wearing a name tag: *Hi, my name is Bernie.* Someone who would take off the name tag and come back, back home, to me.

No, this task of grieving was so much more than missing. It was more like homesickness for a home that was no longer there. A home that had been swept away by a tidal wave, or sucked into a giant sinkhole, or knocked down by a bulldozer to make way for a new Bed Bath & Beyond, never to be seen again. This grieving for my husband was like a permanent exile from that lost home. Like an asylum seeker in a strange land, I would have to learn to live in this world, bereft of familiarity, bereft of comfort. Bereft.

What I would have given to sleep through the night, or at least drive away the nightmares, like the ones where my husband was drowning and I jumped into a churning river to rescue him, knowing it would surely kill me, too, reaching for his hand and missing it by inches as icy waters swept him away. Missing that hand in my dreams every time. More than missing him, every night. Never to be seen again.

―――――――――

MONTHS PASSED. Being a widow didn't get easier. I began to venture out, where the least trigger prompted me to relive what I came to call The Top Ten Traumatic Moments. Somebody's vacation photo brought back the first time I saw that scan of the tumor in Bernie's chest. The sight of a neighborhood restaurant recalled the time he suffered a seizure over dinner at a favorite spot. I tried to talk to friends about some of this, but repeating it mostly fed the panic that was rising in my throat.

I showed up at work, sometimes carting in remains from the party platters to share with the newsroom. I can't remember what else, if anything, I did there. Looking in the archives, I see that I wrote a peppy article about celebrity chefs, so I must have given the appearance of playing reporter. But I was missing another story right under my nose, a story that imperiled my future. Through the long slog of Bernie's illness, I had barely noticed that my job might be disappearing along with my husband as the newspaper industry succumbed to a slow fade of its own. I managed to ignore the evidence, even as co-workers headed for the lifeboats, finding other jobs or quitting to work on their own. But I was still frozen, as I had been in his hospital room, too fragile to face reality, too uncertain to make a change while still absorbing the trauma from such a big one. I couldn't bring myself to consider conditions that would separate me from my job, the one familiar port in my new world of exile. Maybe it was just as well. If I'd left, I would have wound up flat on my couch every day in sweatpants and fuzzy slippers, alone, watching *One Life to Live*. One more life than I had now.

In the evenings, stranded on that couch after work, I sometimes gave myself a break from missing the cancer and missing Bernie, which often coalesced into one overwhelming ache of missing, and turned my attention to puzzling out my new place in society. I'd seen the movies, read the books: Old Widow So-and-So was often an outcast, or cursed. In some cultures, she'd be handed off to the husband's brother like a bag of shabby clothes. I had to admit that my own conception wasn't much more appealing—a sad sack of an old lady, marginal, helpless, irrelevant, ready for assisted living.

That can't be me! I protested. *The only assistance I want in living is from the personal shopper at Barneys!* Here I was—sad, yes, but still able to chuckle when appropriate, still able to wedge into my relatively slinky jeans. I felt as miscast as I did in my rural high school when I played Yente in an all-WASP production of *Fiddler on the Roof.* Applying the word *widow* to *me* seemed . . . unseemly. Rude.

I cast about for possible young-widow role models. There was the dour Queen Victoria, preserving Prince Albert's things as if he might pop back in for tea at a moment's notice. Or the other extreme, Scarlett O'Hara, branded an unfeeling slut for dancing at a ball after her husband died. I decided I should aspire to the impossible grace of Jackie Kennedy while trying to avoid the pitfalls of Jackie Onassis.

Signals from my friends were as mixed as my own jumbled emotions. Some seemed to expect me to live out my life as Our Lady of Perpetual Sorrows. Others promoted casual sex as if it were the new wonder drug from Merck. Should I jump a grief counselor or take up knitting? Cat around or get a cat?

When I made an effort to drag myself to an office picnic or dinner with a college roommate, I recognized that no one knew how to behave in the presence of a young widow, and even more disconcerting, neither did I. Those who weren't tongue-tied might blurt out something wildly inappropriate like, "Don't worry, you're young, you're blonde—you'll find another man."

Everyone from close friends to total strangers started sizing up my desirability and feeling free to comment on it. "Your ass looks amazing in those jeans" became something I heard nearly as often as "I'm sorry for your loss." Nobody, aside from Bernie, had noticed my ass in twenty years. Now it looked as if all the stuff from high school—looks, popularity, condoms—might matter again. It was surreal to contemplate that my entire future happiness might rest on the contours of my behind.

Among my mostly married contemporaries, I felt like a freak. My friends wanted badly to be helpful, and they were. But we were out of sync. It wasn't their fault that they were already overtaxed, with children, husbands, jobs. Did I mention husbands? My buddies tried to fit me in. At dinners with couples I'd known for years, it was heavy lifting holding up half the conversation without Bernie to carry some of the load. My repertoire of cancer anecdotes didn't make for sparkling material, and I had nothing else going on. Still, I knew I needed to get out. On many, many Saturday nights home alone, I felt like the least popular kid in junior high school.

It was on one of those Saturday nights when I formed the resolution to join a widows' support group. After nearly a year and a half of widowhood, I was ready to "move on" in the words of the grief literature; ready to think, maybe, someday, about dating again, taking some vacations on my own, finding some other unattached people to hang out with on the weekend. What I needed, I decided, were knowledgeable guides. I hoped the widows in the support group might help me sort it all out. Those fellow castaways to the land of the grieving might be the only people I knew who could speak my language, show me the customs. They might have discovered the tricks I didn't know—how to change that lightbulb above the kitchen cabinet, or make small talk at that wedding where I was marooned at a table with the geriatric and infirm. How to keep making things happen, necessary things, when I could barely manage to make breakfast. After I got kicked out, I was more confused than ever, utterly flummoxed about what to try next.

I wasn't very good at the role of decorous widow, so I fixed on what I was good at—being a reporter, in essence, finding out about stuff and then writing about it. Only now I wanted to find out what I needed to learn most for myself: How does a human being remake a life when it's shattered by loss?

———

TALKING TO DR. GOLDENBERG, the psychiatrist who helped Bernie during the last months of his life, was a logical first step. He was young, articulate, and well informed, and I knew he specialized in patients with cancer and HIV. He would be up on the latest thinking about people and death. And much as I dreaded meeting him in his East Side office and sitting in the same upholstered wing chair where Bernie had sat, hemmed in by the same bookshelves filled with the same soothing Asian art, more than anything I wanted to learn what Goldenberg knew about this perplexing state of bereavement that I now inhabited.

"You look about as I'd expect." He greeted me with welcome candor, no doubt taking in my freefall weight loss, the sacks under my eyes.

"That's refreshing," I said, lowering myself gingerly into the armchair that had been Bernie's and pulling a notebook out of my bag. "Everybody keeps telling me what a babe I am now."

"People want you to feel better right away," he said. He sat opposite me in an ergonomic chair and switched into his soft, professional psychiatrist voice. "Unfortunately, there's no shortcut." A therapeutic silence filled the room as he waited for me to continue.

"I don't expect a shortcut," I countered. I switched into my professional voice, too. "I know I have to plug along this road on my own. But I don't seem to be following any map. Like the five stages of grief—I can't seem to get the hang of it."

"There *are* no five stages of grief," Goldenberg said sharply. "They're a complete misconception. Elisabeth Kübler-Ross studied people who were dying, not people who were grieving. People who are grieving don't necessarily follow any particular pattern."

"You're kidding me!" I said. "At my support group we had hand-outs! I thought we'd be tested on them later!"

"Somehow, the stages of grief have lodged in the popular consciousness." Goldenberg shrugged. "Even many professionals buy into them."

I nodded slowly. It made sense that these emotions might emerge in a person facing his own death. Denial—of course, Bernie had been incredulous at what was happening to him. Bargaining—yes, we tried everything to forestall the end. Anger—sure, it was tough to accept the unfairness of it. Depression—understandable. And acceptance—ideally, perhaps, a person would want to die at peace with his fate, although I can't say that Bernie achieved that stage. Why should he?

The truth is, scientists had begun a serious study of grieving only in the last few years, Goldenberg said. "They say that the emotions of loss and sadness come in waves, and that the waves become less intense over time."

"That explains why I'm weepy one minute and finding something funny the next."

"Exactly."

I told him about the nightmares and flashbacks. "Are those normal, too?"

"More than you'd think," he said. "Many people worry about succumbing to depression after someone they love has died. But trauma is more common than depression among people who are bereaved. You probably suffer from some degree of post-traumatic stress disorder."

Just what I need, I thought. "But I haven't exactly been waging war in Afghanistan."

"No, but in some ways you and Bernie were in the trenches, bullets whizzing around you," Goldenberg said.

The comparison was extreme, but it made sense, too. I thought briefly about the sorts of excruciating medical interventions Bernie had endured. The toll on those left behind can be traumatic, I knew too well. Visions of robot surgeons and failed rescues from drownings didn't seem much worse than what I had witnessed in broad daylight before he died. I was reliving the horror now in my mind, again and again.

"Also, while you were at war, so to speak, you were surrounded by people who were living a normal life," Goldenberg said. "You were living a double life, and that makes it difficult to adapt. You still are . . . everybody around you is continuing normally while you go through this traumatic experience of loss."

"What should people who are traumatized do?" I asked.

I scribbled on my pad as he answered. It used to be that trauma victims were encouraged to talk about the events that had triggered their condition, to get it out of their systems. But now researchers into post-traumatic stress were concluding that talking about trauma, or even thinking about it too much, can reinforce disturbing memories. "When you have the intrusive thoughts, the nightmares, the flashbacks," he said, "push them aside."

"I thought I was supposed to talk it through. Getting it out there was supposed to help me come to terms with all this. That's why I tried a support group," I said.

"Did it help?" he asked, giving me a knowing look. "Support groups aren't for everybody. Sometimes if there are people in the group who are angry or upset, it can magnify negative emotions for everyone. You can come out angrier, more unhappy, than you went in. It's good to spend time with people who understand you, but not necessarily good to be forced to discuss something that's traumatizing you."

"Isn't that what you do for a living? Get people to talk about what's bothering them? Are you trying to put yourself out of business?"

He looked more amused than solicitous. "I treat people who need therapy," he said. "You are grieving normally."

I felt a burden lift, the burden of conforming to my sorry stereotype of a proper widow. A small smile appeared on his lips, mirroring mine. "You are not depressed," he said. "You don't have it in you."

chapter

SIX

*t*urns out, I wasn't such a misfit after all.

But I didn't take his word for it. My visit with Dr. Goldenberg gave me the first solid evidence that the script I was
following didn't have to play out like some creaky Victorian melodrama. In fact, when I started reading more about bereavement,
I saw that many of our culture's most misguided notions about it
began during that hidebound era, when the widowed forty-two-
year-old queen set the standard for acceptable widow behavior, living out the next thirty-nine years of her life in partial seclusion,
swathed head-to-toe in black.

Well, widow this, Victoria, I thought, feeling oh-so-twenty-first-
century, when I found myself in a spare white room at Columbia
University, punching buttons like a *Jeopardy!* contestant in front of
a computer screen. I had turned up in the university's Loss, Trauma,
and Emotion Lab, epicenter of the latest research, where a team of
experimental psychologists was challenging the once-entrenched
canons of the field. It was my first step toward assembling my

own highly unscientific Saturday night widows' group. But first I wanted to gather a little highly scientific background information, to base the plan on something more substantial than my own defiant hunch. For three hours, I let a couple of doctoral students monitor my facial expressions; time my reactions to happy, sad, or disturbing photographs; challenge me with subliminal messages about Bernie; and generally mess with my head.

I had come there to learn more about what science had to say about how people negotiate the difficult waters of grief and renewal, and I liked what I found. These scientists were conducting research based on evidence from real people like me, and they were concluding that most of the assumptions I'd been contending with up to now weren't true. According to the researchers, losing a loved one is a normal transition in everyone's life. Always has been. Therefore, most of us, they said, possess emotional resources and natural resilience that help us rejuvenate after such a loss, just as we remake ourselves after other setbacks in life. In fact, the process looks nothing like the long-term, debilitating sadness that many seem to expect. The process can even bring new insight and new joy.

One of the experiments I performed, for example, was designed to determine whether I could manage my emotions well enough to lead a normal life or whether I had feelings of grief so severe that they interfered with my ability to function. In front of a computer screen, I focused on a series of photographs of people showing a wide range of emotions—fear, happiness, sadness, horror, surprise. After each picture appeared, a dot showed up on the left or right side of the screen, and I pressed a button to show where I had seen it. Apparently, my reaction times could be affected by the emotions I saw in the photographs. Subjects suffering from prolonged, dysfunctional grief are distracted by the sad photos to the point that it interferes with the assigned task.

What I didn't find out until later was that the screen was also flashing me messages, too fast for me to perceive consciously but long enough to register. Sometimes, the message might have been Bernie's name, or sometimes his name coupled with words relating to loss, words like *separation* or *death*. People with unresolved grief apparently get thrown by these reminders of the people they've lost. People with more functional grief do not, or may sometimes even draw comfort from the names of lost loved ones.

My head was reeling by the time the man in charge of these inquiries met me in the lab, and it didn't improve my equilibrium when I saw what he was wearing: an untucked yellow short-sleeve shirt with an acid-trip pattern of random lines. George Bonanno, a spiky-haired professor of psychology at Columbia and the author of many of the most forward-thinking studies on human bereavement and trauma, wasn't at all what I expected in a grief guru. He offered me a cup of tea as he led me into his office.

"How did you wind up doing this?" I asked.

Bonanno's doctorate in psychology focused on experimental work, but when he was offered a job studying bereavement, he blanched. "I didn't want to do it," he said in a light, slightly raspy voice. "It seemed creepy—you know, gross, old people."

But the scientist in him was tantalized when he realized that no one had applied the sort of rigorous methodology to normal grief that had been employed in the study of other human behavior. "The bereavement literature was woefully out of date," he said. "I wondered where they were getting all these ideas from. And the more I looked into it, the more it became clear that there was no evidence for them."

As a newcomer to the field, Bonanno had no preconceived notions to overcome, and he quickly concluded that most of the notions that were out there before were plain wrong, the Kübler-Ross five stages chief among them. What Dr. Goldenberg had told me was true. Kübler-Ross had posited her theory based on observations of people who were dying, not people who were grieving, and even she didn't regard the stages as some sort of rigid, step-by-step program.

Bonanno and others began to conduct the first painstaking studies of thousands of actual grieving people, following them over time, comparing some of them before and after their losses. Sometimes he'd quiz them while monitoring skin temperatures, breathing, heart rates, facial expressions, fidgeting, or reaction times, as the lab workers did in the experiment with me. He concentrated on people who had lost their spouses and were under age fifty-five, as I was, so he could exclude emotional issues that were unique to aging. His seemingly audacious findings scandalized traditionalists at first, but his scrupulous methodology gradually won them over.

It was easy to buy into what Bonanno was saying, a consolation, even. What he and others were learning about living with loss sounded familiar: It was just what I'd been going through. And it ran counter to many common cultural assumptions, unsupported by facts, that I'd been buying into, assumptions that had been holding me back.

First off, he told me, no one experiences grief in rigid stages. Early in the grieving process, people oscillate between sadness and normality, just as I had, and just as Dr. Goldenberg had told me people do. Over time, the swings become less frequent and less extreme. My ability to crack up with laughter in some of the darkest moments wasn't shameful—it was natural, and helpful, too.

Humor, Bonanno said, is one of the strongest predictors of an eventual return to emotional equilibrium.

Second, there's the misconception that grief is a paralyzing sadness, a despair so overwhelming that it's difficult to return to a normal life, sometimes for many years—or forever. It's what I'd come to call the Queen Victoria syndrome. This misconception, in which grief is regarded as practically a form of mental illness, maybe requiring professional help, is widely held, said Bonanno, but it's never been subject to systematic study. In fact, he has found, most people cope with losses fine on their own.

In one large study, about half of widows or widowers showed little evidence of clinical depression six months after losing their spouses, and two-thirds were in the clear after eighteen months. Only sixteen percent of those in the study who were not depressed before became depressed after the loss. Experts have come to use the term *complicated grief* for the minority of people who suffer an unrelieved yearning that intrudes on everyday coping. For such people, a loss can be shattering, but they are not the norm.

"Most people are resilient," Bonanno said. "Almost everybody suffers—you can't get away from that. But we're wired to do this suffering naturally. It's ridiculous to think otherwise. Because losses are inevitable."

He poured himself another cup of tea and nestled it in his hands, leaning forward. "Only ten thousand years ago, human beings were nomadic," he said. "When you're nomadic, you don't have months to sit around and mope. The tribe moves on."

All the more reason, he said, to reject another long-established theory once embraced by psychologists, psychiatrists, grief counselors, and just about everybody who offered me advice after Bernie died. That theory holds that it's necessary to dwell on the harsh and painful emotions surrounding a loved one's demise, disgorging them through repeated talk. Therapists call this *grief work*, and it can be heavy lifting indeed. Anyone who didn't perform this chore was considered to be in denial, vulnerable to some sort of booby-trapped delayed reaction years in the future. But new research, Bonanno said, shows that people who are well adjusted shortly after a loss are almost always fine years later. "Delayed grief just doesn't exist."

This is especially true for people who suffer from trauma, a central focus of his research. The standard thinking used to be that it was helpful to "debrief" people after a traumatic experience, to encourage them to review disturbing events by repeating them aloud or writing them down. Had I followed this advice, I would have devoted myself to cataloging The Top Ten Traumatic Moments of Bernie's illness, straining to recall every detail. In fact, the research shows—and it makes sense when you think about it—that keeping searing or frightening thoughts ever-present can lead into Our Lady of Perpetual Sorrows territory and make it even harder to conjure up happier, more sustaining memories. Why obsess about Bernie waking in pain from cancer surgery when I could summon him reading the Sunday paper? The same logic applies to support groups—forced sharing of unpleasant memories with other wretched people can make somebody even more wretched. Good old-fashioned repression, it seems, is underrated.

I told Bonanno about my support group fiasco, and he grimaced. "God, that sounds awful," he said. "Support groups that are sadfests are the worst. But that's not unusual. Because when we witness people who are encouraged to express sadness and anguish, we're wired to have a comparable emotion."

"But the loss of a partner *is* devastating," I said.

"Yes, it's a powerful experience. It dramatically shifts our perspective on life." But we are all equipped with emotional tools to make that shift, he said. "Sadness, for example, helps us to turn our attention inward, which we must do to take stock." And looking sad is a compelling signal to others that we need help, drawing them to our side in a crisis. It was the primary impetus, I suppose, behind all those fruit baskets and the compliments about my butt. Even anger, when appropriate, he added, can be functional, allowing the newly vulnerable to stand up for themselves in shifting social situations. As in, "Hey, stop looking at my ass."

Bonanno mentioned another common misconception—the idea that it's helpful to indulge in a serious, long-term wallow after someone dies. "It is adaptive to spend *some* time processing your loss," he said, "but to focus on your grief *all* the time is harmful." People who can modulate their emotions, who can suppress their melancholy thoughts for a time in order to go to a movie or perform at work, for example, can return to normality sooner. And while friends will be supportive of sadness for a while, in time, someone who is an unrelieved sad sack will drive supporters away. It's better to be able to experience some pleasure, even in the worst times.

So what about me? How was I coping? I was burning to know what he'd learned from my hours in the lab, but Bonanno couldn't say. The research was designed to draw conclusions about large groups, he told me, not to diagnose individuals. But there was something I wanted to know even more. "What are the principles that help people like me?"

The good stuff, he said. Flexibility. Humor. Positive experiences. *New* experiences. Bonds with friends. "When people have lost someone, they want to feel connected to other people," Bonanno said. "People want to share some kind of experience and adapt with each other."

"It sounds to me," I said, "like this is the bottom line: if you want to help somebody overcome a loss, you should take her out and show her a good time."

Bonanno laughed. "Not a bad idea." Then he said something that stuck with me: "Grief is a process of finding comfort. It doesn't have to be painful all the time."

I'd been reading a lot of the new research before this meeting, using it to cook up my scheme for an unconventional widows' group. I hadn't planned to share this quixotic plan with Bonanno. Seriously, what would somebody with a wall of diplomas and a couple million dollars in government grants think of an amateur idea from me, somebody who couldn't remember the beginning psych course she'd taken in college? But I took a flier and brought it up.

"It wouldn't be the least bit scientific," I said. "It would be the blind leading the blind. Or at least the bereaved leading the bereaved."

"Nobody's ever studied this," he said, without a hint of academic snobbery. "It's exciting. If the goal of the group is to sit around complaining, that's not good. But if it's to find other ways to share emotion, to build a connection to other people—that could be very positive."

━━━━━━━

BACK ON THE SUBWAY, I considered what I'd learned, itching to bust out into the real world to see if I could put the concepts into practice. I quickly cobbled together a strategy. I would assemble a group of women like myself, women like most of us, as science had now told me, determined to reclaim our lives. We would be guided by equal parts common sense and the principles I now understood for what truly helps those who have become uncoupled: friendship, fun, humor, the flexibility to strike out anew. We'd offer each other the companionship of a traditional support group without the gloom—doing, not talking.

The first step would be to choose some widows ready to move beyond the sharp pain of early grief. According to what I'd read and heard, most grieving people aren't ready to think about much aside from themselves for about the first six months, when they're busy looking inward and taking stock. That's why most support groups, beginning in the early weeks after a death, turn into the sadfests Bonanno was talking about. I decided to look for women who had been widowed anywhere from six months to two years, ready to leave behind the sadness while craving support for the inevitable changes ahead.

I wish I could say that my selection process was more methodical, but I'm not kidding when I say that my project was unscientific. Young widows are rare, so I basically asked around, buttonholing people at work, at parties, practically strangers on the street. I met Tara first, through a real estate agent who had been showing her possible houses to buy. Marcia turned up through a widow who led formal support groups—Marcia had asked if she had heard of any for younger women. Colleagues from work referred me to Dawn and Denise. "You'll like her," said the woman who knew Dawn. "She's a force of nature." A friend of a friend who ran a travel company told me about Lesley, who had gone on a recent trip to India. My sample was more slapdash even than random. But given the women's various backgrounds, I decided, it added up to a kind of Everywoman, although one who'd had some lousy luck.

Along the way, I encountered one widow I decided not to invite. Melissa's problems seemed too tricky for the rest of us, her state too perilous for amateurs like me. When I went to meet her, she picked me up in her car at the train station in her town, and I felt unsettled as soon as I slid into the front seat. There was a photograph of her husband taped to the center of the steering wheel, where she could see it as she drove.

"How long has your husband been gone?" I asked cautiously.

"Four years," she said. She was only forty-nine, a mother of three, but still she had a dull-eyed, fixed expression of sorrow, a sign of the complicated grief that I had heard about at the lab.

As we entered her home, a banner over the door said, *Welcome Home Daddy.* Inside her kitchen, nearly every surface—walls, refrigerator door, ceiling beams—displayed more photos of her husband, and Melissa walked me through them. "This was before he was diagnosed," she said. "This one was after the chemo. See? He put on weight."

Bonanno had warned me that an extraordinary number of photos of the deceased could indicate an inability to adapt, but this shook me nevertheless. Worst of all, no matter what I asked Melissa about herself, her past, or her plans, she turned the conversation back to the day her husband died, in all its piercing detail. Not surprisingly, most of her friends had fallen away.

"At first there were triggers that would send me into a vortex, and I couldn't get out for hours," she said. "Now I can get myself out. But I still get enormous physical pangs."

She said she was seeing a therapist for help. I had no clue how to cope with her, not that she seemed to want me to. She seemed barely to register that I was there. Meeting her was a warning to me not to take grief lightly. It had the power to destroy.

The other women I met could not have been more different. They were mourning, but their moods cycled through the quicksilver changes that I recognized from myself. And something else— I liked them, right away, something no laboratory could quantify.

So I extended the invitation. We would see whether we all found what we were seeking—adventure, companionship, understanding, a more cheerful way to spend a Saturday night. What had Professor Bonanno said? "Grief is a process of finding comfort." Maybe we'd find that.

chapter

SEVEN

*W*e began by finding our rhythm.

Lesley and Dawn were so hooked into a groove that they were cutting loose in giddy riffs. It was the Saturday night of our second meeting, a private cooking class that was spinning off into free-form silliness. Those two, tapping away with their knives on some innocent celery stalks, were the only two women I knew who could find the sexual innuendo in rice pilaf.

"It's all about the rhythm," Lesley trilled, bouncing in time to the knife work.

"Let's see that rhythm, girl." Dawn boogalooed along. "Up... down... up... down..." She dissolved into giggles, then elbowed Lesley and turned fake serious. "It scares me that you and I are always on the same page here."

We had invaded the kitchen of Lauren, a chef and cookbook author, who must have felt like Miss Molly trying to keep order in *Romper Room*. Dawn, vamping it up in a low-cut sweater under her apron, her showy glamour a magnet for attention, and Lesley, her naughty sense of humor fully deployed, were clearly the class cutups. It sounded like a flock of woodpeckers had landed as we practiced our chopping techniques around a central workstation, smacking down stalks of celery to flatten them out and dicing them into tiny bits on our cutting boards. Very therapeutic.

Lauren, no doubt expecting what most people do from a group of recent widows, didn't seem to know what to make of our guerrilla group. "I want us to talk about cooking," she pleaded, barely loud enough to be heard over the chatter.

We'd already heard the reason for Lesley and Dawn's exuberance. In the month since our first gathering, Lesley had moved into the new house she'd bought, the biggest decision she'd ever made on her own. Almost instinctively, she followed up by impulsively asking Craig, the guy she'd started dating the summer before, to move in with her. She was keeping house again, and she was ecstatic about it. Dawn had high hopes of her own, having met a promising widower with two kids the same ages as hers. The two women couldn't contain their high spirits long enough to knuckle down in class.

If Dawn and Lesley were the Don't-Bes, Marcia was the Do-Be, diligently hacking away as per Lauren's instructions. Marcia hadn't wasted any time letting Lauren know her level of skill in the kitchen (nil) and her level of interest (less than nil). Nevertheless, she applied herself with steam-driven concentration, extra credit for trying at all.

"My husband was the cook," she said with characteristic bluntness. "I don't cook. I make breakfast."

Marcia had all of her other meals delivered, and she ate them alone when she got home from lawyering at ten or eleven every night. Yet she persevered with slow if determined chopping, stolid in her sturdy jeans and stiff linen work shirt. I entertained the possibility that Marcia, as intimidating as I found her to be, might also be something I hadn't expected: a good sport.

I gave myself some points, too, for bringing off this evening at all. No one had bailed on this enterprise after our first get-together. In fact, they had all told me that they felt as jazzed up as I had afterward, invigorated by the company of others who could read some of their thoughts and finish some of their sentences. In the four weeks since, Dawn had come into the city from New Jersey for a gossipy one-on-one dinner with Tara, and then a more sober one with Denise. "Human beings are just incredible," she told me when we spoke on the phone. "What we endure and how we move forward! These women are so inspiring to me."

This February night, everyone had made it to Lauren's suburban house through the slushy residue of a snowstorm. Everyone except Tara. The weather had waylaid her at a stopover in the Houston airport. I got a text message as we piled through Lauren's front door and shook the snow off our boots: *so sorry. best to all, xo T.* I worried out loud that maybe she wouldn't stick with the group, especially after her hesitation at the first go-round.

"She wanted this companionship most of all," Lesley reassured me. "She just wanted us to know that whatever she does now, she does on her own terms. I understand it after everything she's been through."

Once our hostess put us to work, I relaxed into the evening, feeling little of the anxiety of our first encounter. The group had made it through the hardest part, our backstories already revealed. This one would be easy. Easier. We'd pick up some cooking techniques as we prepared dinner, and then enjoy a good gossip as we polished off the results.

As an engaging theme for one of our first Saturday nights, I thought, we couldn't do better than food. If grief is a search for comfort, food was comfort itself, nurturing, sustaining, both a carnal pleasure and essential for life. This group needed nurturing, and maybe some carnal pleasure, too—these widows had appetites. It would be useful to learn to make some simple, delicious dishes as a treat for one or an entertainment for others. And food was universal. Despite the various personalities on vivid display in that kitchen, we all had to eat. Simple, right?

As the lesson progressed, though, I felt a growing disquiet whenever I stole a look at Denise. Her inscrutable composure had helped me hold on to mine at our first meeting. Yet tonight she was keeping to herself, at a cautious remove from the banter and horseplay. She quietly chopped and whisked on command, and smiled as if she had sat and practiced it, but her usually mindful presence seemed unsettled, far away.

"Do you like to cook?" I asked her, trying to draw her in.

"I love it," she answered dutifully. "I loved cooking for Steve. But now that he's gone, I've quit cooking, and I've quit eating." There was that smile again as if to soften the message, and then she turned her full attention to stacking her chopped vegetables in a neat Lego-like pile on her cutting board.

Denise, I had noticed before, often displayed the same courteous smile, especially when she was saying something sad. She smiled with her mouth, but her pale, wide-set eyes seemed far away. It was a considerate smile, self-effacing. It seemed to be saying, *Please don't feel obligated to be sad on my behalf. Look here. See? I'm smiling.* Only she wasn't, not in a heartfelt way.

I looked more closely. Her porcelain complexion looked as faded as bone, and even under a loose tunic and trademark yoga pants, she looked thin. Not frail—all those hours of yoga had granted her a supple strength—but there seemed to be less of her this time.

I worried that our unfettered repartee was too much, too soon, too *too* for Denise. Her husband had died at the end of August, and this was only February. I had resolved not to invite anyone to join our group if she was still suffering through the early months of grief, but I had made an exception with her. She seemed so centered, so serene, so in command of herself that I thought she might be ready to re-engage with the world faster than most. She was also the youngest, not even forty. Whether that rendered her more resilient or more tender, I couldn't know.

———

I COULDN'T KID MYSELF, either. Denise was the most recently wounded, and I had seen the signs of it the first time we met, when I asked her to consider participating in my group. She had invited me to her apartment one evening only two months after her husband died. Denise displayed the same measured grace even then, but the expressions on her face were what captured my attention most. When she wasn't turning on that wan smile, when her face was at rest, I could have been looking into a mirror at myself during my earliest days of loss. It was a spot-on impression of a grieving person that I'd seen in some writings by scientists like Professor Bonanno: the face literally sagging, the eyebrows knitted together and raised up, forming a triangle, the jaw slack, the lower lip drawn out and down. "Whether we are aware of it or not, this expression is a compelling signal to others that we may need help," Bonanno wrote. I had brought Denise some take-out food, and it was all I could do not to go all Jewish mother on her and spoon it right into her mouth. I couldn't help myself—I wanted to help. She said she didn't feel like eating, so instead we settled in her big empty living room.

"I've been on the Widow Tour," Denise told me. She flicked on that polite smile for my benefit. Practically everyone she knew had stopped by or asked her out for lunch or drinks or dinner, asking, "How *are* you? Is there anything I can *do*?"

"It was the same with me," I said. "People asked what they could do on a daily basis, but I could never think of anything. It was much better when they suggested something concrete. One of my friends offered to help me write thank-you notes, which was a godsend. I couldn't string two words together myself."

"That was considerate." Denise said she appreciated the kindness, all the invitations, but they were exhausting. "I have to master this performance of being somewhat pulled together, and I have to talk about the particulars," she said. "And my short-term memory is shot, so I can't remember what to ask about what's going on with anybody else."

"Yes, I was just the same!" I said. "I sounded like Mrs. Elton in *Emma*. It was all about me. Or else I'd be sitting there thinking how I've got to say something, anything, but my mind was a blank."

"People want to be kind, but if they are people I don't know particularly well, it's very wearing."

Maybe that included me—we'd just met, after all—but the

"widow" entry on my résumé seemed to grant me diplomatic im-
munity, so we plunged into the dreaded particulars, taking the scenic route through Denise's early life first. Her father, a headmaster
at various private schools, moved the family around a lot—Florida,
Germany, Minnesota. It was there where a tragedy redirected her
childhood when Denise was twelve. Her brother, one year younger
than Denise, died suddenly of a brain aneurysm. Then, over the
next three months, her mother had surgery for thyroid cancer,
after which Denise's grandfather contracted stomach cancer and
died. Denise related these facts to me patiently, without adorn-
ment, without any reference to their effect on her. It was as if she
had been a spectator in a family defined by sudden heartbreak. I
suspected that it was during that three-month period and its aftermath when she perfected a skill at containment, a talent for not
bothering anyone.

"My brother and Steve had the same birthday," Denise said. It
took me a moment to register that Steve was her husband. Denise's
gaze turned inward as she slipped out of our conversation into a
hazy, preoccupied state, her stare fixed on something far away. I
recognized this, too, from Bonanno's description of typical grieving behavior and from my own memories of swinging in and out
of focus after Bernie died. I gave her time to reconnect before I
prompted her to continue.

Denise's response to the tragedy of a brother's shocking death
seemed to be to strive for achievement and perfection in herself,
deflecting attention by never causing a fuss. When she was sixteen,
a teacher suggested she go straight to college, and so she did, never
finishing high school. "It was a good thing for me to start over,"
she said.

She met Steve on an otherwise unpromising day when she moved into an apartment in a brownstone on the Upper West Side. Under her door, she got an invitation to a welcome-to-the-building party, but when she showed up, she was the only guest of an unemployed guy who looked like a member of ZZ Top and kept his shades drawn against the daylight. Single life at its worst.

As consolation, a friend took her out to the All State Café. It was a classic dive bar in the neighborhood, home to a mellow crowd, a jukebox blasting out "Wild Horses" and bartenders with nicknames like Uncle Gig and The Shark. Decades of residue from greasy cuisine coated the dull brick walls, and illegal smoke drifted under hanging lamps dimmed by shades of dark green glass. It was the kind of place where conversations with strangers took care of themselves. Steve, there with friends, spotted Denise risking an order of nachos with her wine.

He asked her about her camera, a Canon ELPH that she'd placed on the table.

"You probably think I'm old-fashioned, because I still shoot with film, not digital," she said. Of such lines are romances born.

Steve was a professional photographer and a film fanatic, too. Before he left, he took some pictures of Denise with his ever-present Leica. A couple days later, their first date made a detour into home improvement when he stopped at her new place to pick her up and saw that her electrical outlets were shooting sparks. He rewired all the outlets. "Now you're safe," he said.

They never made it out of the apartment that night. Nor on the next date, when she had a cold and he brought her flowers and juice. Denise, the girl who had grown up too fast, reveled in being cared for.

That was August. By December, they were engaged. By the next

August they had moved into the apartment of their striving dreams, a neglected mess when they bought it, but with great bones. Steve bought them unisex uniforms, matching coveralls made from stiff gray cotton, and they changed into them when they replaced the wiring, rehung the doors, or installed new ceiling fans. Gradually, they turned the apartment into the showplace the group saw at our first meeting. The next summer they married in a simple ceremony with thirty friends. The decorations were blowups of the photographs Steve took of Denise the day they met.

They hoped their next project would be to have a child. But the following August, a year after the wedding, Steve was gone. "We only got three years, pretty much to the day," she said. That smile again, briefly, and then another moment lost in introspection.

At five thirty in the morning on the day he died, Steve woke Denise and said he wasn't feeling well. She listened from bed as he went into the shower, and when he came out, she heard a crash in the hallway. Denise ran out. He gasped out his last words—"Help me"—and collapsed on the floor.

"I knew he was dead," Denise said. She called 911 and began CPR, but he didn't respond. Ambulance workers arrived, too late. Police treated her apartment like a crime scene, leaving his body there all day, covered, while they waited for the medical examiner to take it away for an autopsy, required in the case of an unexplained death of such a young person. Steve had been fifty. Once again, Denise kept to the facts in telling me this story, periodically smiling her don't-worry-about-me smile.

Somehow she had the composure to speak without notes at the funeral. "I couldn't speak at Bernie's," I said. "I didn't think I had the strength. That took nerve."

"Or just adrenaline. I felt like I had to. It was my only chance."

Afterward, wallowing in grief was not an option. Denise had started a job as a senior editor at a publishing house only six months before. Bad timing—it takes at least two years to prove oneself as an editor, and none of her books would come out for another year or more. The pressure was on to find successful books and edit them quickly. She couldn't let up, forcing herself to concentrate on reading entire manuscripts at a stage of widowhood when I could barely follow a paragraph in the newspaper. I had been able to get by on my salary, but for Denise, the near-impossible burden of paying the mortgage by herself loomed. She stopped eating. She stopped sleeping. Yoga classes helped her hold herself together. They were tranquil, familiar, conducted in the presence of others, but somehow private, too. And she was good at yoga. It gave her a crucial sense of mastery when her husband was lost and everything else that mattered—job, home, bank account—was hanging by a thread.

Meanwhile, her striking outward composure led people to make the strangest comments. Some acquaintance said, "Now you can go out and have sex with whoever you want," which defied all explanation. Or this: "Don't you find it disgusting that he died right in your apartment?" And another weird one: "You'll see, in six months you'll be pregnant."

"It provoked a lot of self-analysis," Denise said. "Have I ever said anything like that to anyone? Ugh, I hope not."

Impressed by her equilibrium, I invited Denise to join the group. And after the first meeting, everyone else told me they admired her self-possession as much as I did. It hadn't occurred to me that a cooking class might cause her distress. But what happened that Saturday night at the cooking class would make me doubt what I knew about Denise, about widows, about what constitutes comfort in or out of the kitchen.

LAUREN, OUR TEACHER, was eager to embrace our widow-hood dilemmas. She had devised a menu with all that in mind.

"It's unfortunate when people don't feel entitled to cook unless they have another body around," she said. She handed each of us an apron in her impeccably equipped kitchen, punctuating a relentlessly buoyant tone with the gestures of a majorette. A rambunctious Labrador retriever, Mango, fishtailed wildly around our knees. "Eating and sharing and smelling good food cooking are incredible pleasures in life."

Marcia tied on an apron with a brisk tug. "That dog needs a sedative," she said.

Lauren scooted Mango out the swinging door and described the menu. All the recipes, from lamb chops slathered with a chunky fresh tomato salsa to fudgy chocolate-chocolate chip cookies—just about the right amount of chocolate, as far as I'm concerned—were designed to teach basic skills: measuring, chopping, braising, and grilling. We could make any of the dishes for one or for a crowd, helping us repay the awkward social debts to people inviting us out on the Widow Tour.

First we mixed cookie batter, a deep, decadent chocolate hash made more sophisticated with hints of cinnamon and espresso. It was Lesley's job to roll the dough into logs. Lauren explained that they could be stored frozen that way, ready at short notice to be cut into individual cookies, the better to accommodate a widow treating herself to a fresh-baked indulgence on her own. She could also pop the whole batch into the oven at once for a party of friends, or mainline the entire stash in one orgiastic bender, I thought, a perfectly plausible option that went unmentioned. Lesley pulled up the sleeves of her silk blouse and made a show of stroking and caressing the mixture into a long, smooth cylinder, seizing the opportunity for bawdy repartee.

Widowed the longest, aside from me, Lesley seemed to take it as her duty to set an example, to demonstrate that a widow doesn't have to be a saint. She also seemed to have gotten the memo from George Bonanno that humor is the best balm for grief, and Dawn was only too happy to follow that lead. High spirits aside, I saw that they were both competent cooks. After years of meal prep for their families, they had the most confidence and the loosest posture, joshing and wielding their tools with abandon as the room filled with the tantalizing scent of baking chocolate and we turned to chopping onions, smashing garlic cloves, and whisking salad dressing. Marcia and I, more accustomed to surviving on takeout, mimicked Lauren's motions with serious concentration in an effort not to embarrass ourselves. Only Denise, with that Mona Lisa smile, remained impossible to read.

We stationed ourselves at cutting boards while Lauren circled us like a border collie, prodding us with suggestions and correcting our techniques. "Keep your shoulders down when you chop," Lauren advised me. "And brace your belly against the counter." Hands busy, we slipped easily in and out of cooking and widow talk, and I took pleasure in the group's enjoyment. When I had visited George Bonanno's emotions lab, the researchers analyzed my expressions, looking for what is called a Duchenne smile, named after a French anatomist who discovered that true, happy smiles always involve contracting the muscles around the eyes. It's an involuntary crinkling absent from polite, deliberate smiles, and noticeably absent from Denise that night. Bonanno found that the more widows laughed and smiled these genuine smiles, the better they would feel during the early years of bereavement.

Lesley and Dawn would have satisfied Monsieur Duchenne handily, Lesley with her constant look of merry surprise, Dawn with her easy, buoyant laugh. Marcia's smiles were far more difficult to discern—no eye crinkling, just an infinitesimal upturn of one side of her mouth. Her face barely moved at all. I didn't know whether Marcia was still grieving intensely, or whether she had always been someone who held her emotions with a tight fist. She kept her distance from the hijinks—hijinks were not Marcia's thing—but that tease of a smile hinted that she might be amused by others performing them.

At least she was picking up the rhythm of the class. With Denise, the beat was off. While she steered clear of the conversation and made her best effort to remain unobtrusive, our teacher stepped in often with advice and corrections.

"Try holding the whisk lower down on the handle." Lauren gripped her hand over Denise's to demonstrate. Denise complied obediently. A minute later, Lauren returned. "You see, you are in much more control. When you do it like this, you become much less timid."

"I'm not timid," Denise said, quietly.

"You need to get down farther on the handle again," Lauren said brightly.

"Get down, get down," Lesley sang, gyrating along.

"I'm getting distracted by the commentary over here," Denise said crisply.

The more Lauren intervened, the more disconnected Denise became. Was it the class? Was it us? Something was rattling her.

"Let me show you this," Lauren said later, when Denise was chopping celery.

"I'm doing it wrong again?" She smiled, her eyebrows still in the woebegone position.

"I think what you need to do is slice it a little closer together."

"I can't do it that way." Denise kept working without further explanation. I said nothing but kicked myself for pressing Denise into a Saturday night of enforced activity when she probably would have preferred a solitary yoga marathon at home.

"Maybe it's because you're left-handed," Lauren concluded, moving on. She addressed us in the spirit of a pep rally. "You guys are doing great! I have to tell you, I'm so proud of you all. You are doing amazing!"

Denise cut out the chopping, raised her eyes to meet Lauren's, and smiled with particular care. "What happens when people aren't doing amazing?" she asked faintly. "What do you say then?"

Our knives stopped tapping and our whisks stopped swirling. Dawn wiped her hands on her apron and chuckled nervously. Lesley leaned over and gave Denise a squeeze.

Lauren, perplexed, said, "I . . . I always say that."

The kitchen filled with a bosky plume of smoke from the lamb chops as we plated the food to carry into the dining room. I untied my apron and stood aside for a moment, watching the scene and thinking about the lesson. Denise seemed to wish she could disappear. And the more she did, the more Lauren tried to make her more visible, to pull her back into the lesson. Lauren couldn't stop trying to help. She seemed to be driven to it, like a herding dog nudging a wayward lamb back to the flock.

Then it hit me—the Help Me look. Those were Steve's last

words, but they also described the expression on Denise's face, the mournful expression that I'd employed once to great effect myself. Lauren was hardwired to react to it, to help Denise any way she could. As long as Denise had that Help Me look, people were going to try to help her, whether it was by sending her fruit baskets, inviting her out on the Widow Tour, offering wacky reassurances about her future, or showing her how to hold a whisk. Human beings are programmed to help those in visible distress. It's an emotional symbiosis, as ingrained as attraction or a mother's care, and it is probably one of the more admirable characteristics of the human race, even though it may not always seem that way to the person on the receiving end of the cooking tips or the Harry & David Deluxe Sympathy Basket With Pears and Havarti Cheese.

Whether she was aware of it or not, Denise was sending the Help Me signal, and people were going to respond. Whether she wanted to or not, she was projecting a message: Take care of me. Make me safe.

chapter

EIGHT

*d*enise broke her silence during dinner, but it wasn't
until afterward that I understood. That all the nour-
ishment on the table could do nothing to fill the void
she was feeling now. That her grief was stronger than I knew. It
humbled me.

Lauren worked overtime to make us comfortable in her family
dining room, her husband banished to the multiplex for the night.
She presided at the head of a long, formal table set as if for a state
dinner, with pink roses and crystal candlesticks. Denise chose a
chair at the opposite end, as far away as possible, and the rest of us
settled along the sides.

Lesley was even more animated than usual, flush with the pleasure of having a new man under her roof again, and while the
ostensible topic for the night was food, she couldn't resist the far
more enticing subject that filled her thoughts. "I'm a homemaker,"
she chatted up Lauren as we began the meal. "That's what my job
is, and I love my job. But after my husband died, I stopped cook-

ing. Now that I've met somebody else, I've been able to experience being in love again in a different way, and I'm cooking again. I've found that part of me again." She radiated such happiness—sitting across from her, I lapped it up.

Caring for a family, Lesley had told me, was her life—her vocation and her joy. I wasn't surprised that she wanted to fill her new house and feed that part of her again. "This is what I do," she said to us. "This is what I do well. It would be a shame to waste it."

Lauren warmed to parallels between cooking and romance. "Cooking is a connective sport," she said. "There are not many things in this world that you make with your own hands and ask somebody to put into their mouth, roll it around, and swallow. How many things are there? That are that intimate?"

Lesley nodded. "This guy thinks I'm so much sexier when I cook for him," she said.

"That's because of what you're thinking about when you're doing all that cooking," said Dawn. They grinned at each other like co-conspirators.

"It's such a gratifying thing. I did it for twenty-seven years, because I loved it and my family enjoyed it. But now, the second time around, the pleasure, the intimacy . . ."

"You lost it and now you're getting it back," said Dawn.

I knew when I started the group that some of our members might fall in love, but I hadn't expected it to happen so soon. I peered around the table to assess how the others were taking the news. Clearly, Dawn was as glad for Lesley as I was. Marcia, inscrutable as ever, was harder to read, and Denise, nearly lost at the distant end—I wondered where this development would leave her.

Lesley's fast-moving love life underscored for me how everyone here was at a different juncture, how there were disparities that could make us root for each other or allow jealousies or resentments to intrude. My plans for this particular Saturday night had been motivated by the connection between food and comfort, but I'd overlooked that there was a flip side to this connection, too. Food shared and food unshared were two entirely different meals. There were those of us who had someone to share their tables— Dawn with her children, for example, and now Lesley with her new love—and those who did not.

"I really am enjoying cooking the second time around," Lesley chattered on. Her husband, like her, had been South African, she said, and South African men, at least back when she got married, tended to expect home-cooked meals from their women. "Now I'm with an American man—he's never seen anything like this. Seriously, I can cook *nothing* and he thinks it's fabulous."

Dawn and I laughed heartily. Dawn's husband had been South African, too, as it happened, so she understood the different mentality. Marcia chuckled, and Denise executed one of her careful smiles.

Thinking of Denise, I asked Lesley how she had felt about food in the early days of her loss, in the more uncertain state where Denise still resided.

"I didn't even want food in my house, and I sure didn't want to cook," Lesley said. At first she lost a ton of weight. But then she and her girls sank into the big, soft living room couch for what seemed like weeks, while their Jewish friends carted in copious provisions every day. Lesley called it the Sitting Shiva Weight-Gain Program. She never changed out of a pair of sloppy sweatpants.

"Then one day I woke up and said, 'The dryer is shrinking my underwear!' I couldn't understand it. Because of those sweatpants, I had no clue that my waist was widening and my panties just didn't fit anymore."

That got the rest of us talking about our own experiences with eating or not eating, the changes wrought on our bodies by the physical impact of grief.

"I had lived a traditional Manhattan life where you go out to dinner all the time," Marcia said. "Or my husband made food and I'd eat when I got home. So nothing has changed."

"Except that now you're eating alone," I said. "The social element is gone. When I started eating alone, I read a magazine to keep from going bonkers with boredom." For two decades, dinner had been the time to talk over the day with someone who cared about my take on the Iowa caucuses or the new Terrence McNally play. Bernie's empty chair mocked me with an indifference that all the come-ons in *Condé Nast Traveler* couldn't dispel.

"Read a magazine, that's what *I* do," said Denise, taking an interest.

"I eat in front of the television," said Marcia. "The news, whatever. I don't even use my dining table." I envisioned her alone in the apartment that she found so small and isolating, grimly absorbing updates from the Weather Channel. "I don't even *like* to watch TV."

"It's company," said Lesley. "It's the jibber-jabber in the background."

"I fall asleep with the radio on now," said Denise. "If I fall asleep, that is, which I don't. I can't sleep, and I can't eat. I've lost twenty-seven pounds in the last six months."

We gasped. I'd been attributing Denise's all-yoga-wear fashion choices to her all-yoga fitness regimen. Now I realized that the stretchy gear was low-maintenance camouflage, like those sweat-pants of Lesley's. I should have known. In the first months after Bernie's death, I switched to nothing but dresses after a pair of pants dropped right off my bony hips. Food tasted like ashes to me then. I needed big glasses of water to flush it down my throat.

Dawn told us that she had lost weight, too, but food was re-emerging now as a source of pleasure. "The widower I just met is a good cook," she said. "We met at a sports program where I take my children. He says I should come over to his house and bring the kids, and he'll make dinner for us." She turned the color of the tomato salsa she was spooning onto her lamb chops. Lesley clapped and made little fox terrier sounds.

"A widower!" I said, as if she'd drawn four aces. "I always thought it would be nice to meet a widower, somebody who understands what we're going through."

"I dated a divorced guy before this," Dawn said. "He said that in some ways I was better off than he was. I don't want to say it's bet-ter, but it *is* different. We don't have to deal with the ex—who's got the kids, who got the house, all the stuff that people get so worked up about."

"We have all kinds of roiled-up emotions, but they aren't angry emotions," I said.

"I hope never to know what a divorce is like," said Dawn. "I'm sure it's horrible. But when you've gone through what we have, it's hard to tolerate people who are caught up in pettiness. You want to say, 'You know, you could die tomorrow.'"

"Nobody else looks at things like us," said Lesley.

"It's funny..." Dawn said. She often started sentences with "It's funny." Like Denise's smile, I noticed, the phrase often preceded a sentiment that was anything but. "It's funny, this widower's wife died nine years ago in an accident, when their kids were toddlers, a boy and a girl. When he said that to me, it took my breath away." She made a horrified face and quickly shook her head to fend off the memory. "Now I can relate to how people react when I tell them about me. I've never been on the other side like that."

We all nodded. We'd all seen the look. We knew our power to strike the fear of early death into everyone we met.

"I met a widower, also." Denise resurfaced at the far end of the table, where she had been picking here and there at her dinner.

"Woo-hoo." Lesley nearly jumped out of her chair like a kid who's opened a present, her eyes and lips forming perfect circles.

"Completely, completely randomly," Denise added quickly. The peculiar smile had washed off her face, and she looked pleased, in a careful and tentative way. She was supposed to meet a friend who never showed up at a restaurant, Denise said, so to kill time, she started speaking to a man at the next table. "His wife died four years ago. He has a twelve-year-old daughter. He loves to bring me groceries every day." She glanced around the table, almost sheepish. "Nothing has happened between us, but he brings me groceries every day."

"I'm liking this twist," Dawn said, grinning.

"He's worried that I don't eat."

We had met only a month ago, and already more was going on with this crew than with all my other friends combined. Lesley had moved Craig into her new house; Dawn had found a promising widower; and now Denise, fragile Denise, had met someone who brought her groceries every day.

"He's not being pushy. Or being sexual."

"As a widower, I suppose he knows what it's like," I said, feeling protective. "Sex may be too much to handle right now."

"I didn't ask for this," Denise said, half apologetically. But still she looked half pleased, maybe a little more than half.

The widower and his groceries reminded me of Denise's first encounters with her husband, Steve, how he had cared for her when she was sick and fixed her faulty wiring. Denise was projecting a quality of wanting to be cared for again, and why not? She couldn't eat, she couldn't sleep, she couldn't escape the pressures of money and work. Plenty of faulty wiring to fix, more than ever before. This widower of hers sounded nurturing and caring. He brought her stinky, runny cheeses and Kalamata olives and crusty baguettes, tempting snacks, because he knew she didn't want normal meals.

"That's really good," said Dawn. "Take it slow."

Could it be that Denise had achieved what many a widow dreams of, finding a simpatico man, a no-pressure man who could fill some of the emptiness so that she didn't have to endure a pro-tracted span alone? Could she even cope with it now if she did? Hard to say.

I couldn't help worrying about her. "Why are you still losing so much weight?" I asked.

She performed one of those seismic mental shifts I'd seen her make before, lost in her thoughts while we waited for a reply. The widower and his groceries were forgotten.

"I always used to cook for Steve," she said finally, driftily. Then she took a detour into another story about food and the weight it can bring to bear on a psyche. It was a couple of months after Steve died. A friend, going through a divorce, was staying with her, and the atmosphere in the apartment was heavy with doom. How to dispel it? The friend had a magnanimous idea. She'd roast Denise a chicken. It would be ready by the time she got home.

Denise took one look at that succulent bird and broke into tears. The aroma of rich melting fat mingled with lemon and garlic, so reminiscent of candlelit Sunday dinners, hit her with a force that shattered all of her carefully cultivated poise.

"That was the last thing I made for Steve before he died," she gulped.

Denise smiled again, that mirthless smile that I had come to know, the smile with the pleading eyes, only this time tears poured down her cheeks. Instead of wiping them away, she sat at the end of the table with her perfect posture, hands folded in her lap, smiling, the tears flowing, unashamed.

"I can never eat roast chicken again," she insisted.

I couldn't think of a thing to do to stanch the tears. The others held their tongues, too, until Lesley, bless her, blew past the awkwardness with a story of her own. It wasn't going to be another one of her funny stories—that was apparent in the forthright set of her face.

She borrowed Dawn's "it's funny" phrase. "It's funny," Lesley said, her voice at a low and even pitch, "we all have these things. The day Kevin died he knew I had an appointment for a facial. Now, I was always at home, never on any particular schedule, so he could never know when I wouldn't be there. But he knew I had this appointment, and that I'd be out for an hour."

Before she left, she asked him what he would like for lunch. She was the homemaker. That was her job. A Subway sandwich, he said. That meant Lesley would take some extra time after her appointment to stop by the Subway shop.

"So I got the Subway, and when I came back, he had taken his life."

Unlike Denise, Lesley didn't smile. She was setting an example again: Tell your story. Don't let it rattle you. "I can never eat Subway now. It's like your roast chicken."

Dawn followed Lesley's lead, seeking a way to show Denise that she had more company in her distress. "I'm trying to think if I can associate anything like that," she said, casting about in her mind. "Not food, because we were apart when Andries died. But I'm thinking about a song. I was driving along the New Jersey Turnpike a few months ago, or I thought I was, and suddenly I realized I was on the wrong road." Her voice rose unintentionally, more force- ful and slightly shrill. "I didn't know how that happened. I saw a sign that said Route 301. Where was I? What was I doing there?" Dawn threw her whole body into the story, lots of hand gestures— operatic. "And this song came on the radio, a John Denver song, 'Country Roads,' which Andries always liked. 'Country roads, take me home to the place I belong, West Virginia . . .' And that's where Andries died."

Dawn hit the dial. She pulled off the road, stopped the car with a jerk. "All I could do was say, '*Oh my God. He's really not coming back.*'"

Everyone at the table stiffened. Recognition. And triggers, those simple, familiar sights and sounds and tastes and smells that spark feelings sharper than any in the sensory world. For Marcia, they included an Italian restaurant that she passed almost every day. For me, there was the briny tang of freshly shucked oysters.

"It's a shame when you associate something you enjoy, like a food or a song, with a person who is gone and you feel you have to give it up," I said. "I loved eating oysters with Bernie, but if I didn't force myself to eat them now, I'd never get to have one again. What would that accomplish? But it took me a while. I felt too guilty doing things without him that he used to enjoy."

"I have no guilt at all," said Dawn. "Because Andries wouldn't want me to. If you have guilt, it's an excuse to hold on; you're not ready to release."

Denise's tears stopped, and she seemed embarrassed, apologetic. "I'm sorry I told that roast chicken story," she said. "I cannot tell that roast chicken story, ever again. That roast chicken story, it's terrible."

"Believe it or not, it won't always be." Lauren, the one outsider, bravely ventured a comment.

"I make a good roast chicken," said Denise.

"I'm sure you do," Lauren said. She hustled into the kitchen and returned with an abundant heap of chocolate cookies, pungent with cinnamon, still hot from the oven. We clapped with appreciation and passed them around.

"Denise," Lesley said, "after our last dinner, when I went home from your place, I couldn't sleep, so I went to Craig's and talked to him the rest of the night about . . . oh, everything. I told him that I was just blown away by where you were at that point, only five months. You are doing what you should be doing, with grace and dignity."

"I tell my friends, just ignore me if I start crying," Dawn assured Denise.

"Denise, look at you, you can function!" Lesley said. "I don't think I could function at that point."

"I think all of us functioned," I said, remembering my fumbling attempts at work. "In a daze, sure, but we all *looked* functional on the outside."

"I don't want to wake up every day with a panic attack," Denise said suddenly, more tenuous again.

Dawn reached over and took Denise's hand. "The first six months are very hard. I'd have to convince myself not to get all panicky and weird."

"It's really helping me, talking to all of you," Denise said. I couldn't tell whether she meant it. I might have felt better if she wiped that proper smile off her face.

Marcia checked her phone—the New Yorkers would just make the last train home. Dawn set off on her own while I gave the rest of them a lift to the station, Marcia riding shotgun. I heard Lesley in the back, talking to Denise and holding her close in the cold. Lesley, who lived to take care of others, threw herself into full gear now. The two women were less than ten years apart in age, but she spoke in the voice of a mother, mellowed by two decades of ministering to the scraped knees and prom-date letdowns of three growing girls. Lesley, I could tell, drew comfort by offering it herself.

"This is why we're all here," she said. "This is how we're going to learn from each other. I know for sure that you're going to see a side of me where I just blub, and Dawn, too. Those of us with the big mouths and the bravado are going to have tough times, too."

Denise didn't answer.

"Just last month, when I learned that I got the house I bought," Lesley continued, "I sobbed and sobbed and sobbed. It was because I was so proud of what I'd accomplished on my own. But it was also because it didn't have to be this way. But it is."

ON MONDAY MORNING, I heard from Denise, her feelings still in disarray.

"Everyone is in such a different place," she said. "There are those who do the chatty, funny, sexual-reference thing, which is funny. Those who have people in their lives and those who are totally alone."

Maybe, I said, this whole project was too much like a traditional support group, excavating unpredictable, unwanted emotions. Maybe I shouldn't have thrown such a new widow into the mix. The first few months of loss might be better suited to introspection than engagement with others, however well intentioned. Or maybe food, with all its intimate associations, all its sensory cues, cut too close to home, firing the receptors in our noses, eyes, ears, and tongues and lighting up memory neurons deep in our brains that were better left to rest.

Denise questioned whether she could make it through a year of this. "Here I am with these people I like," she said, "but when we talk about this stuff, I get jerked right back to August and how I felt then. It's emotional time travel. If that is going to happen to me once a month for a year, it is going to be really hard."

She didn't have to say more. I treasured the solidarity of the group, but I was as wary as she was about the emotional expense, for myself as much as anyone. The right balance between sharing our common pasts and leaving them behind was a fine one, perhaps too fine for a group of amateurs to calibrate.

I hung up realizing that I had taken grief for granted. I had thought that food and the nurturing it implied would be a consoling motif. But grief has a way of invading the simplest things, the most everyday things, the happiest things, sometimes more than the sad ones. It can take a roast chicken or a song on the radio, the most familiar details of a daily routine, and turn them into symbols of what can no longer be.

Grief, in its rawest form, is a state in which the everyday can become a torment rather than a comfort. I understood that now. For Denise, that night had been a reminder not of what sustained but of what was lost. I only hoped we hadn't lost Denise. I had a month to come up with a better plan.

chapter

NINE

i should have known better. Over the next days, I remembered how I would have felt if somebody had dragooned me into an evening of rowdy kitchen shenanigans when I was newly widowed like Denise—traumatized, spent, unable to sleep, unwilling to eat. I had wanted nothing more than to curl into a protective crouch. I remembered when my fondest wish was to leave all the horror, all the sensory stimuli behind and check into the local Marriott, all alone.

I began this unnatural fixation on a room at the Marriott even when Bernie was still alive. He and I used to pass the hotel near the Brooklyn Bridge every time we took a cab to the hospital once he was no longer able to navigate the subway. I had never been inside the hotel—still haven't, in fact—but the exterior was just bland enough, just generic enough, that I fantasized about finding someone who could care for Bernie for just one night while I took a room there. In my fantasy, the room was always beige—beige walls, beige bedding, beige carpeting, beige curtains, which I would draw tight, and a beige telephone, which I would unplug. Nothing could happen in that three-hundred-dollar-a-night beige vacuum, nothing at all. If I slept, which was unlikely, I would dream beige dreams.

The thought of actually spending a night there came to me when we traveled to radiation treatments for the tumors in Bernie's brain, tumors that began their relentless march by stealing his short-term memory.

"Where are we going?" Bernie would ask, genuinely curious, as if we might be embarking on a vacation.

"To the doctor," I would answer.

"Where are we going?" he would ask a moment later.

I would take his hand and answer again.

Ever more clearly, I envisioned that beige room, that sanctuary where nothing could happen, when the memory loss started to intermingle with generalized confusion so that Bernie began to imagine developments worse than, or at least different from, what was real.

"Where are they taking us?" Bernie would ask with growing agitation, over and over, never specifying who "they" might be.

"To the doctor," I would answer, over and over, in my most reassuring voice, wishing there were some way to keep him safe for just one night while I holed up in that tantalizing hotel. It was all just too much, and that room at the Marriott would be blessedly too little.

One morning before a trip from Brooklyn into Manhattan, I had made the mistake of leaving the news on television while a report of a terrorist atrocity aired.

"Where are they taking us? Are they going to cut off our heads?" Bernie asked in the car, frantic with alarm. The driver and I exchanged nervous glances in the rearview mirror. No answer could comfort Bernie. He had to live in that terrorized state, hostage to preposterous demons, again and again, and I had to witness it, again and again, unable to assuage his irrational fears, unable to assuage my rational ones. I tried to tamp down my own panic, keep my answers as smooth as the gentlest surf, but my fantasy of the night in the Marriott wasn't strong enough to blot out the vision of where they were taking us next.

Once Bernie was gone, I gave up on the beige fantasy and tried to live it instead, residing alone in my echoing apartment, but in many ways seeking an even emptier place. A place insulated from pain at a time when everything, as mundane as Denise's roast chicken or a husband's sweater still folded in a drawer, had the power to inflict pain. After a few months, to keep myself from becoming Miss Havisham, I donated most of Bernie's things to charity, retaining a few of his T-shirts that I wore to bed. I didn't tackle his office for almost a year—his work had defined him more than his possessions. When I did, I found notes he had written to himself in scratchy script as his memory failed, information he was desperate to retain. *Home:* followed by our address. *Wife:* followed by *Becky*. I wanted to check into that hotel all over again.

After my first year of grieving, I knew that I needed to re-engage with humanity. What was the alternative—marathon phone calls with Mom? Solitary forays through the gulch of Saturday night? I devised elaborate campaigns to avoid it, booking excursions weeks in advance and keeping lists of which friends tolerated goofy comedies, which were up for a museum or a concert. Nobody signed on for visits to the better restaurants—those were reserved for lovers celebrating anniversaries. It was pub food or pan-Asian tasting plates for me.

Fine, fine—I was all for keeping it small. Determined to insulate myself from pain, I vowed never again to become close enough to anyone to risk the anguish if that person were lost. Anything— loneliness, lack of popularity, solitary confinement—would be preferable to going through that again. I chose as my mantra the vaguely Buddhist concept, "Attachment is suffering." My theme song, courtesy of the Everly Brothers: "Love Hurts."

Some of my research into what it means to lose a husband, I decided, justified my approach to seek a wide community of less involving companions. Sociologists came out with a study around that time that showed Americans were spending more and more time with their spouses and engaging less and less with friends or community, leaving us all without networks to fall back on if the marriages ended. I swore I wouldn't let that happen to me. My cal- endar was chockablock with engagements. I volunteered to tutor kids after school. They were perfect: a couple of hours of company and someone else assumed their care.

Dating, in particular, was out of the question during my first two years of widowhood. Oh, I might have accepted a gift of food had it been offered from somebody like Denise's platonic widower, but the thought of pursuing a true relationship made me anxious. Zombie anxious. Never again, I vowed, would I view attachment as essential to my well-being. It became vitally important to subscribe to a definition of happiness rooted in remaining alone. If that meant giving up sex for now, so be it. I couldn't risk kick-starting endorphins that might make me feel attached.

Looking at it later, I wondered whether I'd been influenced, back when I was the only widow I knew, by societal attitudes that frowned on our seeking new love. Was I editing my behavior ac- cording to the cruel limits that mourning places on a woman in her prime? I found a survey from 1970 that showed a third of the public approving of a widow remarrying after a year, but a similar survey thirty years later showed only nine percent approval. More than ever, it seemed, people preferred the chaste Jackie Kennedy to the remarried Jackie O, the devastated woman to the recovering one. It seemed that attitudes toward widows had become more restrictive in the thirty years between those surveys, and I considered why. Perhaps the more death occurs away from home, hidden away in hospitals and nursing homes, the more power we ascribe to it. Death has become unmentionable, and therefore unimaginable, and if unimaginable, therefore unmanageable. It should be impossible to recover from, we think, a mortal psychic blow.

Many assume that a widow who manages to move ahead and be happy again probably didn't love her partner much in the first place—the Scarlett O'Hara syndrome. But when I met Professor Bonanno, he debunked that theory. One of the first studies he was involved in followed 1,500 married couples for a decade, and over that time, some of the spouses died. The study found no connection between the closeness of the marriage and the depth and duration of mourning. Those with healthy, happy relationships were well positioned to go on with healthy, happy lives.

In my case, though, there were a couple of years when I couldn't make the leap. After all I'd seen, all I'd done and failed to do, I couldn't imagine having the will again to take on responsibility for another person. The idea that I might stand before my friends in a white dress and pledge to love someone else in sickness and in health? Unthinkable.

Nevertheless, a little more than a year after Bernie died, I obliged a couple I was close to by joining them for an attempted fix-up with a friend of theirs. The four of us met at a restaurant, the kind of boîte that serves real entrées instead of pan-Asian snacks. The couple had told me that the man was successful at his business; they had told him I was pretty.

My intended suitor was a suburban man with a pleasant face, a recent widower, so recent, it turned out, that he redirected all conversation toward paeans to his wife's favorite pursuits—gardening, antiquing, shoe shopping—following up with questions about whether I shared her interests. It was like a job interview to determine whether I could fill the shoes, literally, of a valued employee. His wife had been a devoted gardener, and he was so befuddled over what to do with her vast beds of tulips and nasturtiums that he had hired someone to spread hundreds of cubic yards of mulch to put them into some kind of order. Unless I heard him wrong. It might have been hundreds of cubic *feet* of mulch. I had no idea the quantity of mulch one needs to do whatever it is that mulch does for flower beds.

"Do you like to garden?" the mulch man asked me, while the other couple at the table hung on my answer.

"I have window boxes at my apartment," I answered with careful neutrality.

His wife's antiques also needed to be repaired and polished, and she owned a lot of those shoes that he didn't know what to do with. "Have you ever restored antiques?" he asked.

"I bought an old cabinet at a flea market once," I said. "I think it may have been a fake."

"Are you interested in shoes?"

I felt the anticipation of everyone at the table while the question led me astray and I entered one of those altered states that I witnessed later when Denise lost the thread of a conversation. Was I interested in shoes? I was so interested in shoes that once when Bernie was in the hospital for a one-hour procedure, I busted out of the waiting room, ran outside, jumped into a cab, hightailed it to Barneys, whipped through the shoe department to ogle pumps and platforms and flats, and then repeated the whole escapade in reverse, no one the wiser, all before Bernie's procedure ended, and all simply to remind myself that somewhere there existed a parallel universe where people concerned themselves with the delicious folly of placing something exquisite on their feet. It was a trip to the far side of Pluto and back, all in the course of an hour.

I realized that the mulch man was waiting for my answer. "Sorry," I said. "Not interested." I'd rather keep that room at the Marriott.

chapter

T E N

*d*awn was the last to show up. Most people disappear into the bustle of the Metropolitan Museum, but Dawn's arrival was more of an entrance. Heads didn't just turn, they swiveled when she strode past, confident in a pair of black suede boots, jacked up on heels that few would venture to wear for two hours of tramping through some of the world's most cavernous galleries. As we set off, visitors looked away from stupendous frescoes and statuary, Dawn's flash of blondness too irresistible a distraction. If people come to museums to watch each other as well as the art, Dawn was giving them a helluva show. Her kinetic presence hijacked attention, and she was conscious of all the darting looks. But Dawn *paid* attention, too. She took in everything, making connections, making them hers. Dawn was a woman both fully engaging and fully engaged.

It was the lotus blossoms that brought her to a full stop.

Locking into those blossoms, Dawn lost any awareness of herself and redirected all her scrutiny to a collection of drawings and watercolors that depicted them. A sound, like a purr from a Persian cat, came from somewhere deep in her throat.

The lotus blossoms were sequestered in their own room away from the crowds, but they were no dainty, ladylike flowers. As depicted by the Chinese artist Xie Zhiliu, they were strong, forceful blooms with palpable erotic power. Their colors, virgin white or red like the lipstick of a whore, emerged with muscular force from some murky depths. They were beautiful, too, of course. But these watercolors weren't just for show. They had something more, something penetrating to say. Dawn looked at them like someone trying to work something out. Something, something *else*, was up with Dawn.

"I want to start here," said our guide, Katie, a slender art history student with long, pre-Raphaelite ringlets of fawn-colored hair, "in part because it's more peaceful than other galleries on a busy Saturday night, and in part because lotus blossoms are highly symbolic in many cultures."

We stepped closer. The works captured fleeting moments in the lives of the flowers. Some bowed gracefully. Some stretched toward the sun on tender stems. Withered ones dropped their seeds. "The idea for the artist was that no one of these was *the* lotus blossom," Katie said. "It's necessary to see the various facets of the life cycle to understand the flower itself."

Everyone in our group moved from one painting to the other, respectfully silent, drinking in the sinuous forms, the bold lines like calligraphy, the showy eruptions of color.

"Lotus blossoms close their petals at night and reopen in the morning, so there is also the idea of perpetual resurgence and renewal, of reinventing themselves," Katie continued.

"Ahh . . . renewal," Tara said, casting a meaningful look toward Dawn, who was still transfixed.

"That red is so vivid," observed Lesley.

"And they can surge forth and be beautiful and pristine in a muddy, difficult environment." Katie finished and stepped to the side, leaving us to soak in the essential qualities of the blossoms, their splendor, their drive, their strength.

Dawn could hold her silence no longer. "I can't believe it," she blurted out in a croaky rush. "It sits on my desk, that picture."

"This picture?" I asked, pointing to the one in front of her, the most colorful one in the room.

"No, no, my own picture." Dawn spun away from the painting toward the rest of us, lit up by the coincidence. "I have a photograph of a beautiful lotus blossom on my desk. I look at it every morning." It was a gift from her husband, who took the photograph on a trip through the bush in Africa. "Sometimes Andries and I liked to go off and do our separate things. He liked to rough it as though he were in the army. It reminded him that life could be taken away in a minute."

Dawn didn't know anything about lotus blossoms when he gave her the photograph six months before he died. She asked him why, of all the glorious sights in the wild, he had chosen this image of a lotus, rooted in an inky swamp, for her. "It is because a lotus blossom will grow and perfume and flower," he said, "even in the muck."

Everyone made that same contented sound that Dawn had uttered before. We got it, all right. All of us—Denise, Dawn, Marcia, Lesley, Tara, me—we were blooming in the muck.

FOR OUR MARCH OUTING, I had come up with this excursion, away from the everyday, like cooking, and into the sublime. The roast chicken train wreck had made me leery about my skill at planning activities for our group, so I consulted Camille Wortman, a research psychologist at the State University of New York at Stony Brook. She had kicked off much of the new research about grief with an attention-grabbing paper back in 1989 called *The Myths of Coping with Loss*, setting the tone for others that followed. She recommended that people who are grieving throw themselves into positive experiences that fully engage their interest, what psychologists call *flow*. I told her that going with the flow at the cooking class hadn't been so easy for everyone in our group.

"If I lost my husband, going to a cooking class would be very hard for me," she told me when I visited her office. "I cook a lot. My husband cooks. It's something we do together." For her, she said, "Cooking would be a zinger."

A zinger, Wortman explained, can be any unexpected reminder of loss, like Denise's chicken or Dawn's John Denver song. It can strike a person with spooky intensity, even causing difficulty breathing or heart palpitations. Obviously, we had stumbled onto this third rail of zingers with Denise and food.

I was chagrined, but Wortman was otherwise reassuring. Unlike Bonanno in his Hawaiian shirts, she had that precise appearance that you look for in a scientist, very neutral—short brown hair, pale skin, tan pants, tan shoes, a red and tan paisley blouse. Her work as a research psychologist involved interviewing thousands of couples before and after bereavement, for as many as ten years, to assess their ways of coping, and she had uncovered the benefits of positive experiences. Walking the dog, going shopping, just about any activity that generates some enthusiasm, she said, can break the grip of negative thoughts and offer a respite from depression, anxiety, anger, or guilt. So she was all in favor of our planning these regular outings.

"But if you are sponsoring a group like this, it might be good to screen for zingers," she advised. "Of course, it would be hard to know what they would be. They could be different for different people. They could be anything."

WHICH IS WHY I nearly suffered breathing difficulty and heart palpitations when, ten days before our get-together, I found out that the museum had organized what I can only call an all-zinger tour for our group, a tour so lacking in positive engagement that Denise would be begging for roast chicken as an alternative.

Once again, I had come up with a plan deceptive in its simplicity. I heard that for a reasonable sum the Metropolitan Museum of Art would put together a private tour on the subject of one's choice. I requested a survey of artworks that reflected on the subjects of loss and recovery, a tour for a group of young widows who were intent on remaking themselves; a Saturday night tour that would be positive, even inspiring in tone, revolving around rebirth, renewal, and change. Perhaps naively believing that the Met would understand what I had in mind, I thought my planning was done. I relaxed for a couple of weeks and reflected on how art was the ideal antidote to grief, how art in many forms had served that function for me.

I wanted our group to find the same solace I had found in art during my own low patches, when my life was so stripped of interest and significance that I hungered for the ideal rather than the real, the abstract rather then the actual, when I wanted to see the world filtered through someone else's interpretation, trusting it more than my own. Art—and I'm using the term broadly here, music or painting, theater or movies, high or low—allowed me to experience emotions I didn't get to feel in my real life anymore: a good chuckle, the warmth of close connections. I no longer lived in a place where I had a man to love, but I could listen to *"O soave fanciulla"* from *La Bohème* or "I Got You Babe" from Sonny and Cher and visit that place, if only for a few minutes.

Art helped me find order and meaning at a time when I couldn't find them elsewhere. Like religion, I thought, art offered a connection to a world where stuff that happens makes sense. A few weeks after Bernie died, I had seen a reproduction in the newspaper of a painting by the California conceptual artist Ed Ruscha. It depicted an orange vortex on a gray background, and in the center were the words *I WAS GASPING FOR CONTACT.* Too done in to visit the Whitney Museum to see the painting for myself, I tore the image from the paper, referring to it again and again. At that moment, the painting spoke to me more than the daily details of my life, details like canceling Bernie's credit cards, pretending to work. Gasping.

So I was primed for a meaningful evening at the museum until ten days before the date, when I realized that I hadn't heard back yet from anyone there. I called the manager of tours. "We're having a little trouble," she said, "putting together your tour on, let me see . . . death and dying."

Zing. "Stop right there," I said. "Death and dying! No! No! I wanted loss and recovery, emphasis on recovery."

I asked to speak to someone directly in charge of choosing the art we'd be seeing. Minutes later, she was on the phone.

"I've been mulling over your topic," she said with abrupt

authority before I had a chance to speak, "and I think recovery is not something you can show very well in a painting. A painting may bring a sense of recovery to someone who is viewing it, but that is in the eye of the beholder."

I could see her point: people's reactions to art might vary. "What are the sorts of pieces you would show us on death and dying?" I wondered.

Roman sarcophagi, she said. Egyptian funerary objects. A sculpture of the antihero in Dante, Ugolino. "He is imprisoned with his children and they are begging him to eat them to save his own life, and he is biting his fingernails and going through questions about what to do."

I knew how he felt at this point.

"And Christian iconography of, you know, crucifixion, resurrection. We have a sculpture by an American called *The Angel of Death*. A painting by Homer of a guy on a boat called *The Gulf Stream*. He's on a raft, really, in the ocean with sharks circling him. We have the statue *The Burghers of Calais*, where they're in chains, about to be put to death. David's painting of the death of Socrates. It's pretty monochromatic."

I was crushed. Graphic depictions of people going to a horrible demise—"this is the opposite of what we'd want to see," I said. Out of more than two million works in the Metropolitan Museum, she couldn't come up with subject matter that might be more comforting or inspiring?

"This is not really something an art historian can lead without knowing your group," the manager said. "I think you need more of a psychological counselor than an art historian, to be totally honest."

Up to now, I'd been willing to cut her some slack. But did she really think that the death of a loved one was such an unheard-of occurrence that only a mental health professional could address the subject? Was she patronizing us because we were widows?

"Let me explain," I said. "These women are past the initial stage of grief, and they are remaking their lives."

"Mm-hmm," said the voice on the other end.

"This takes strength. It takes optimism. It even takes humor. So what I have in mind is something much more ... uplifting."

"I don't know how much these widows know about art and appreciate it," she said. "You might be better off with just a highlights tour. I talked to a few colleagues and they were baffled by this project also."

"What about images like the phoenix rising from the ashes, or images of strong or beautiful women?"

"There again, our major strong women are more like Salomé with the head of John the Baptist. Or Judith slaying Holofernes."

Women beheading men. Did she think we'd killed our husbands? "Nasty strong women," I said.

"Yeah, exactly," she said. "Look, maybe you just want a tour of women in art and women artists. I mean, that's pretty attenuated."

Attenuated—I know what that means, I wanted to say. I know what *obtuse* means, too. My zinger needle was banging in the red zone. "It doesn't sound like this is going to come together at the Met," I sighed. I signed off in despair.

Now I was in trouble. A little over a week until our gathering, and unless I was prepared to brush off my pointillist memories of Art History 101 and guide this jaunt myself, we had nothing prepared. I quickly Googled "private art tours" and came up with a company that employed art history students.

"I ran your idea past some of our guides," said the head of the company, only four days before the date. "Katie is very young, but she was moved by your request. She proposed some works that you might enjoy."

"Such as?" I braced for the worst.

"Well, one of them is a beautiful series of Chinese watercolors of lotus blossoms. She chose them because they bloom even in the mud."

"Stop right there," I said. "She's hired."

chapter

ELEVEN

*i*t took a goddess to stop the show after those lotus blossoms. A gilded statue of Diana glowed high on a plinth made of stone in an interior courtyard flooded with late-day sunlight. Katie held us at a distance, heightening the drama, the better to take in Diana's golden form. All certitude, she balanced on a single toe, her slender arms aiming a bow and arrow. Her body was strong, not ripped as if she'd been to the gym, but purposeful—a delicate, feminine strength. We felt the tension in her bow, shaped like a pair of lips.

"It's hard to see her up close, because she's placed so high," said Katie. The statue, cast in 1928, was a replica of the scandalous nude weather vane by Augustus Saint-Gaudens that perched atop the old Madison Square Garden. "She is the goddess of the hunt, athletic and strong. The myth is that she assisted in the birth of her twin brother, Apollo. So she is associated with the idea of women helping other women."

Tara and Dawn cut each other knowing glances, while the rest of us nodded approvingly.

"She is also associated with anyplace where three roads meet, helping travelers find direction. So the idea of Diana on a weather vane is beautiful and special."

"She's got a normal body, which is kind of nice." Lesley craned her neck toward the goddess. "She's in good shape."

"All that running around and cavorting with her nymphs," Katie said.

We laughed, appreciating more than the humor. It was uncanny—Katie had a precocious ability to know what would speak to us, to understand that we might have been widowed, but that our interests were defined by life rather than death, that we were at a crossroads, seeking whatever guidance Diana might provide. Katie's first two choices were so spot-on that even money said we would follow her anywhere.

Denise, to my relief, had joined us again, and I noticed she was more cheerful this time, her expression less strained. I was grateful that she was giving us another chance. Art seemed to grant her a more comfortable distance from her troubles than food had, and she had changed out of her perpetual yoga getup into a belted black dress with a loose swinging skirt. I was glad that Tara had returned, too. She and Dawn trailed behind, deep in conversation about whatever was on Dawn's mind. She talked up a storm, something about a man in her life, and Tara nodded thoughtfully, interjecting measured bits of advice. I was happy to see them forming a bond.

Katie, divining that romance was on our minds, brought us to a voluptuous Titian nude of Venus, goddess of love, painted in 1565. Recumbent before a lush landscape, languidly receiving a crown of flowers from a cherubic Cupid, Venus directed her gaze outside the frame, contemplating, what?—her own fabulousness, it seemed. She didn't engage the viewer. Like Dawn, she didn't need to work to attract admiration. Venus would never deign to wink at someone on Match.com.

Being women past the age of puberty, we couldn't help evaluating the state of Venus's pearly flesh.

"She's got perky boobs," Lesley said.

"If only we lived in an era when big hips were considered ideal," I lamented. "Think how easy it would be."

Having shown us a strong woman and a beautiful woman, Katie introduced us to an accomplished one, Adélaïde Labille-Guiard, a painter admitted to the French Academy in the eighteenth century, when membership for women was limited to four. In a self-portrait, she captured herself in the act of painting, gripping a palette and brush while sporting a shiny silk dress in aquamarine, the color of Lesley's silk blouse, that set off creamy skin, pillowy décolletage, and a killer stare. Adélaïde's dainty embellished shoe looked like one I'd seen at Miu Miu, and her audacious hat could blindside the paparazzi at a royal wedding.

"She's saying it's okay to be feminine and frilly and still be creative," noted Lesley. She sized up the dress the way Holly Golightly sized up the baubles at Tiffany's.

"Absolutely," Katie agreed. "She maintained all her feminine charms while having a prominent and important career. She's based the composition on a fashion plate."

I would have thought that Dawn, a businesswoman and a fashion plate in her own right, would have felt an affinity for Adélaïde, but when I looked around, Dawn lagged several yards behind. She had waylaid Tara in front of a sculpture, gesturing toward it with flamboyant flourishes. We scuttled over to form a crescent around her.

"Why are you blushing?" Lesley asked. It didn't take a keen eye to see how deeply Dawn was affected.

She actually fanned her fevered face. "This kind of thing always happens to me." She gestured toward the life-sized statue. "I have a replica of this sitting on the mantel in my bedroom. Andries gave *this* to me, too."

The sculpture was blushworthy all right. Blatantly erotic, *Cupid and Psyche*, sculpted by Antonio Canova around 1800, depicted love of the most rapturous sort. Cupid, portrayed as a winged adult, whooshed into his lover's yielding arms, cradling her face. Talk about sexual heat, all soft surfaces and entwined limbs. But I couldn't help noticing the tender look on Cupid's face. He treasured her. Any woman on the receiving end of that look would never have to doubt. His love was certain. *Their* love was certain.

"Dawn, I didn't know Andries was a god," I said.

"He sure looked like one," she said, her face still on fire. "I was looking at pictures the other day. He was so freakin' gorgeous. Where do you go from there? I can't imagine a man coming along and filling even a quarter..."

Her voice trailed off. Tara scootched in next to her, and Dawn dropped her head onto Tara's shoulder with mock melodrama. When she picked it up again, her eyes had taken on the appraising hardness of Adélaïde's.

"I don't know what to do about this guy I'm seeing now," she said. He was Adam, the widower she had told us about the last time we gathered. They'd begun to date regularly, but just that morning, she had felt him backing off. He had even put forward the one strategy guaranteed to throw ice water on any budding relationship. "'Friends with benefits,' he said. Ugh. No. That is *not* my thing."

That was what she'd been confiding to Tara.

"It *is* nice to know that you are desirable to other people," Lesley offered.

"To have a little physical contact, maybe until the next level comes along—maybe that's not so bad," Dawn said with a wistful look at Cupid. "But in the past I was always with people I really cared about and who cared about me. Even if it didn't always work in the end, it didn't feel empty."

"How long have you been seeing each other, six weeks?" Lesley said. "Maybe he's just being cautious."

Dawn looked doubtful. "Nine years after his wife died, he still has all her stuff. It's everywhere." She glanced back at the idealized lovers in the sculpture. "I believe I had a great thing. I want a great thing again."

I followed her gaze. As Dawn might say, it seemed so freakin' unfair that after basking in the warm assurance of her marriage, she had been tossed out into the chilly reality of guys who didn't look at her the way Cupid looked at Psyche, the way the gorgeous Andries had looked at the gorgeous Dawn. The statue hadn't quite been a zinger for Dawn. It didn't bring her to tears or feel like a defeat, but it was making her think, casting her current choices into the context of her marriage.

"*Psyche*, of course, means *soul*," Katie informed us. "And Cupid is love. The reciprocity of their embrace is the recognition of love and soul coming together."

Harder than it looks, I thought. Not everyone comes equipped with wings. I could tell there was more that Dawn wanted to say, but we continued through the galleries, finding more parallels between art and our own circumstances, notably at a familiar water lily painting by Claude Monet. I had thought there would be little new to say about this much-reproduced work, but Katie found a way to rivet our group. Not only did the painting depict the lilies, close cousins to our friends the lotus blossoms, floating in some serious purplish depths, but Katie's story of its creation lent itself to reflection, too.

She explained that after Monet's first wife died, he remarried and moved in 1883 to Giverny, where the new couple blended its two families and built a house and water gardens, the subjects of his most acclaimed work.

"In this second part of his painterly career, he focused on what really moved him as a painter, which was on painting exactly what the eye sees," Katie said. She pointed to the complexity of the images, how the viewer couldn't be sure whether some green tendrils were willow tree branches reflected on the surface of the water or lily stems growing up from beneath.

"How old was he when his first wife died?" Lesley asked.

Everyone hung on the answer. "I think he would have been around forty."

"So he was a *young* widower." We exchanged looks.

"Yes. With a young son. His first wife had been the model for many of his paintings, so it was a devastating moment. He had to reevaluate what he wanted as an artist and as a parent, but it let him get to where he wanted to be." I saw the others pondering this progression of events.

"Beautiful," said Marcia.

Our next stop proved more polarizing. A small terra-cotta

sculpture from Mali depicted a seated figure the color of clay, a man, I assumed at first, curled in on himself, his head resting on his knee. His eyes were downcast, his mouth slightly open, curving down. Katie didn't need to tell us—he was in mourning. He looked as if he were rocking himself, comforting himself. I found him eloquent, dignified.

"This sculpture is from the thirteenth century, but it looks very modern to me," Katie said. "We've been looking at a lot of things about strength, but this one is resolutely about grief and nurturing one's self. The shaving of the head is part of the mourning ritual in this part of Africa, so it's not clear whether this is a man or a woman. The face and positioning of the body are so expressive that it doesn't look like a particular individual so much as an evocation of sorrow."

Lesley and Dawn backed away from the glass case as if it held a live grenade, while Tara drew her face close and pulled on her reading glasses. "It's extraordinary how well preserved it is."

"The protective posture really protected the sculpture, too, as an object," said Katie.

We went quiet as some of us circled the figure with respect and others pulled farther back.

"I'm not comfortable looking at it for too long," Lesley said, "because . . ."

"Well, look at that face," said Marcia.

"I want to give him a hug," I said.

Dawn kept her distance, shaking her head. "How many times a day have you felt like that yourself? I mean, that is grief, right there in front of you."

"I feel voyeuristic," said Tara, still peering through the glass.

"There's something about it that seems really private," Katie agreed. She led the group deeper into the African galleries, while three of us fell behind.

"That really traumatized me, that grief thing," said Lesley.

"What traumatized you, sweetie?" Tara asked.

"Didn't you two do that at some point? Get into the fetal position? When you were just too sad?"

"Sure," I said. "The fetal position is a very comforting little position."

"I rocked," Lesley said. "Rocked and rocked. It was the rhythm for me."

So the sculpture had been a zinger for Lesley, but not for Tara, apparently. "It had a powerful effect on me, too," she said in her sonorous voice. "It was a human being with elemental, fundamental, primal grief . . . but it was strong, too. Think about it . . . seven hundred years old, and it didn't break. Dawn and I were talking about this." She paused. "Sometimes, in order to get strong, it's necessary to . . . face the pain."

Lesley wasn't buying it. "It gave me a feeling I'd forgotten—that I didn't want to remember."

"Then why go back there?" Tara said.

I hadn't been able to read Denise's reaction to the work—her expression was as opaque as usual. But when we caught up, she was intent on an African mask, demonstrating more enthusiasm than I'd ever witnessed before. Worn by women in Sierra Leone when they initiated each other into a society of healers, the mask had idealized feminine features, wide-set eyes, and a small, composed mouth—very much like Denise's face, I suddenly recognized.

She declared it her favorite piece of the day, and I asked why. "See? This is how *I* feel," she said, pointing to the enigmatic expression. "Pretending everything is normal for the benefit of others."

Our tour had achieved its goal. Each woman was finding insight through the idealization of art, sharing it with the others. Perhaps it was fitting that the final stop spoke most to me and my aspirations for the group itself.

"I thought we would end with a celebration of beauty and the giving and receiving of gifts and favors, which is something that all of you do for each other," Katie said as she steered us toward *The Three Graces*, a Roman marble sculpture from the second century. The piece depicted three women, handmaidens to the goddess of love, in a dancelike pose. "They are known as beauty, mirth, and abundance, and the interlocking of their physical forms is also about the interlocking of these ideals."

The Graces were missing their heads and a few arms, too—they'd been through it—but their sisterly affection and camaraderie remained. Our group had yet to forge such a fond alliance. I wondered if we would.

"You won't believe this," Dawn said, by now accustomed to coincidence. "I have a statue of this at home, too."

Figured.

***

DAWN, YOU SEE, believed in fate rather than happenstance, that things were meant to be, that she was following a path, that the world, in short, made sense. This system of belief, rooted in her Roman Catholicism but fed by an embrace of all things spiritual, granted her such an outlook of optimism that her friends called her Sunshine.

Whereas many of us tend to believe that we are, for the most part, at the mercy of the irrational forces of the universe, Dawn believed that Somebody Up There could have been paying close enough attention to draw up a plan that led me to hire a last-minute museum guide who picked out three works of art that Dawn happened to own in some form or other and that she looked at and drew strength from every day. She was capable of believing that they had been placed in her path now, because that Somebody meant to grant us wisdom and encouragement, not because random luck had brought us Katie, the best possible guide for a group of ladies in our searching state. Dawn believed she inhabited a world of meaning. The coincidence of the three works of art spooked me enough that it seemed worth considering Dawn's point of view.

But what about the death of Andries? Was that part of Someone's master plan? I couldn't accept it, and I wasn't sure Dawn could, either.

Otherwise, destiny had blessed her with beauty, grace, abundance, and so much more: her sunny nature, her knockout body, her business acumen, her ability to hit the sweet spot between work and family. Which is probably why, when I first met Dawn, I assumed that things would go easily for her, that she would know how to take the conundrum of young widowhood and hit that right down the line, too.

"Wait a minute. This is *not* who I am." The first time I heard her emphatic voice over the phone, I had just told Dawn that I was interested in talking about her experience as a widow. "Don't use the W-word around me," she commanded.

That threw me for a momentary loss, until she rescued me with her full, free-floating, throaty laugh. "Unless you mean the W Hotel. They have the Bliss Spa there, and it is *just* the *best*."

A few days later, she met me at a screaming-loud Italian restaurant on the Upper East Side. As she approached the table on high-altitude heels, I immediately realized that here was walking, talking proof that a widow doesn't have to be the old Italian lady in black in the back of the church, which was how Dawn said she thought of her. A master of the feminine arts, Dawn looked the way all of us think we could look if we quit our jobs, relinquished our family responsibilities, and dedicated ourselves to hair, makeup, nails, the works. It wore me out to realize that she managed all this while running her company, mothering her children, and leading a spirited social life with a passel of girlfriends and, for all I knew, maybe a boyfriend or two, too.

Confronted with this brute glamour, I took stock. Like Dawn, I had blond hair that fell below my shoulders, but hers was screen-siren platinum and perfectly in place. I've maintained myself well enough that I'm still game for bathing-suit season, but Dawn's figure was the stuff of year-round male fantasies, with feminine curves cantilevered over a taut little torso. I believe in maintaining appearances in the limited time I'm willing to allot to the task, but her nails were impeccable crescents of white polish, her makeup airbrushed to a fine glow. I know my way around a sample sale, but Dawn's creamy white cashmere sweater with a blousy top and trim little waist looked like a full-price find to me—and what mother of young children hazards white cashmere? Please!

It wasn't all surface sparkle, either. Like a movie star before a camera, she could blaze with an inner light, and she understood her effect.

"I think I've challenged a lot of people to look at me and say, 'Wow, did she really lose her husband?'" Dawn said. But she was determined not to let social expectations dictate her script. His death, she said, left her thinking, "If this can happen in my life, I'm going to live *every single second*. I can almost hear him saying, 'Dawn, go out and do something fun. What are you sitting there for?'"

Yes, I thought: Here she was in the flesh, the ultimate *widow provocateur.*

Dawn had never concerned herself with culturally sanctioned behavior. She filled me in while we split some sautéed shrimp and a salad. "I was a bit of a rebel, right from the beginning," she said. Her upbringing was Catholic, but she never believed in confession. "It was too dark and scary for me. And what can a seven-year-old child confess?" She told the nuns, "I can just talk to God myself."

Her self-reliance served her well growing up on the wrong side of the tracks in a mostly Italian American New Jersey town. After her dad left the family, Dawn pretty much ran the house and looked after her younger brother while her mother supported them. She got an associate's degree in business management, burning to strike out on her own. She baked cheesecakes from her mom's recipe and sold them to restaurants. Then she and a partner went into a venture together, providing two-way radios to police and fire departments, but with an eye on entertainment events. She became a fixture backstage at concerts, where top rock-'n'-roll acts hired her to manage communications. It was hard, exacting work, star-struck work for some, but the thrill for Dawn was in building her company.

She paid a personal price with the constant travel. In 1996, though, amid the backstage hubbub at the MTV Europe Music Awards, a handsome blond South African who set up the generators struck up a conversation with her. It turned out they had been working the same tours in the same places for years but hadn't met before. "As fate may have it," Dawn said, "when you're in alignment with the universe and doing what you're supposed to be doing, it's almost like the universe paves the way." This remark, I gradually learned, was what Dawn's friends call a Dawnism, a statement of such over-the-top positivity that it could only come from her.

She and Andries married, and he left the road after his last tour with the Rolling Stones to run a division of Dawn's company. They both scaled back their travel as the company grew, especially after they had kids. She savored the memory with a satisfied smile and then came up short. "Yeah...anyway."

Anyway. Andries and Dawn sometimes went separate ways on weekends. He was a robust outdoorsman, a risk taker, a guy's guy, whereas Dawn was a girl's girl, no apologies. "I am not sporty, not an ounce of me," she said. Which is why she stayed home to host a family party one weekend while he went gunning through the forests of West Virginia on all-terrain vehicles with some friends. One of them called to break the news that Andries had careened over a cliff. He was forty years old. Dawn was forty-four.

"I don't even try to ask why Andries died, because it will make me crazy." Dawn's voice was uncharacteristically soft. "I don't think I'll ever have *that* answer."

She tried to spin a Dawnism even out of this. "I always think that when bad things happen, it's because something better is coming." But, for once, her perpetual sunshine failed her. "I can't imagine it being any better than what we had. I'm not being negative. But anybody who knew Andries would agree. Where do you go from here?" Her voice jumped an octave. *"Where do you go from here?"*

Throughout lunch, Dawn played her voice like a musical instrument, finding the right tone for the emotion, ranging from husky low notes when she began describing how she first met Andries to the full-throttle high of that impossible-to-answer question. Scientists had told me that the bereaved can benefit from the ability to express genuine emotions so long as they don't dwell excessively on the negative, and if so, Dawn was right on track. She let her feelings rip, looking for the bright side, the humor, ever ready for a laugh. And when things turned dark, she instinctively looked away.

For the first months after Andries's death, she considered selling her stake in the business. Seeing his closed office door, hearing others cry at their desks, made her sick to her stomach. But she had a family to feed. The children kept her spirits up. It was important that she keep their father alive for them, telling them he would be proud of them, keeping out pictures and photo albums. "They would be the first to say that Daddy is watching over us. I believe he is, too. No one will tell me different."

On holidays, she and the children hosted his family, surrounding themselves with people who looked and sounded like him. And she maintained Andries's active philosophy, keeping busy, surrounding herself with happier friends. On a weekend trip to a spa in the Poconos six months after he died, she met a guy who was going through a divorce. He asked her out, but she said it was too soon.

A few days later, she was on the phone with her mother-in-law, a widow who warned Dawn, "The holidays are coming up, and it's going to be awful, and I just have to prepare you." She paused for dramatic effect. "It. Doesn't. Get. Any. Better. Ever."

Dawn got off the phone as fast as she could, and the next day, she called the guy from the spa. "I told myself I was getting right back on that horse." Her gestures as she told me this were so big, so over the top, that she nearly knocked over a water glass. She asked him, "What do you want to do?" He said, "Anything you want." Dawn fired back, "Okay. Let's go."

She smacked down her palm. A deep flush suffused her face. "There's that saying—there's good, and there's good for now. And the good-for-nows can actually be better." Dawn's irrepressible laugh cut through the noise in the restaurant.

I relished her defiance of convention. "Do you ever worry about social pressure?" I asked for myself as much as her. "That if you date someone else, that if you don't seem miserable all the time, people will think that you didn't love your husband?"

"Life is so short," Dawn said. "I say, when you've walked a mile in my shoes, come talk to me."

Her fling with the spa guy had been a lark, but that didn't satisfy her larger mission. Those kids felt the absence of a father acutely, and her goal was to fill that absence. Good-for-now wouldn't cut it for long.

Days before our lunch, Dawn's daughter had drawn up a wish list for Christmas. "Mommy, all I want is another Daddy," she said, with pleading eyes. "It's at the top of my list." She handed it to Dawn and pointed. "Look, I have an arrow here, next to the word." *Daddy*.

"Honey, Mommy can't just go on the Internet and find one," Dawn explained. Actually, Mommy can, she acknowledged to me with a laugh, but she couldn't be assured of the quality. "Mommy is very open to this, but we have to make sure it's the right person. It has to just happen. It has to come from God."

chapter

TWELVE

hether through God, the Internet, or some other higher power, most of the women when we first met seemed bolder than I had been about finding love again, or at least an occasional good-for-now. But the question was how. Attractive, available, age-appropriate men seemed as rare as plutonium and possibly just as dangerous. After we said good-bye to Katie and convened for dinner at a museum café, Tara told us that in the last month she had survived the mortification of one of the great trials of the midlife single person—the public fix-up.

We found a table near big windows looking out over Central Park. The sun had yet to set, and outside we saw little buds beginning to bloom in the dogwood trees. Appetizers arrived—small plates of roasted eggplant, shrimp arancini, cocktail meatballs, red beet ravioli, and red pepper hummus—while Tara slowly recounted the excruciating details.

Two longtime couples had invited her to join them for dinner at the home of a single man, a keen woodworker who had recently built a new recycling bin. Ordinarily, Tara might have declined, but Lesley and Dawn had convinced her there was no harm in accepting the attentions of a gentleman more than a year after her husband died. Nevertheless, this being a public fix-up, we groaned at the possibilities for embarrassment—the intimate setting, the implication that Tara and the recycling-bin guy constituted a third couple, the witnesses standing by like laboratory scientists eagerly awaiting evidence of romantic combustion.

Tara did her best. She brought a bottle of wine—recyclable! She praised the museum-quality bin to the skies. But over dinner, Recycling-Bin Man asked her, "How old are your children?" His were six and eight.

Tara told him that both her girls were out of college. Silence descended over the table like the dirigible in *Black Sunday*.

"How young is he?" Marcia said.

"Forty-seven." Tara was fifty-four. A meaningless difference if the man had been the older one, but even in this enlightened era, dating a younger man was still, apparently, a stretch.

"That's what I want," said Marcia, who had just turned fifty-eight. "A younger man."

"Well, this guy . . . freaked out." Tara dragged out the suspense with her protracted way of speaking.

Dawn tried to salvage the story. "He was probably thinking, 'I can't believe she looks that great and she has kids that age.' You are feeding into your fears."

Tara's expression shut her down. "It got worse. Afterward, my friends critiqued me. They said I didn't show enough . . . interest. I didn't . . . flirt enough." Her alto voice had dropped a full register. "I was . . . *dying*."

I told her about my failed public fix-up with the mulch man, and Lesley weighed in with one she'd endured. Through the alchemy of retelling, these episodes seemed funnier than they had at the time.

Nevertheless, Tara had decided that the best approach to this strange new phase in her life was not to think about romance, but to concentrate on upgrading everything else about herself. Perhaps, as a side benefit, she might draw a man to her from some uncharted, outlying sphere on the sheer force of her newfound magnetism. If not, so be it. She was making undeniable progress. Since leaving her job at an educational foundation, she had been casting about for something new, and that dusky voice of hers had opened an unexpected opportunity. A friend who performed voice-over work, reading scripts for commercials and industrial films, recognized her potential and invited Tara along on an audition. Competing against trained actors, she gave it a shot, more for laughs than anything else, and she was thrilled when she began to field some offers—a callback for a drug commercial, a script for a business conference.

"I've had so much fun," she said. "Not . . . a whole new career, but it's a nice little bit of . . . icing on the cake."

Lesley asked Denise how she was faring since the gathering at the cooking class. To help with the mortgage, she told us, she'd been considering a couple of candidates to rent the second bedroom in her apartment. A midlife roommate, unappealing as that sounded, was probably necessary. But the helpful widower was still buying her groceries. "He's getting me laundry detergent right now," she said, discreetly pleased. "It's not romantic, though."

"Has he done anything more, like touch you or kiss you?" Lesley asked, watching with sharp eyes.

"No, he hasn't. I don't want more right now."

"Let me say this as gently as possible," I said. "When I was first widowed, I needed all kinds of help—you know, reaching a high shelf, painting the bathroom ceiling. In my experience, the guy who wants to help you is the guy who wants to get into bed with you."

"I can't say I disagree," Lesley said.

She filled us in on how everything was humming along in her live-in relationship with Craig. It wasn't as simple as her marriage had been, when she and Kevin, young and unencumbered, made their home and started a family. Craig was divorced and had custody of a thirteen-year-old son, so the boy was now living with Lesley, too. They were cautiously negotiating protocols on vegetable consumption at dinner and the proper volume of an electric guitar. It sounded as if Lesley was winning over Craig's son, cautiously extending affection, stepping into her homemaker role, with or without green beans. In her rush to share her home with Craig, she admitted, she hadn't thought through all the implications of caring for his boy, too, but she was reveling in having company in the house again.

The sky grew dark outside the windows, and a waiter lit candles on our table. It was easy to talk over the soft undertone of other diners scattered nearby. While we waited for the main course, I passed around my frayed clipping of the Ed Ruscha painting *I Was Gasping for Contact*.

"Contact," Lesley said, nodding. "That was the thing I missed the most from being married to Kevin. I missed touching somebody. Think about babies, how they thrive on touch. You stroke your baby, you touch her head. This is what we need to thrive."

"It's tough," I said. "In our culture, touching is considered sexual, so if you're not in a sexual relationship, nobody ever touches you. All you get is a quick social hug, or a peck on the cheek."

"All day I'm around tons of people," Marcia said. "They work and go home. It's not the same. It's not intimate." Listening to Marcia, I began to realize that she wasn't so much inscrutable as brief. She cut right to the point—blink and you missed it. As this one sank in, I understood that Marcia, with her all-consuming career, might have fewer opportunities for meeting love interests than the rest of the gang.

"Marcia, we need to get you on Match.com," Lesley said.

"No," Marcia scowled. Point made.

Lesley rattled on, undeterred. "Craig touches a lot," she said with a grin. "If I'm in a room full of people, he'll walk past me and touch me, just to let me know he's there. I go *woooo-hoooo*, like I'm having an orgasm. Those are things you forget."

"Also, it's different now," said Dawn. "You know what you've lost."

Something in her expression caught my attention, something fragile. She, too, was wrestling with the matter of needing or wanting touch, but this new relationship with the widower was stirring up more, reviving a longing for the union of love and soul that we'd witnessed in *Cupid and Psyche*. Dawn told us that she and Adam had carried on a three-hour discussion that day, starting at breakfast and stretching through the morning, trying to sort out what limits to place on their relationship, what to combine and what to keep separate. Dawn was drawn to Adam and his children, but he was resisting.

"I don't think he wants to feel *anything*," she said. "He said he thought the reason it worked between his wife and him was that they didn't need each other. They were independent." But Dawn told him, "It's not the *need*. It's the *want*." She turned her eyes on all of us, trying to explain. "It's the *wanting*."

Her voice built to a whine. "Everything feels so freaking *calculated*. Is it ever going to be like it was *before*? Is it ever going to happen where you just meet someone, you love each other, and then you sort everything out *later*?" She looked at each of us imploringly. Her next words sounded discouraged. "With him it's all about what works and what doesn't."

"Because you know things now that you didn't know when you got married," Marcia said.

"Just this morning, I said to him, 'It's just freakin' easier to be by yourself.'" Dawn banged her hand against the table and made the silverware bounce.

"I took a different approach with Craig," Lesley said. "I jumped into this living together without thinking too much. But here's what I did think: things with Craig are good *right now*. They might not be good next week, but what the hell, I'm having fun. I'm willing to take that risk. If it doesn't work next week, my heart will be broken, but you know what? I've overcome much."

"But it's different for Dawn," Marcia said, bringing her analytical mind to bear. "She has to worry about young children, hers and his."

Marcia, as usual, had hit on something. None of us thought there was anything wrong with casual affairs, but easygoing romance was harder to pull off when children were involved, especially children who had recently lost a parent and longed for stability.

The children had met already, Dawn said, her boy and girl and his boy and girl, hitting it off immediately. They played together at

Adam's house as if they had known each other forever, getting all muddy in the yard. She was more touched than she was prepared to admit. *This is a family,* Dawn looked at them and thought, *the family we don't have anymore.* The kids scurried upstairs to clean up, and Dawn followed after a while to call them down for dinner. She came upon Adam's little girl sitting alone at a child-sized vanity table, rows of nail polish neatly lined up on top, all the girly things belonging to a girl in a family with only a brother and a dad. She turned a hopeful face toward Dawn.

The sight hit Dawn with heart-stopping force. "I almost lost it," she said. "I thought, *oh my God,* this little girl doesn't have a mom."

All the emotions that she wouldn't let herself feel for herself, that she wouldn't let herself feel for her own fatherless children, all the emotions that she suppressed to be the happy mom for her family, came to the fore. "The whole situation," she said, her voice leaping and swooping, "I don't know if I was feeling it for myself, or feeling it for them, or maybe feeling it for myself vicariously through them. All I know is, this triggered a lot of my own stuff that I probably didn't experience in my own way. Because you know what?" Her voice squeaked. "I was twelve years old, just her age, when my dad left."

We waited, full of thoughts, while Dawn explored sedimentary layers of feeling in her mind.

"Is it normal to be so nervous about all this?" she asked.

"Yes," everyone promptly agreed.

She took a measured breath. Later that night at home, she said, as she put her children to bed, her son posed a question. "Mom," he said, "what if we meet a family where there is no mom, and we're a family that has no dad, you *knoooow* . . . ?" Dawn drew out the word to leave the question hanging in the air. "Can you imagine?" he said. "What if the kids don't even know each other's names?"

"You see?" Dawn said. "He's thinking about it. He has all these fears."

One day soon after, her daughter told Dawn she had had a dream. "It was a dream about Daddy," the girl said, "but then all of a sudden I turned around, and it wasn't my daddy. It was some other man."

It sounded as if the possibility of a new husband, a new father, a whole new family, was just too strange for all of them to wrap their heads around. Our minds have to approach such jarring transitions indirectly, I thought, through dreams, or art, or through the lives of others, such representations sometimes being the clearest mirrors for puzzling through changes so big we can't face them without the distance. This trip to the museum was driving home the point that it might be easier to contemplate something outside ourselves in order to understand something inside ourselves.

Dawn was thinking the same thing. "I look at my own kids and myself and I think we're in great shape," she said. "Then I look at this man's family and it triggers so much emotion that I can't even tell you. But we're in the exact same position!"

It pained me to see Dawn contending with so much, and it forced me to re-examine my assumptions about her. Naively, I had thought that her beauty, her faith, and her optimism would smooth her way toward a happy destiny. I had thought that men would flock to her, that she and her children would flourish under her buoyant guidance, and that it all would happen quickly for her, snap-snap. I had fallen into the old presumption that attractive women have the world on a string. Uniting her family with another one just like it would have been just the quick, gratifying ending I would have predicted for Dawn. But here she was, involved with a man who wanted to keep her at arm's length even as his children wanted to embrace her. Even those who are blessed with much, as I understood it now, have their work cut out for them when forced to reorder it all in the middle of their lives.

Even for Dawn, it wasn't possible to carry on the way we all had in our youth, before marriages and families and mess intervened. Remaking a family, as opposed to making a family, was a much taller order than finding some great guy when both of you are young and unattached, marrying him, and letting the dice roll. I took a hard look at Dawn. Like the lotus blossom paintings, she might have been showy, but she wasn't just for show. She had deep roots. She had a striving spirit. And her way forward right now was a murky one. I could only hope that the goddess Diana was out there somewhere, poised to guide her.

━━━━━━━

LESLEY CHANGED THE SUBJECT back to art. Her favorite piece, in fact, had been Diana, who offered direction to those in need of it.

Dawn, of course, was drawn to the lotus paintings. "But tonight I noticed *The Three Graces* more," she said, brighter, "for what they stand for." She looked at each of us in turn around the table. "I always tend to look at life in the way of grace. I've had so much of it."

The waiter brought Dawn a bowl of ice cream and a spoon. She was the only one who'd ordered dessert.

We set off through the largely empty museum, wandering unseeing past more great works, having had our fill. Lesley changed the subject again. "We have to do something about a name," she said. "People ask me what I'm doing, and I have to say I'm going out with my widows' group. I can't do it."

"I was thinking of one—the Diana group," said Tara. "But it sounds like a reference to the Princess of Wales."

"I don't like it," said Marcia.

"So what about the Lotus Blossoms?" Tara said.

"Oh no, please," I said. "People who don't know our story will think we're a bunch of little flowers—which we are anything *but*. They'll think that we sit around talking about crystals and drinking herbal tea and channeling the positive energy in potted plants."

"Who cares what they think?" Tara elbowed me aside. "We're blossoms. We're blossoming." Dawn beamed her approval.

"And we've all been in murky waters, haven't we?" Lesley added.

I opened my mouth to object, but too late. The others had settled it between them. They were calling themselves the Blossoms now, ambling arm-in-arm, exchanging hugs, sharing conspiratorial whispers, making plans to keep in touch until the next gathering. We passed *The Three Graces* again, and I lingered, alone, delighting in the similarity between that friendly tableau, the way hands fell softly on shoulders of ancient marble, and the women embracing ahead of me. What about The Graces, I thought, The Six Graces? That's a name I could live with. Beauty, mirth, and abundance times two.

But the others had moved on without me. And that was it, the moment when I realized that this group was no longer *my* group, that it didn't matter anymore what I wanted to call it, even what I wanted to do with it. I held my tongue. What do you call six widows with nothing more to lose? *Anything they want*, I thought, *anything they want.*

chapter

THIRTEEN

a month later, I found myself slathered in some kind of celestial ooze, bound in a full-body straitjacket, unable to free my hands to lob a votive candle at loudspeakers that were playing a pan pipe loop of the *Titanic* theme that would lodge in my head for the next six days. Yes, I had succumbed to a weekend at a spa, a place in the mountains of Pennsylvania where Dawn had met the spa guy. No, a spa was not my sort of thing. Why did I do it? Because the ladies in my group—don't make me call them Blossoms—wanted us to go.

I could hardly object, because I had been belaboring one of the primary purposes of our group, which was to engage in new experiences together, emphasis on *new*. This one would qualify for me, and I hoped my willingness to compromise would set an example and help avert a crisis. Ever since our first meeting, I'd been lobbying for us to plan a far-flung trip at the end of the year. I was holding out for a wild adventure, something that would challenge us and take us where we'd never thought of going. Others were resisting or pushing destinations that were predictable and sedate. Marcia, ever the lawyer, insisted we wouldn't leave the spa until we hammered out an agreement. This had the potential to turn boisterous, even contentious, disrupting the high-minded, vaguely Zen calm of our weekend retreat. I'd let the spa attendants baste me in butter sauce and sauté me if it would help avert a showdown.

"Ladies," Tara said with full solemnity on our arrival, "this is . . . serious. Our leader . . . has never been to a spa before."

She and Dawn, veterans of such indulgences, promised to guide me. First we changed into fluffy white robes and matching slippers like escapees from a virgin-sacrifice slumber party. Then they directed me toward the spa services, which included this Soothing Herbal Body Wrap that was turning my skin—and possibly my brain—into custard. Algae-scented custard.

They explained to me the purpose of a spa—equal parts chakra-aligning relaxation and drill-sergeant-sanctioned self-improvement. We would achieve a higher state of being through pampering, exercise, and food so healthy that I'd considered smuggling in my own stash of bourbon and Mallomars.

I wasn't opposed to healthy per se. I knew that healthy was crucial for anyone overcoming the loss of a spouse, because such a loss can have devastating consequences for the survivor. Men and women who have experienced the death or divorce of a partner have more chronic health problems later, including heart disease, diabetes, and cancer, even if they remarry. The stress of uncoupling damages chromosomes all over our bodies—researchers have seen it through their microscopes. So I recognized the value of spoiling ourselves a bit, eating properly, maybe even getting slimed with a soothing algae wrap or two. Our chromosomes might thank us.

Nevertheless, normally when I traveled, I chose options not likely to extend my life for long. Back when I vacationed with Bernie, if I wasn't faceup on a beach somewhere with a book, I might fancy a dose of Paris, where the regimen was more my style than the soy-based menu at the spa. But experts had told me about the benefits of novelty in breaking the cycle of grief, and my own experience reinforced that message. In fact, there was one particular exploit that had turned me into a convert, in large part because it was unlike anything I'd ever done before. It was the single episode most responsible for helping me to turn a corner and heal. And it was truly, at least for an office-bound city girl like me, a far-out adventure on the far side of the world.

———

IT HAPPENED A FEW MONTHS after my misadventure with the widows' support group that rejected me, a far-out experience of a different sort. There I was, a year and a half after Bernie died, still out of place among my contemporaries, out of place among other widows, too. Maybe that's what led me to sign up for a trip to a place that I'd never considered visiting before, a place, in fact, that had never interested me in the least.

I had worried that my first vacation alone after Bernie died might be not only lonely but boring as well. I didn't care how empowering it was supposed to be for a woman to dine alone in a restaurant—I'm a slow eater, and I like having somebody to talk to. And group travel? I envisioned myself stuck on a bus with Iggy Pop and Mrs. Schreckengost, my high school home ec teacher. Breezing around the Internet, I came across one last opening on a trip to the

Galápagos Islands. I saw beaches and a sailboat. I somehow over-looked the fact that the water temperature was fifty-five degrees.

After minimal research, I decided that this excursion might be the fix for my travel problems. The Galápagos, I vaguely recalled, were famously populated with creatures that had washed up alone in a harsh environment and had to learn to adapt and evolve. I could relate. And to protect the islands' unique environment, visi-tors were required to travel with a group and a licensed guide. That way I'd have company over dinner every night and something to talk about after spending days trailing around after peculiar wild-life. The romantic in me liked the idea that the trip was really out there—in the middle of the Pacific Ocean, far from everything in a daily life that now was such a challenge.

Oh, I got challenge, all right. The trip involved ten days of hik-ing, sea-kayaking, and snorkeling with twelve strangers, all orga-nized by an adventure travel company known for African safaris and Himalayan mountain climbing.

I recognized the scope of my mistake at the first rendezvous with my fellow travelers at the airport in Quito, Ecuador. I was wearing clothing appropriate for the snack bar at Cap Juluca. They were wearing *gear*—ultralight, water-repellent, moisture-wicking, mesh-and-spandex actionwear in blazing colors that gave conspicu-ous definition to their lean and sculpted bodies. They frisked about in the waiting area like racehorses at Churchill Downs. We intro-duced ourselves. One woman let me know that she had completed marathons on all seven continents, including Antarctica, where her husband, equally fit, had shoveled the snow off the course. This same couple had scaled some of the highest peaks in the Andes on their last vacation, hiking to safety when their bus veered off a mountain road. Another imposing figure had sea-kayaked through Papua New Guinea on her most recent trip, sleeping on floors of mud huts. She swam every morning in the icy currents of San Francisco Bay.

I'd spent much of the last five years in hospital waiting rooms. Thinner than thin and frailer than frail, I didn't even belong to a gym, and my writing job hardly required feats of strength. Because I had signed up for the trip only a week before, I had assembled a mishmash of sporty togs from the recommended packing list on a last-minute shopping spree that I called Survival of the Fittings. My Puma cloth sneakers provided no shock absorption, torsion stability, or functional support of any kind, but I held out hope that my new wetsuit, a size too small and strained to the point of snapping, made me look like Lara Croft. Once, I reminded myself, I had been a competitive swimmer, even though now my foremost association with water was the series of drowning nightmares that were all tied up with Bernie's death.

Our guide handed out the itinerary, jammed with activities several grades beyond my endurance level. There was also a list of our fellow travelers. I had signed up too late for my name to be included. Someone had written in ink only this: *New York Woman*.

Unlike the seasoned adventurers in the group, I hadn't done much reading about the Galápagos or Charles Darwin or nature in general, for that matter. Our guide, Klaus, filled me in on the plane. A true action hero who looked the part, with sun-bleached hair and a square jaw, Klaus was skilled in surfing, scuba diving, and mountain climbing. He explained how the barren mass of islands had been formed by relatively recent volcanoes. The only creatures that lived there were descended from birds that could fly hundreds of miles without a place to rest, or land species like turtles that were capable of surviving long sea voyages on tree branches or other floating debris. Over time they had morphed into just the right configurations to keep themselves alive and attract their mates, some two thousand species that existed nowhere else on earth. I looked out of the window as we landed, catching my first view of the islands' craggy black landscape, peppered with scrubby plants, looking about as hospitable as the surface of Uranus. This wasn't St. Barts. It was a land of misfits, home of living things that didn't really belong there.

If the animals living in the Galápagos could manage for centuries, surely I could suffer through ten days. I settled into my billet on the sailboat that would carry us from island to island. The first morning, I groaned with horror at the six a.m. wake-up knock. But I told myself that I had become, however improbably, a woman who owned a fanny pack with Velcro closures. It was time to strap it on. Soon I found myself scrambling over jagged lavascapes, my ankles wobbling as I struggled to find my balance and keep up with two other single women. We took each other's pictures next to whatever oddball bird or reptile we ran across. There were three-hundred-pound tortoises; marine iguanas that were genuine leaping lizards, diving into the sea for food; and flightless cormorants, swimming birds whose wings had withered to useless stubs. Pairing off throughout history, mating couples had produced these freaky mutations. Some species, Klaus explained, like the albatross, were monogamous for life. What happens to the ones whose mates died early, I wondered? Where did they fit in?

Thanks to my dormant swimming expertise, I kept pace better in the water, where the multicolored fantasia on snorkeling excursions carried me far from such thoughts. I sloshed through the frigid sea to spy on penguins, sharks, spectacular schools of colored fish, and, one day, two manta rays—six and eight feet across at least—gliding elegantly by. I don't know which impressed me more, the beauty of their graceful progress or the fact that I was lapping with them at six thirty in the morning.

One day as we were hiking along some tidal pools, Klaus stopped to point out something really special, a fish called a four-eyed blenny, with quirky gills that processed air and fins that allowed it to pull itself up on the rocks. We gathered close, straining to follow Klaus's pointing finger. I couldn't make out the fish at first. It was tiny, Klaus said, and its mottled scales blended in with the crusty rocks. I tried again, and there it was, my soul mate: a genuine fish out of water.

"Hang in there, little guy," I said.

By the last day, I had become so nimble in my high-fashion sneakers that the others took to calling me, only half kidding, Action Girl. In fact, they were still teasing me after our final snorkeling foray as our skiff skipped across the water on the way back to the mother ship. I looked toward the horizon and spotted a large school of fish leaping into the air a hundred yards or so away.

"What's that, Klaus?" I shouted over the engine.

"Those are skipjacks," he shouted back. "Swimming with skipjacks is the most incredible experience. Do you want to try it?"

"Yeah!" I didn't even know what skipjacks were. I later learned they were a fast-moving fish, related to tuna, but just a couple of feet long. Waiting for no one, I flung myself off the boat.

What was I thinking? We were out in the deep, wide-open ocean. We had seen hammerhead sharks only minutes before.

When I put my face down, I saw nothing but black. For a moment, I gasped and sputtered. All those drowning nightmares crowded my mind, pulling me down. I pushed them away. Something in me wanted this adventure. And something else: by now I felt safe with my group. I sensed the impact as they hit the water beside me.

I took off after those fish, tapping some lunatic strength to churn across the surface of the sea, punching into the choppy waves. I spotted some skipjacks up ahead, just a few of them at first, and then more, and then even more, and I was thinking, *Damn, these fish are fast, but I'm as fast as they are.*

Unaccountably, it was true. I was slicing through the water with preposterous ease, leaning into it with everything I had, feeling the rhythmic force of my breathing and the surging, unexpected power of my arms and legs, the pure euphoria of acceleration. The water buoyed me up and carried me forward. Soon the shiny, silvery skipjacks were flashing all around me, hundreds of them, maybe thousands, tens of thousands for all I knew, yet they also moved as one, switching directions through some mystical telepathic connection, and I was right there with them, in a swirl of iridescent motion. I could have been arcing through the air with a flock of shimmering birds. I felt blessed to possess whatever it took—my old swimming skill, my aqua-dynamic physique, or maybe a fear-juiced shot of adrenaline—to be alive to that wonder.

Out of breath, I stopped and looked up, all alone in the deepest water I'd ever been in. I was astonished to see my friends scattered far behind. No one but me had caught up to the fish.

"Becky," Klaus exclaimed when he reached me at last with the boat. "You are an incredibly strong swimmer." He reached out a hand to pull me in.

"Trust me," I said, as surprised as he was. "I'm not strong."

"You are incredibly strong," Klaus said again. I could swear he was looking behind me to see if I had an outboard motor attached. The others were equally agog.

"No, I'm not," I insisted. Dripping all over, legs all wobbly, I pulled off my mask. I felt the rigid muscles in my face let loose into the biggest smile I'd put out there since Bernie died. "It's this place. I seem to be well adapted to it."

And that was how I took a trip to the Galápagos, Land of Misfits, to discover that I was stronger than I knew, that I could tackle something new, even in the wrong clothes, the wrong shoes, the wrong body. That I, too, could evolve. My newfound Action Girl persona, I understood, wouldn't be much use back home amid the trials of work and loss. Most days I would still feel like that four-eyed blenny trying to drag myself by my flippers onto dry land. But like the strange, adaptable species of the Galápagos—birds that don't fly, iguanas that swim, fish that walk—I had seen that I, a wife without a husband, could bring my own grab bag of strengths and weaknesses to an alien situation. And that I might not be the fittest, but I could survive. Maybe even thrive.

chapter

FOURTEEN

*i*f only Bernie could have been there. We'd still be talking about it today. Anyone who has ever been married knows that among the many perks—companionship, affection, reliable dinner conversation—one of the least appreciated is a well-curated stock of memories, the ability to turn to a longtime partner and say, "Remember the time . . ." I hadn't given much thought to this when Bernie first died, but gradually I realized that now there was no one there to fill in the blanks. I had stored up a lifetime of adult memories that nobody remembered now but me. Without the sharing, the memories were slipping away. What was the point of attending that avant-garde production of Coriolanus in the rain if Bernie and I couldn't laugh about it later?

That was part of my reasoning in forming our widows' group. It wasn't enough that we widows get out there and take on a husband-less new world. We needed to take it on with new companions, making not only new memories but new friends to share them with.

This was on my mind at the spa when I met up with the group

at the *Gotta Hoop* group fitness class, a hazing ritual masked as play that involved a lot of hip-swiveling with heavy fluorescent hula hoops. I expected to be left in the dust from the get-go. In the time since that trip to the Galápagos, I had engaged in a somewhat higher level of daily activity, but I still associated the term *group fitness* with the terrors of fraternity hell week.

In a carpeted exercise room with a view looking onto a lake, the instructor revved up some too-cute remixes of Beatles songs. Remembering my mission for the weekend—openness to new experiences—I planted a hoop around the midsection of my drawstring pants and started to spin. The damn thing banged against my pelvic bones, clattered down my legs, and hit the floor with a thwack. I tried again: same result. And again. No amount of pop music could mask what was going on here: I had just been defeated by something I could do when I was ten.

I sneaked a look at Denise. Stripped down to form-fitting spandex that put her midriff on display, she seemed most likely to occupy the top of the food chain here, but she fared no better than I did. Most of the others, managing a little more seductive hip action in the latest clingy gymwear, kept their hoops up for half a minute or so at best. "I Should Have Known Better" taunted us over peals of embarrassed giggling.

Then my eye caught a blaze of billowing motion over by the window. It was Marcia, looking even more stolid than usual, dressed in black sweatpants and a square gray T-shirt with the New York Giants logo. She had on her best game face, too, and had adopted the stance of a longboard surfer riding a perfect wave, legs planted firmly apart, arms up, elbows out. But she was rotating that hoop with the reliability of a metronome.

"Get 'em, Marcia!" I called out. The others hooted their appreciation.

Marcia's face registered the compliment, one corner of her mouth twisting ever so slightly to the side, but she didn't break stride. She kept chugging around the room, forward, backward, and sideways, literally twirling circles around the rest of us. The only change I noted was that sideways skewing of her mouth. She fought to keep her lips in the straight line that rarely varied for her, but this was a look of scrupulously suppressed glee, the kind I'd seen before only when she talked about crushing a rival in a business deal. It was a sight to remember, worth every bruise on my pelvis and knees.

Tighter abs and silkier flesh aside, it was everything I'd hoped for from our weekend at the spa, in fact, from any of our gatherings—a new experience, and a shared memory. Marcia had just sealed one of those moments for us. After the weekend at the spa, all we'd ever need to say was, "Remember Marcia and the hula hoop?" and we'd be back in the moment, together, relishing her triumph over gravity.

———————————

I HEARD THEM before I saw them. And that's saying something, since the ladies clustered around a crater-shaped fire pit out by the lake, faces like carnival masks lit by leaping flames. But there was so much hilarity in the air that I knew as I approached it could only be our group. The day had been balmy, unseasonably warm for a first weekend in May, and the fire took just enough raw chill from the evening air. Marcia had brought wine from home, the primo vintage stuff, so we could conduct a formal tasting after our low-fat, low-salt, low-expectations spa dinner.

Tara's voice carried mellifluously through the tamarack trees and out across the glassy water. "What does LMAO mean?" she asked, peering at an iPhone buried in her fist.

"Laugh my ass off," Lesley was quick to reply. "When Craig and I met, we did flirty texting all the time," she said with a wicked spin. "Or sexting, as we called it."

"What do I answer?" Tara looked panicked but thrilled, too. Dawn huddled with her to compose a response.

All of us were thoroughly marinated and tenderized by Lavender Garden Body Polishes and Delaware River Stone Massages, but no one could match Tara's glow that night. I had never met anyone whose appearance changed so dramatically with her moods. She was thoroughly transformed since our first meeting, excitement giving her high-cheekbone features a radiant beauty as she flitted around the fire. She had switched out of her customary classic black cashmere for this occasion into white capri pants paired with a glittering orange, gold, and white tunic, accessorized with dangling beaded earrings and a big silver cuff bracelet. Everything shone.

She and Dawn had become bona fide buddies by now, sharing private glances and inside jokes. We pulled some wooden rocking chairs up to the fire, and the two of them filled us in on the guy at the other end of the texts.

"He asked me out on a date this weekend..." Tara said.

"But she said no, because she was committed to us," Dawn cut in. "I figure that will make him more interested."

"We met last week at a casual dinner with a few old classmates of my husband's," Tara continued. She wasn't speaking slowly this time. "They were in the same class, but I had never met him before. His name is Will." Unlike Recycling-Bin Man, she gave this one a name.

"She likes this one." Lesley rocked forward, giving us all an arch look.

"And before I left for here, I got a call to have dinner this Saturday night."

"She fancies him," Lesley sang.

"Yeah . . . a little." The fire caught Tara's flushed expression.

"Look at her eyes." Lesley couldn't have been more pleased if Tara had won the Mega Millions jackpot. "Did he smooch you good night the night you met?"

"God, no!" The thought seemed to terrify Tara.

"Do you see that look?" Lesley asked the rest of us. "You always know when you see that look." We saw it.

"He texted Tara this morning," Dawn told us. "He said he wanted to see a picture of her at the spa." So in the afternoon, Dawn and Tara slinked into the spa's Whisper Room, where clients zoned out after massages and such. Dawn scooped some cucumber slices out of a water pitcher, plonked them onto Tara's eyes, smeared some cream on her face and snapped a photo of her recumbent on a chaise longue, then showed her how to transmit the image on her phone. *LMAO* had been his response. Tara was passing around the picture when the iPhone lit up again. She snatched it away to read his latest text, keeping it to herself.

"Now what do I write?"

"TTYL," Lesley said. "Talk to you later."

Tara's thumbs went to work. She cackled. "I'm not sure I ever want to go out on a date with him. I would just like to keep doing this." She hit send. "Because then the bubble bursts."

Dawn exhaled in frustration. "Have I taught you *nothing*! Take it back."

"Honestly, I'm trying to be realistic."

Everyone jumped in. "Don't be negative!" Marcia ordered.

"Oh! Oh!" Dawn wailed. "You are causing me physical pain!"

"I'm sorry, sweetie, I'm sorry," said Tara, embracing her friend. "You know what I'll say to you? I'll say: This is wonderful right now. This is fun right now. I haven't had fun in a long time."

"Fun! Fun!" Dawn fixed Tara with a look and thrust both arms at her as if she were casting a spell.

Six other women had settled into chairs across the fire and watched us with open curiosity. Tara, more chatty than I'd ever seen her, soon learned that they were five daughters and their seventy-year-old mother, celebrating her birthday.

"You seem so close," the youngest daughter said. "How long have you all known each other?"

"Just since January," I said.

She looked shocked. "*How* do you know each other?"

All six of us blurted out in unison, "*You don't want to know.*" Our collective impulse set us off laughing.

We went quiet for a moment, and I could hear bullfrogs croaking by the lake. I knew why none of us answered. We knew what the reaction would be, that pitying look. It wasn't so much that we minded them knowing, even minded the sympathy, but everyone was having such a good time around the fire, and we knew our story would bring them down. It's not easy being a walking, talking buzzkill.

Tara owned up, but added, "We are not what you think. We are not like widows who go to depressing meetings."

Besides, here in this largely female sanctuary, there were ample reminders that husbands weren't the only source of fulfillment. As we returned to our own conversation, the moms among our group boasted about the accomplishments of their offspring, and others relayed the satisfaction they drew from full-tilt work. Denise talked about a novel she'd signed up and how absorbed she became in bringing order to a muddled manuscript. "Editing is like the card game Concentration," she said. "I can remember where the two of hearts is when I see it in the pile."

Dawn asked our advice on another business she might launch. "Another one?" I asked. "Don't you have enough going on?"

"I live for the thrill of starting businesses," she said, looking as tickled as Tara. "It's a more reliable thrill than a man, let me tell you."

Whether through parenting or work, we were finding happiness in the flow that psychologists had told me about, the immersion in tasks that both suited and challenged us, the gratification of goals set and met.

Still, Dawn said widowhood had brought a new perspective to bear on her career. "I want to keep building my business, but have fun and keep it light. I don't think I'll ever again be as serious as I was."

It was Tara's birthday that weekend, but there was plenty more going on with her. Since we last saw her, she had set a price on her house, the suburban family house, having decided that she wanted to sell it quickly and look for something smaller, maybe in the seaside town where Lesley had moved. If Tara didn't find someplace new in time, Dawn had offered a room at her place. We asked Tara if it was hard giving up the home where she had raised her daughters.

She thought for a moment. "I find it liberating," she said. I could see the relief on her face at the prospect of being unburdened of too much space, too many things, unburdened of her past.

"It shows," said Lesley. "You are looking so lovely. Since January, I see you getting stronger and stronger."

"Hmm," Tara said. "Dawn and I were talking about this today. Should you feel liberated? That you got a second chance? Or should you feel guilty for the sense of liberation you feel?"

Whatever her feelings, Tara was turning a corner, making some moves, forcing changes. Why now? Why, fourteen months after her husband died, four months after she'd looked so burdened at our first meeting, why now did she feel this elation, so visible in the firelight? Tara had been puzzling over the same thing on her drive to the spa. The easy answer was that she had met a man, from her description a funny, charming, viable man, both interesting *and* interested, but she dismissed that before she hit the first on-ramp. It was likely his regard was a mere flirtation, most probably leading nowhere.

Tara savored the monotony of a long trip. Two or three hours on the open road would give her time to reflect in the splendid isolation of her car. She thought about how she would turn fifty-five on Sunday. Fifty-five, no big deal. She had so much life ahead of her, and a responsibility to do something with it.

She eased onto the busy bridge over the Hudson River, reflecting on how she had weathered some miserable birthdays in the last few years, some birthdays mired in family turmoil, some tucked into bed with Dude, her Pekingese. This birthday, she thought, could have been a repeat performance. Instead, she told herself, *I am going to be with friends, supportive friends, and we are going on a journey.*

Halfway across the bridge, she had an open view of the water rolling below and the vast sky arching above. As views go, this vista might seem puny in contrast, say, to the Great Continental Divide in Montana, but for those of us in the swarm around New York, it's the best we've got, and crossing the Hudson heading west can feel supremely liberating. Tara felt the sensation of a curtain opening onto a wider world. In the last year or so, she realized, she was living behind that curtain. Closed off from a wider life, she had been forcing herself to go through the motions of recovery, looking within, taking care of family business. It was all thought out, structured, devoid of joy. She had never lived behind such a curtain before alcohol claimed her husband's life. She had been an extroverted person, a person who acted with her heart and her gut. Driving west, alone in her car, she realized, *I am beginning to return to who I really am. I'm letting my personality and my instinct take over again.* She hadn't achieved this state intentionally. It had arrived when she was occupied with everything else.

She steered her car beyond the suburbs and crossed into Pennsylvania, where the highway melted into shaded country roads. She wondered, as I did: Why now? What had changed? Time had passed, certainly, since the loss of David. She had made the hard decision to let go of her house and find someplace new, someplace uniquely hers. She was fielding more requests for voice-over work, a talent she had never suspected she possessed before. The understanding companionship of the other Blossoms, as she called us, made her feel safe, inspired her to do better. And she mulled over her growing friendship with Dawn. The connection had been quick, impulsive, but Tara knew it would last. Dawn's infectious optimism reminded Tara that her own nature was essentially optimistic. The hopeful, confident spirit had been there all along, waiting for her on the other side of the curtain, and Dawn reassured her that it always would be. They were beginning to share a vocabulary, and Tara found herself repeating some classic Dawnisms.

That weekend, Dawn was cheerleading Tara through her budding courtship as Dawn continued to debate the merits of her relationship with Adam and his children.

"We may go out when I get back Sunday," she said with a shrug. "He may not be the forever guy. I make sure to tell the kids he's just a friend. It's touch and go. We'll see."

"Baby steps for baby feet," Tara said, a Dawnism if I ever heard one.

The lodge, tucked into a forest, seemingly far from home, was turning into a refuge from everyday concerns, a chance to find perspective and get back in touch with happier selves.

"This is the first time I've been away since Steve died," Denise said, breathing the smog-free air and leaning back into a rocker. It was also the first weekend in months when she didn't have to read or edit for work. She still felt pressure to sell her apartment and find a cheaper one, but instead she had rented out the second bedroom to an acquaintance who wasn't there much, fortunately. That would give her some financial relief, although she still needed to earn extra money helping out at a yoga studio to pay the mortgage. "I can't tell you how good it feels to get some space, not to feel like everything is closing in on me." She smiled a normal smile, almost a Duchenne smile. "What a gift."

"Denise, what happened with that guy?" Lesley asked. "The one who brought you all the food."

Denise winced. "Disaster." She had been enjoying their platonic attachment, when, after he treated her to dinner at a fine restaurant, he announced, "I think I'm falling in love with you."

"Well, hello?" Tara said.

"I was horrified," Denise said. "It was less than two months since we'd known each other—way too fast for me." She didn't answer him, and the silence was thunderous. He repeated what he'd said as if she hadn't heard.

"Oh, God," Tara said. "Crawl under the table."

Denise cut the evening short. "I'm not in that kind of place," she told him a couple days later. "If you are looking for a response, I can't do that now."

He kept calling and e-mailing, but Denise stood firm. To her credit, she didn't seem too shaken by the loss of the friendship. Having the mettle to let an uneasy connection go, I thought, was a form of corner turning, too.

Tara's phone lit up again, and she handed it to Dawn to read in the dark.

"Nice ... serene ... hope it never ends."

"What's he reacting to?" Marcia asked.

"A picture of all of *us*," Dawn said, "at the fire."

"That was really sweet," Tara said.

Lesley was right: Tara fancied him.

Marcia yanked the cork out of a bottle of a full-bodied Spanish Granache and got down to the business of her wine tasting, pouring sips into glasses and handing us each a printed form to note our responses in categories like color, smell, and taste. I took a critical sip and wrote *dark cherry* next to color and *raspberry* next to taste.

"What are you doing?" Marcia said indignantly. "You're not supposed to write words. You're supposed to rate them with numbers, one to ten."

The rest of us were baffled. "How do you rate a color in numbers?" I asked.

"You rate how pleasing it is," said Marcia.

We couldn't help but laugh. Only Marcia among us would try to quantify something as subjective as taste and smell. I randomly wrote down some sevens and fours. Is cherry a five? Maybe an eight. But Marcia filled in her form with certainty. It was Marcia's job to establish the worth of things, their worth in numbers, anyway. Her work done, she sat back in her rocking chair and let us tease her about the forms for a minute as I wondered whether anyone else she knew had the nerve to make fun of her. Her husband probably had. I saw her mouth move to the side as she fought the urge to grin. It was the half grin I'd seen before when she talked about work, the same one I saw when she triumphed in the hula hoop class, the one I'd been seeing as she watched the rest of us kid around by the fire. Marcia waited for an opening to raise something new. She was trying to turn a corner, too.

"Guys," she said, "I saw an apartment a few months ago. I put a bid on it, but the guy wouldn't negotiate with me. He won't come down, and I really want this apartment." She was fighting to keep her mouth straight, fighting that grin. "If I want it, I'm going to have to overpay."

Marcia cave on a business deal? Unthinkable. It would violate every tenet of her creed. And yet. She was looking at Tara and

Dawn, watching for reactions, and they saw what I was seeing. Marcia wanted this place. Marcia wanted it so much that she was considering paying more than it was worth. She wanted it so much that she was considering going against her very nature. She wanted it so much that she was looking to Tara and Dawn for advice.

Buying this condo, she said, wouldn't be sensible. There were a lot of built-in shelves, so there might not be room for a mahogany bed from her husband's family. Not such a downside, we thought. We did a quick survey—everyone else but Denise so far had replaced the bed since her husband died. The marital bed was a zinger, for sure.

I thought that would be the end of it. But Marcia repeated, "I really want this apartment. It has this great open view over the city. It's got"—she chuckled, half embarrassed at the frivolity—"a pool on the roof. There's a steam room, a Jacuzzi..."

"I think I paid more for *my* new house than it's worth," Lesley said. "But it came down to this: this is where I want to live. I haven't looked back."

Tara began, "If you are going to be happy there..."

Lesley broke in. "Marcia, is your life about money or passion?"

The question seemed new to her. "You know, that's an interesting point," she said. "I make enough that it's not a big issue."

"It sounds like you would have fun there," I said. "You can hula-hoop on your roof, the whole city at your feet."

Everyone whooped at the image. Marcia's eyes crinkled, and her mouth tried to curl up into a full-blown smile as she fought the impulse. The effort showed, but she succeeded. This was serious. She was measuring the value of pleasure.

"I'm trying to be disciplined," she said. "I'm a lawyer. I do this all the time. When you do deals, you decide on an amount, and you won't cross that line."

"But this is personal," said Dawn, pleading. "Personal is different."

Marcia looked obstinate. I feared that a year from now, she would still be living in that depressing dorm-like apartment, scoring a victory for business over pleasure. The chance of Marcia giving in where money was concerned? I rated it a two.

"All I can think about," Tara repeated, "is Marcia in that hula hoop class."

Maybe a four.

chapter

FIFTEEN

*i*t depended which Marcia showed up at the table—the one in the Politburo suit, or the one in the kick-ass cowboy boots. From what I'd seen of Marcia up to now, it was the unrelenting dealmaker who usually dominated, and I do mean dominated. I still remembered how she cowed me during our first telephone conversation. She interrupted me with brusque asides to her assistant. "Tell him I'll call him back in five minutes," she barked. Or: "I don't even know who that *is*. Take a message."

I tried to explain my theories about overcoming grief, and she cut me off there, too. "I heard you are starting a group. I want to join your group." Bottom line.

She knew what she wanted, but did I? I doubted whether Marcia would fit in with what I hoped would be a merry gang. I could almost hear her saying, "Let me in the group. Cross me and I will crush you." My resistance crumbled, and I heard myself agreeing to meet her for dinner at a plush expense-account place near her office, around nine, after she wrapped up at work. She ordered foie gras to start.

Marcia reminded me of one of those Galápagos tortoises, a thick shell protecting her from unwanted scrutiny, a blunt tenacity compelling her to thrive. She wasn't like anybody else I knew. But as we set aside our menus and began to talk, her head poked out of that shell, just a bit, and I saw the gentle gaze of a tortoise that is visible only up close. This formidable woman had loved her husband, and for the first time in her life, she felt uncharacteristically weak. "I want to join your group" was less a command than a plea, however it sounded.

Her cryptic expression gave little away as I coaxed out her life story. "I knew that whatever I did with my life, I had to use my intellect," she said of her childhood in New York. But I began to discern an essential dry humor as well. After law school, she briefly joined a litigation practice with her father. "We'd butt heads all the time, because he was pigheaded and I was pigheaded." So she headed into corporate law instead, negotiating contracts. Even now, she often found herself the only woman at the conference table, but no one dared to patronize Marcia. "Even if they are inclined to in the beginning, it takes them about twenty minutes to change their minds," she said, gratified at her power to intimidate. Her sharp mind knew its stuff, and her sharp elbows defended her turf. After a merger with another company, she and a new colleague overlapped in expertise. "They had to separate us before we killed each other."

She never lost her temper, she assured me. "If I go after the other side, it's very calculated. If you want respect, you have to stay in control. I'm by nature, as I'm sure is apparent, very controlled."

Very apparent. We were halfway through sculptural French-Asian entrées at that first encounter before I saw the first crack in her shell.

"I *love* doing a deal," she told me. "The excitement—it's amazing." In the heat of negotiation, she allowed herself to be consumed by the action, but there were also constraints. "You don't want the guys you're dealing with to identify you as an emotional woman," she said. "You want them to see that you're stable, that nothing's going to crack you, that no matter what happens, you're not going to break."

Her description of her husband, Martin, hinted at another side. He was a holistic healer with an advanced degree in biology and the jovial host at their weekend parties in the country. He also hung out in local pubs with John Lennon and Harry Nilsson, two of the biggest carousers in rock 'n' roll. Marcia's father had set the unlikely pairing in motion after he conducted a legal negotiation with Martin's father, who had brought Martin along. He had a soft way with his stubborn parent, could get him to yield without going at him directly. He seemed like the perfect counterbalance for Marcia. "You want to meet my daughter?" her dad asked.

This union of opposites flourished for twenty-nine years, but the last five months, following Martin's diagnosis of stage four colon cancer, were fraught with friction. "He desperately didn't want to do chemo, even if it meant he was going to die," Marcia said. It was too late for surgery, so she went along with his plan for alternative treatment, wanting him to have a better quality of life, but when the disease progressed, she was all for blasting those tumors with the strongest stuff traditional medicine had to offer.

For the first time since she and I sat down at the restaurant, Marcia's assurance wavered. "The last few months were really tough. Because not only was he dying, but our relationship . . . there was a lot of tension in it. I was trying to get him to appreciate that the treatment wasn't working."

"The cancer had already metastasized to the liver," I said, wanting to reassure her. "The odds were against any other route curing him."

"I always tell myself that," said Marcia with the same crisp assurance she adopted when she spoke about her job. "Otherwise I'd go insane."

Marcia and I shared some of that ability to suppress emotions, along with a sense of displacement once we were widowed. Her friends, like mine, were married. Like me, she had no children. She was close to three nephews, nearly grown up, her godsons on Martin's side, but she wasn't close to the rest of Martin's relatives, who no longer included Marcia in family events. She worried that she and the boys would become estranged now that Martin was gone.

She joined a widows' support group, but the others were older, and none of them worked. For Marcia, now more than ever, work was everything. Weekends were bleak, so, like me, she planned ahead. She took an advanced photography course, learning to operate a super-complicated camera, but everyone in the class was younger. Younger people, older people—like me, Marcia had difficulty finding people like her.

I dithered over whether she belonged in the group I was forming. I explained that we were supposed to be freeing ourselves from the past and freeing ourselves from grief through adventure and experimentation. Everyone needed to be open to change. On the surface, Marcia struck me as someone wedded to routine. But I saw that she might engage her drive and intellect in what we were doing if she viewed it as a project, that the idea of participating in an experiment based on ideas might appeal to her. She weighed the logic of my argument, and then warily said she would give it a shot. I warily agreed to include her, half kicking myself that Marcia would forever be the odd woman out.

———————

I'LL GIVE HER CREDIT; for the first few meetings, she dutifully followed the program. The spa was a little more free-form. It would have been easy for Marcia to hole up in her room reading legal briefs. We had negotiated a sweet group rate that included all sorts of vigorous or not-so-vigorous self-improvement activities, so the morning after our fireside wine tasting, we went our own ways. Denise headed for back-to-back yoga sessions. Lesley signed up for a hike. Tara and Dawn kept up an all-day patter through fitness classes and facials and pedicures.

I took a kayak out on the lake, pondering how to raise the prickly subject of the final trip I envisioned for the fall. I'd spent the last few weeks talking to adventure travel organizers, salivating at the options, and I'd sent potential itineraries to the others, but no one had breathed a word about it since we arrived. It looked like I'd have to force the issue. But first, I let Denise talk me into getting in touch with my inner something-or-other at *Meditation to Quiet the Mind.* Forty minutes of envying Denise's posture and trying not to fixate on how the lotus position aggravated my knee only confirmed what I'd long believed—that remaining perfectly still while thinking about nothing was not my idea of entertainment. I repaired to the pool and hot tub, wondering what Marcia was up to.

She had shown up at breakfast in her full athletic ensemble, her agenda crammed with so many activities that I suspected her assistant must have booked them weeks in advance. She took on all comers: yoga with Denise, swimming with me, and something called *Barefoot Dancing* with Tara and Dawn, where they learned a pastiche of provocative moves that left the rest of us begging for mercy around the fire that night.

"I'm telling you, girls, all I needed was a pole," Dawn said.

The three of them demonstrated what they'd learned, which seemed to involve a lot of revolving the hips as if using one's tush to scrape cake batter from a bowl.

"Left, left, double, double, right, right, double, double," Tara purred, taking charge. "Now do the *whole* bowl." She and Dawn, despite potentially crippling laughter, translated these ridiculous directives into pure seduction, while Marcia moved around off to the side like a stiff apprentice in an actual cake-baking class at Le Cordon Bleu.

"I don't understand the instructions," she grumbled.

"You're not supposed to," Tara commanded. "It's all in the attitude."

Marcia kept at it, assuming something akin to the stance that had worked for her with the hula hoop.

"My favorite is when you slink down," Dawn said. "I can't do it now in my heels." She tried anyway and pulled it off. "I love the little wiggle on the way up."

"You have no shame!" Lesley cried. In a flash, she joined the line. "I want to try this when I get home."

"How am I supposed to remember all this?" Marcia asked.

Tara and Dawn turned to her. "Marcia," Dawn ordered. "Just do it. Just do it."

"Let loose," Tara piled on. "Don't overthink!"

"I actually like it," Marcia shrugged, flashing her secret grin.

They danced a bit more, Dawn and Tara and Lesley looking like headliners on the night shift at the Pussycat Lounge. Denise and I joined the lineup, too, swearing that there was no one else on earth we'd allow to see us in this ludicrous state. All the while Marcia kept giving it her all, the odd woman out, the woman who promised she never cracked. Marcia, the great lawyer, Marcia, who rated her wine by numbers, who ran her life by numbers—Marcia had a killer swivel. She slowly peeled back the façade, one stiff outer leaf at a time.

We collapsed back into the rocking chairs. Marcia hunched toward me, cryptic expression restored, and cupped a hand around her mouth. "I get a kick out of these women," she said.

Our weekend was wrapping up, and the whole crew was still scrupulously avoiding the matter of my push for an ultimate trip. I seized the Kumbaya moment in hopes of striking a deal. "Did you look at the possible itineraries?" I asked the group.

Silence descended, and the five of them stole guilty glances. They had been talking behind my back.

"What about Nepal?" I said. I envisioned glorious views as we tramped through the foothills of the Himalayas. The others looked as if I'd proposed a tour of the subterranean railyards of the subway system. "The scenery is spectacular," I tried.

No one spoke for a moment. It was as if I'd thrown a firecracker into a circle of cats. "I wonder how good the hotels are," Lesley said slowly.

"And the flight would take forever," said Dawn. "I was thinking maybe a beautiful beach somewhere, where there's a Four Seasons."

"But I want us to have an amazing, transcendent experience," I said. "I'd like us to feel a sense of accomplishment. This has to be different from any other trip we've ever made. What about Machu Picchu? It's one of the wonders of the world. Imagine entering the Gate of the Sun at sunrise." I tried an incentive. "The first night would be at a five-star hotel."

"In Peru," said Marcia.

Dawn suggested we hire a boat to take us along the coast of Turkey, but Marcia had gone there on her honeymoon. I wanted us to visit a place where none of us had set foot before. I suggested the Galápagos as a compromise. Even though I had been there, no one else had. "We'd travel on a boat," I pointed out, weakly, trying to play on Dawn's longing for sun and fun. But I felt obliged to note that there would be nature walks, bordering on the educational.

"I'm more of a people person than a nature person," said Lesley.

Almost everyone pushed for a barge trip in France, with a stop-over in Paris, of course. Only Denise kept her opinions to herself. "I want us to discover a culture completely different from our own," I implored. "That's what being a widow is all about: navigating a foreign land, triumphing over adversity."

Their faces went dark, and it wasn't due to the fading fire. They weren't looking for adversity, and why should they? Their lives were foreign enough. They had reveled in the pampering at the spa. They wanted a respite, not a forced march through intimidating terrain, a room with a lumpy mattress. This strenuous trip was my loco idea, not theirs. If forced to be honest with myself, I'd probably choose a Four Seasons, too. Still, I was crestfallen.

"Morocco might not be bad," Lesley conceded, sensing my misery. "The flight is shorter than some."

"There would be a four-day camel trek through the desert," I felt obliged to mention.

Marcia grew rigid next to me. "We'd have to sit on camels? I can't ride a camel."

"You're allowed to get off and walk."

"In sand?" yelped Dawn, the four-inch-heels girl. "I cannot walk in sand."

"And where would we sleep?" Marcia demanded.

"In deluxe tents."

"What's *deluxe* about a *tent*?" Marcia was horrified.

That got everyone worried about bathroom facilities. My assurance that there was a separate toilet tent did little to reassure them. Cries of "I cannot pee in the desert" rang out in the night.

Tara silenced them with authority. "I can pee … anywhere," she said. "Maybe Becky can keep all of our comments in mind. Maybe she can present some … other choices."

Right, I thought. Play personal concierge to the dancing divas and devise an adventure trip with no walking, no camping, no nights on sheets with less than a six hundred thread count, and no peeing in untoward locations. I retired to my room, all benefits of massages and body wraps evaporated, and spent a tortured night. It was me against the, uh, Blossoms, and they weren't about to wilt. No question, some of the women had been seriously unhappy at the prospect of the trip. I feared if I pushed it, I would tear the group apart.

---

chapter

SIXTEEN

i hadn't been looking for a bunch of docile widows, and I certainly didn't get them. In the days after I returned from the
spa, I looked at the bright side: they were turning corners,
beginning to flourish, rediscovering themselves. They were asserting themselves, too. If they were rediscovering that they didn't like
adventure travel and asserting themselves with me, I might have to
redefine my strategy.

But I wasn't going to give up without a scuffle. All that talk of
turning corners at the spa was heartening, a reminder of how I had
turned a corner during my mind-altering trip to the Galápagos. I remembered that after I returned, I no longer drowned in my dreams.
Instead, I choked. Trust me, it was a step up.

One night after that trip, approaching the two-year mark after
Bernie died, I dreamed that I was seized with a fit of choking. I
stumbled forward, gripping the sides of a mirror, an antique that
had belonged to Bernie's mother, in the entrance hall of my apartment. Something was wedged in my throat, cutting off my air. I

retched and coughed and fought for breath, struggling to expel the deadly obstruction. Still it would not dislodge, and I felt my legs grow weak, give way. I was alone, of course—no one to save me. Then whatever it was that was choking me popped out of my throat and landed in the palm of my hand.

It was a bee. A freaking honeybee. But it was hard as a stone. I took a breath; my lungs swelled and relaxed. I turned the bee over in my hand, lifted it to the light. It was fossilized in some way, encased in amber, every color and detail perfectly visible. It was exquisite, a thing of wonder. My fear melted away as I cupped it in my palm, held it up to my face, and delighted in the discovery of a phantasmagorical treasure.

The front door of the apartment opened, and Bernie walked in. In every dream I had dreamed since he died, the Bernie who appeared had been the sick Bernie, the Bernie who was lost and confused and needing my rescue, my rescue that always failed. But in this dream, I saw immediately that this was the well Bernie. His eyes were alive with mischievous pleasure at seeing me again, his body alert and erect. He no longer needed me. I needed him. He opened his arms, and I ran into them, sobbing with joy. He swept me up and we landed somehow on a fold-out couch where we never sat during his life.

Even in the dream, I knew that Bernie was dead. I knew that we were being granted an extraordinary visit. It was more than I had dared to hope. The well Bernie had returned, if only in an incandescent dream.

When I awoke to our half-empty bed, I felt joy nearly as intense as any I had ever known. Crazy, I know. I knew that Bernie was gone. But the dream had seemed realer than real, a high-definition,

Technicolor immersion in what we once had. Seeing him again, well and aware, as I had forgotten he once had been, made me so euphoric that I wept like a teenybopper at a Beatles concert.

I was thrilled to be allotted what little I could get, a memento of who Bernie had been before he slipped away, bit by bit and then all at once. I had been struggling to forget the sick Bernie and remember the well one, and the dream brought him alive again in my mind's eye and my mind's ear and touch. I could hear his voice the way I could before it became hoarse, talk to him as I could when he had filled my head with ideas, hold his hands when they were strong. From that moment forward, I knew, I could summon this fresh memory of Bernie as he really was. I could carry it with me as I tried to carry on.

I told the bee dream to the women at the spa, and I welled up with emotion when I reached the climax, when the healthy Bernie appeared. I was supposed to be the observer in the group, but here I was, only the second of us to shed a tear at our gatherings.

"Wow, look at that," Marcia said.

Tara reached across the dinner table to take my hand and began to puzzle through the symbolism of the dream. The bee had been encased in amber, she said, like a relic from the past. "It was a symbol of memory," Tara said. "Your unhappy memories were . . . choking you. Your memories of when he was ill. But when you were able to cough them up and see them in the light, you saw the beauty in the past again."

"That's when my memory of the well Bernie was restored to me," I said, "when he came back to me in the dream."

"The bee represented both sides of your memories, the happy and the sad," said Denise. "It makes sense, because bees are a yin-yang symbol. They sting, but they also make honey. Your memories of Bernie had been painful up to then, but you recognized that they could be sweet, too."

And bees perform a sort of alchemy as they transform nectar into honey, I pointed out. I was in a state of transformation. Perhaps I was ready for a more creative phase in my life, perhaps ready to retrieve my true voice, now that my throat was clear.

I understood the significance of the fold-out couch, I told them. It meant that Bernie was a guest who could not stay. After he disappeared again, all that would be left was the beautiful bee, the memory of a past before cancer and decline and death took him away. Left on my own, I would need to hold the sweet memories close, let them supersede the painful ones. The bee dream held the secret for how I could be happy. And it marked a genuine turning point for me. I seemed to stop choking and learned to breathe again.

When I told the bee dream to the others, they assured me that I was not alone. They had experienced meaningful visitations from their husbands, too. Lesley revealed that for a long time she felt that Kevin in some form wandered into her bedroom at the same time every night. Her Staffordshire terrier, spooked, would run into the hall, but Lesley found the visit reassuring, in her way, sensing that her guy was checking up on her. Tara said that a week after David died she sat up most of the night conducting an imaginary talk with him, speaking aloud into the emptiness. "After that," she said, "he was gone ... and the demons were gone, too."

I told them that the sensation that a departed loved one is present, whether in dreams or even waking visions, is pretty common among people who aren't necessarily crackpot paranormalists. A survey found that sixty-three percent of widows or widowers felt their spouses were with them at various times; forty-seven percent thought their spouses were looking out for them. Thirty-four percent said that they held regular conversations with their spouses. Once, any such ongoing connections might have been considered loony at worst, maladjusted at best. Theories of healthy grieving from Freud on down decreed that it was necessary to cut all emotional ties to the departed. Out of life, out of mind. But observations of bereaved people by a team of researchers in the nineties found that continuing bonds in healthy moderation provide support and sustenance. We didn't see our husbands as scary ghosts—we were glad for their company.

I'll admit I made occasional remarks to Bernie's photo and sometimes greeted him aloud on the beach near where I scattered his ashes. But it was in the bee dream where I felt his presence so acutely that it seemed as if he were really there. Apparently, that's fairly typical. Researchers even have a name for it—the visitation dream. It tends to be more vivid than normal dreams, and those who are reunited in them hold conversations and come to understandings.

The rationalist in me had to wonder. Did our husbands still reside in some parallel dimension from which they dropped in on us at will? Did they follow our progress, offer encouragement, maybe slip us an answer in the crossword puzzle on occasion? Or were we the living merely dreaming or hallucinating, summoning our own wishful visions from a recess of longing? Never much of a believer in stardust, I tended to view my ongoing connection with Bernie as arising purely from memory, and that had to be enough for me. My bee dream, and my one-way conversations, were all the comfort I had, lacking more concrete means of gratification.

I POPPED OUT of bed the morning after the bee dream, fully awake. My seven-grain toast tasted like eight; the water in the shower hit me like the surf on Maui. My body felt alive, my mind sharp. Seeing Bernie again with blessed clarity had cleared not only my vision, it cleared all my muzzy senses. It was the sensation that Tara described, how she had been living behind a curtain, and now it was opening onto something more. I'd been cowering back there for nearly two years, two years of looking inward. Seeing Bernie as I did in the dream swept the curtain away, granted me a view that was familiar yet hyper-real.

As I dressed for work, I could see again who Bernie had been when he was well—and who I had been, too. I remembered how much I had enjoyed my marriage, my job, the world in general. Whether I had the bee dream because I was beginning to remember this already or whether I could remember this because I had the dream—who could say? But it all started to come back to me—my bedrock of optimism, my dormant ambition, the incurable curiosity that drove me to seek out the news and succeed in New York, the open heart that delighted in my husband.

The day had come to become myself again. I threw the deadbolt on the front door of my building, scooped up my copy of the *Times*, and advanced down the street like the self-assured woman I once had been. Seeing Bernie had fired up my resolve. It was time to put my head down and go. It was time to get on with it, to Move Forward After Loss. It was time to stop thinking about what I'd lost and think about what I wanted.

It was only minutes later when my eyes shifted focus and

blinked with dismay. I was settling into the saggy seat of a train for an hourlong grind to a suburban industrial park that I called the Gulag. I was heading to a job that was a shell of what it had been. Without taking much notice, I saw as plain as I had seen that bee that I had allowed my career to wither away.

While my mind was elsewhere, my beloved job in my beloved city had disappeared along with my beloved husband. *New York Newsday* had been a scrappy upstart in Manhattan when I started there two decades before. I was preoccupied with Bernie and cancer when the Internet began to spell doom for newspapers, at least the ones that weren't nimble enough to compete.

Newsday changed owners not once, but twice, and later a third time. Austerity—and dejection—set in. New managers shut down the city edition, leaving only a suburban Long Island version behind. After Bernie died, they shut down the New York bureau, too, so I worked mostly from Bernie's old desk at home, doubly lonely, missing the relentless banter of the old city room, trudging out to the main office in the Gulag as little as I could get away with. Scores of my colleagues hightailed it to other jobs, other careers, but I had clung to the health insurance while Bernie was sick and to the faded familiarity of a job I could do in my sleep after he was gone. The paper's new mandate was quick takes on local stories, the sort of thing I wrote when I first got out of school.

The entire impetus of my adult life had been to escape my small-town upbringing and make it in New York. I lived for the challenge. I lived for the flow. I gazed out the sooty train window at the bleak suburban sprawl. It was a winter morning, and the landscape, in between the strip malls and tract houses, was bereft of color. I was going through the motions, covering my ass to keep my paycheck now that I was squeaking by on my own. It was a pinched existence. I saw with dismay that I had become a drone.

I suddenly felt certain what Bernie would say if he could see the person I had become: "Who made off with my wife?" The one who thrived on meaningful work. The one who wouldn't hesitate to rethink her career, rethink her life, if it no longer satisfied. My whole persona as a no-bullshit, independent woman had gotten lost during those months of mourning. I had thought that my goal as a widow was to get beyond grief and return to the status quo. But now the status quo was as gone as Bernie was. I would have to reinvent myself from scratch.

It would take some serious reassessment and nerve. But I saw it clearly now: the world was changing around me. If I didn't change with it, I wouldn't recognize myself anymore.

The bee dream jolted me to remember something else with electric clarity, something even more distracting. It was the pleasure I had taken in marriage. I squirmed in my seat and felt a long-suppressed grin play on my lips. The thrill I got when Bernie came through the door was a charge worth feeling again. I might not be ready for a new attachment, but a frisson of attraction wouldn't be bad. It was time to start thinking about the benefits of attraction. Attraction to another man.

chapter

SEVENTEEN

*i*t was a Sunday morning, one of the least threatening slots on the calendar, in the lobby of the Museum of Modern Art. Safe territory. Lay a hand on the art, lay a hand on me, either way, the alarms go off. Still, I masked my dread with a goggle-eyed stare. I had on the same green flared skirt and tank top I'd worn to the widows' support group. If I got kicked out of the museum, the outfit was going in the Dumpster.

I scanned the top of the crowd, trying to spot him first. At five foot nine, I figured, he should be two inches taller than me. I watched for thick graying hair, dark eyebrows, a certain thoughtful expression.

"You must be Becky."

The voice materialized from somewhere below my chin. I peered down onto a magnificent bald spot. Here in the glaring light, the thoughtful expression read more as defeated. I relaxed, buoyed by a surge of sympathy for this guy who had felt his only hope was to lie. I squinched down helpfully. Give the guy a break. This wasn't easy for any of us. My romantic exploits, Act Two, curtain rising.

Finally. Months had passed since my resolve to seek companionship again, and more than two years since Bernie had died. My long-married friends were thrilled, frothing for details. I would be their entertainment, relief from marital monotony. Unfortunately, they were no help. I began my odyssey by quietly informing them that I was now Ready. If they knew any appropriate, available man, I would be open to an introduction. I'd have been better off asking for an unsecured loan. No one came through.

Plan B involved accepting any invitation to go anywhere, anytime, on the theory that George Clooney wasn't loitering around my apartment. I attended the opera, where the average age of the audience was 103. Parties, where well-upholstered couples traded tips about mutual funds and restless leg syndrome. An architecture tour, rife with college students from Sweden. I became the most cultured, outgoing, and architecturally knowledgeable person in my circle, but still the only widow. Anyway, my flirting skills were dripping with cobwebs. I had interviewed dignitaries all over New York, but once, at a rare event when an attractive screenwriter asked me to join him for a drink, I tried to say, "I know a nice little wine bar around the corner," but it came out as *"b'dab b'dab b'dab b'dab."*

Thank goodness my longtime friend Fred kept me entertained. Fred was a writer specializing in opera and Italian food; his business card read "Pleasure Activist." Sometimes I was lucky enough to join the cause, sharing his box at Carnegie Hall or sampling all the desserts at San Domenico. So long as I kept myself occupied with the opening night of *L'Elisir d'Amore* and other sensual pleasures, maybe I could tune out the rising crescendo from my libido.

One night over antipasti at a trattoria, Fred broached the subject. "I know someone I think you should meet," he said with just enough mystery. "I don't do this often, but when I do, it always works."

He seemed to know everyone in New York, but—my luck—this man lived in deepest darkest Connecticut. Strike one. "You know I love New York," I bleated. "And my job is in the Gulag now. I could never get there from Connecticut. Any chance he would move?"

"He has custody of his daughter. She's thirteen. I doubt he would change her school." Strike two. "He has a dog, too." Strike six.

On to Plan C. Natural methods having failed completely, I dipped a toe into the Internet, where I demonstrated my ambivalence by signing up for a dinky dating website that limited itself to graduates of a few colleges. There were hundreds of women in my age category and only a few dozen men. One described his ideal Sunday thus: "Morning, sex with you. Afternoon, Bills game. Later, more sex with you." Unfortunately, I wasn't that into football. But the rest of them boasted a smorgasbord of sensitive-man interests—books, museums, travel, and, surprisingly, opera, lots of opera.

I told this to my sister when she called for an update. "The Bills fan sounds more realistic," she said. "Most middle-aged men I know are only interested in a wide-screen TV and a bag of Doritos."

Undaunted, I sent a note to my first choice. An academic, he professed avid enthusiasm for opera and adventure travel. His ideal woman, he said, was everyone's favorite literary heroine Elizabeth Bennet, and he described his ideal relationship by quoting George Eliot: "the inexpressible comfort of feeling safe with a person, having neither to weigh thoughts nor measure words." No Connecticut, no daughter, no dog. Although I suspect it was the word *safe* that hooked me.

Like a genie popping out of a bottle, he answered my e-mail in minutes, inviting me to meet him at MoMA. This was almost too easy! I showed up ready to discuss Verdi versus Puccini, rock climbing versus deep-sea diving—I already owned the wetsuit. I soon learned that he had attended a few operas years ago with his wife but hadn't returned since she crushed him in the divorce. The closest he had been to the sea was Chicken of the Sea. His hangdog expression showed he knew I was on to him. We put in some time at the museum, and then he invited me to lunch. Two steps up from coffee, only one step down from dinner. He even had a restaurant in mind. I slumped along to minimize the height differential as he led me into the morass of Times Square.

He'd chosen a Scottish pub with a tang of stale beer and a sticky floor from the night before. In the middle of Sunday afternoon, we were the only customers, perched on high stools in the gloom. He dug into a basket filled with chips, craning toward a television above the bar. The Jets were losing. I tried to perk him up by telling him that this was my first date in way too many years.

"I've been on the website for . . . a while," he said glumly. "Most of the women don't seem serious about a relationship."

Ah, the wit of Austen, the wisdom of Eliot. We both knew where this was heading. The check arrived. I reached for my wallet, but he waved me off. "This is on me." He pulled a piece of paper out of his pocket and smoothed it on the table as if it were an ancient scroll. A gift certificate he'd won in a raffle at work.

"Sorry, I can't give you change on that," the waitress said. He put up a fight, then conceded defeat with dejection so deep that I feared he might throw over dating altogether for life in a Benedictine brotherhood.

Bernie had treasured me, and now my company wasn't worth the full value of a Groupon. I couldn't let myself think that way. That way lay monsters.

All circuits lit up when I got home, everyone clamoring to hear about Becky's First Date. Hedging, I told them it wasn't that bad. I was scared, he was scared. Our complete lack of attraction guaranteed that we'd get nowhere near what really scared me—emotional engagement, sex, entanglement in someone else's life, sex, responsibility for anther person, sex. Love, marriage, illness, death, sex. Oh, and did I mention sex? This business of mediocre, sexless dates could be a harmless time killer. I'd view it like my job: interviewing people, finding out what made them tick, walking away.

There were a few others. A perfectly presentable social studies teacher who made me feel the way I'd felt in social studies class. A doctor who told me he was seeing someone else but, in case that fell through, he would like to keep in touch. Sorry, no touching of any kind. Still too fragile. Some investment guy who said, "You don't look too sad for a widow." An ad executive who, upon learning that my husband had died, asked, "Don't the guys you date find that creepy?" These guys may not have been right for me, but they weren't all that different from me. They were befuddled and shell-shocked by whatever midlife disaster had sent them back out onto the playing field of embarrassing disclosures and good-night handshakes.

Back when I was twenty, I didn't know how good I'd had it. Virtually everybody I met was available, but now, when prospects were few, I began to wonder whether I'd face a disagreeable choice— remain single forever, or settle for someone less than ideal.

The ad executive, I decided, had short-term possibilities. Tall, athletic, with a zany sense of humor, he peppered me with diverting e-mail messages. He kept asking me out, even though on our first date I packed in a stack of pancakes and half of his, too, while I chattered manically about Bernie's illness and death and explained my theory that it had given me post-traumatic stress disorder.

"You'll never settle down with another man," he said, "because no one could compete with your husband."

"Surely it's not a competition," I said, reaching for his home fries. "I don't believe there's only one person put on earth for each of us."

For a second encounter, he invited me to a restaurant written up as "lovely for long gazes over superb cuisine." "Casanovas," the review continued, "call it the ultimate high-end date." That gave me the willies, but it also got me thinking. I would never love this guy. I didn't even *like* this guy. He was glued to his BlackBerry during meals, admitted that his chronic lateness made people nuts, made pompous pronouncements about how a widow was supposed to behave and feel. But if I wanted to "get back on that horse" as Dawn would later put it, what would be the harm?

My friend Jackie called as I was zipping up my little black dress. "Help! What am I getting myself into?" I asked.

"A good meal," she said, "and some long-awaited dessert."

Couples all over the restaurant were canoodling away when the waiter whisked away the remains of a chocolate tart. I felt a knee brush mine under the table. "You have a quality that is very important to me," the ad guy said earnestly. "You have the loyalty of a lioness toward someone you care about, and the courage of a lioness, too."

Taxi!

———

BACK TO PLAN B. I threw on the little black dress for a dinner invitation from Fred. He was hosting a couple dozen food industry people at a restaurant uptown, where an Italian vineyard was introducing new wines. The menu promised nirvana, the crowd not so much: mostly couples, I saw, and a smattering of unattached women. The room was chilly during the pre-dinner mingle, so I shrugged on a bulky cardigan. Three twenty-something Italian women, identical triplets related in some way to the owners of the vineyard, greeted me so effusively that they knocked me back a pace. The sight of them alone would have done the trick. They towered above me in shiny stilettos, and they clearly hadn't got the fashion memo that if you show some skin somewhere, you should cover up somewhere else. I didn't know where to look first—long legs, big hair, gravity-defying breasts made from the same material as a Tempur-Pedic. I was already entertained.

They moved on and I found myself in conversation with Fred's mother, a retired schoolteacher, about education policy. A final guest slipped in the door. He was a man roughly my age, wearing a sleek black suit, but he looked more like a jeans guy. His hair, prematurely silver, was bedroom tousled, and he carried himself with easy amusement, more so when the Italian Glamazons zeroed in, all six missiles pointed right at him like the entire Iranian weapons arsenal.

He modestly looked aside, a hint of panic in his eyes, and caught me watching. He mouthed a silent word in my direction: *Help!*

I laughed and turned away.

Fred gave a charming little talk about Pinot Grigio and Cabernet Franc, then gestured for me to sit to his right. His mother claimed a seat two more down. The chair next to me pulled back. It was the *Help!* guy.

"You must be Becky," he said, offering a firm handshake.

"How do you know my name?" I demanded, my flirting no better for paltry practice.

"Fred told me," he said. "I enjoyed the article you wrote last week. You really drew me in."

"You're interested in potato farming on Long Island?"

"No, actually. I was interested in you."

It took a moment to sink in. This was Fred's guy. I unconsciously leaned away. "Do you live in Connecticut by any chance?" I should have known: I was in the middle of a dreaded public fix-up. Ambushed. No escape.

Nice move wearing the dowdy sweater, I thought. I considered shucking it, decided to let it be. A plate of risotto landed in front of me, and I dug in with antic zeal. "This stuff is total decadence," I blubbed, mouth full.

The guy took a careful bite and lit up with pleasure. He and Fred swooned over the ingredients. Parmesan, they guessed, and pears and balsamic vinegar for sweetness. This was no Doritos guy.

"You know about food?" I switched into reporter mode: get the story, walk away. I took care not to make direct eye contact.

"I love to cook, sure. Fred and I met about a zillion years ago, traveling around Sicily with Julia Child for some articles I was writing. We had a blast, but I'm still trying to lose the weight."

It didn't seem like he needed to, not that I was noticing.

"You know Fred well?"

"I don't get to see him much—I live too far away. But he's taken me to the opera a few times."

"You actually went?"

"Yes." He looked confused. "But I'm a rock-'n'-roll guy at heart."

This may have been an ambush, but it was shaping up as one I could survive. At least I'd have a diverting evening. I uncovered more details. For some lucky woman who lived in the right state, this guy—let's call him Bob—had definite cool boyfriend potential, if you could say that about someone who played with Bruce Springsteen when he was an opening act. Bob had left the music business to become a writer, publishing some highly regarded biographies, most recently of the Beatles.

He kept me laughing with self-deprecating stories about cooking disasters and single-dad mishaps, and he seemed to find my tales of the Gulag more amusing than the reality. We were rudely tuning out the rest of the table, where diners diplomatically assessed the wines and Fred and his mother discreetly watched over us like hens with their chicks. By the time some braised duck turned up, we had moved on to personal matters. Bob had decamped from the city to Connecticut nine years ago. A well-ordered life, everything in its rightful place—a wife, a daughter, a dog, a mortgage—five years later it all turned out a mess. His eyes grew wary and distant when I asked about the divorce. He seemed to take it as a personal defeat.

"I take it you're single, too."

So Fred hadn't told all. "My husband died," I said, bracing for the reaction.

"I'm sorry." Bob considered this slowly, observed me with deeper curiosity. "That must have been an incredible blow. How do you go on after something like that?"

I found myself telling him all about it, the miserable support group, the strange dislocation from my peers, the gasping for contact, the few pathetic dates. I was halfway through an animated travelogue to the Galápagos when cackly laughter broke out across the room, where the Glamazons were holding court.

"Sorry to rattle on. That sounds like the fun table," I said.

"Nah, I caught their act on World Wide Wrestling," he said. "Seriously, they're basically kids. What would we talk to them about? I like a woman with something to say."

His eyes trailed lightly over my face. Strange, I couldn't tell whether they were brown or blue. They darted imperceptibly to the side just before mine did. Shit, shit, shit. This guy was doing something to my follicles.

By the time I turned back again, he was excusing himself to phone the babysitter. It would be well after midnight before he got home. Daughter, dog, home in a remote location. Here was a man with obligations. And I was a woman without, with visions of pain and loss that shadowed any impulse toward attachment. I should do him a favor and hit an afterparty with the Glamazons.

Bob returned, considering what to say. "You got me thinking, Becky. When my life got shot to hell, that's when I found out what mattered to me. My daughter, my work—I try to stay true to that. I spent a lot of lonely nights talking to the dog, trying to figure it out. As David Bowie would say, 'Turn and face the strange.' But all those ch-ch-changes . . ."

He smiled and shrugged. He was injured, same as me. "I guess in the end they weren't all bad."

I regarded him directly. Hazel, that was it. His eyes were hazel.

*i*t's the craziest thing I've ever heard of." I had just asked Professor Wortman, the grief expert from Stony Brook University, why she thought my group wanted to go lingerie shopping together. "I can't imagine," she sputtered. "It's the *last* thing I would want to do." We were about to go seriously off the grid.

I saw her point. In my first couple years of widowhood, even during my first wan stabs at meeting a man, I felt about as sexy as a grilled cheese sandwich. Put me in a push-up bra and a garter belt, and *voila!*—you'd have a grilled cheese sandwich in a push-up bra and garter belt.

Maybe what I needed was a dose of Lesley and Dawn in a lingerie shop. It might have spared me a couple years of celibacy. Maybe some of those Internet guys would have got lucky. Maybe when I met Bob at Fred's dinner, I would have made a preemptive move.

The lingerie outing in June was Tara's idea, not mine. I didn't entirely understand the appeal of trying on underwear with a cheering section of friends, but the rest of them, except perhaps Marcia, were dizzy with anticipation. I was glad for another opportunity to demonstrate my team spirit. If I agreed to squeeze myself into a negligee and matching thong for them, I hoped they might venture a night in a desert tent for me.

Tara breezed into the glossy white La Perla shop in SoHo on a steamy day, happy to explain her reasoning to the rest of us. She thought we should throw something into the mix that celebrated us as women, something that was also silly and fun. "And honestly . . . get ourselves out of the Mummy pants," she said in her most sultry voice. She gave an approving once-over to the profusion of lace and satin on display. "Think of ourselves outside the dreadful box we've been in."

We'd been dancing around the topic of sex ever since the first meeting. It was time to give some serious consideration to where we all stood on the matter. What role did we want it to play in our lives, and what roles were we willing to play to make it happen?

There was only one subject scarier, and that would be love. A subject for another day.

Today would be all about pleasure. First we cheered Marcia, who had returned from our spa weekend determined to overcome her qualms and buy that apartment she'd been mooning over. She met her real estate agent on the roof at sunset a few days later and made a deal. Maybe it wasn't the best deal she'd ever negotiated, but it was the best deal for her, with the location, the view, and the pool fusing the pleasures of city and country that she'd relished with Martin. She'd be moving in the fall.

Then we turned to the lingerie. Lesley flapped her wings with delight when she spotted a hanger holding a garment, if that's what it was, assembled from strips of nude-colored mesh and a few strategically placed feathers. It could have been the illegitimate love child of a slingshot and a feather duster.

"That makes a statement," I said.

Lesley lifted the item off the hanger with a finger, one eyebrow raised. "Yes, it says, 'You are a new woman.'" Indeed. "It says, 'Try having sex with someone new, after thirty years with someone else.'"

She held it over her T-shirt and gave a wiggle. "Craig tells me the only place for sexy lingerie is on the floor," she mused. "But he did ask me to look for a teddy. Is this a teddy?"

I didn't answer, too busy trying to envision the *Belle du Jour* lifestyle of the woman who on a daily basis wore underpinnings that cost more than a trash compactor. Surely no one in the feather getup would ever have to shovel a driveway or meet a payroll. Just as surely, that was part of the appeal. I had to hand it to Tara. The La Perla shop, with its soft-core allure, captured her aesthetic of subtly withholding chic. No bordello décor, nothing sleazy or garish. The place had the spare ambiance of a first-class lounge at LAX. I felt a kind of dull lust kick in, a lust for objects of desire way beyond my financial standing. This place was a total tease.

Dawn was savvy enough to ask for everything that was on sale in her size. Then she and Lesley disappeared into dressing rooms in the center of the store with an ample stash. It wasn't long before they whipped aside the curtains and flaunted their finds to appreciative shrieks.

"Dawn, you can't buy that," Lesley said. "You're going to give some guy a heart attack."

She was right to worry. Dawn's look-at-me figure strained inside a black mesh slip with a few satin ribbons slashed across some high-risk territory. I remembered some dialogue from *Body Heat*, when Kathleen Turner wondered why William Hurt suggested she shouldn't wear an outfit and he answered, "You shouldn't wear that body."

Lesley pirouetted in a silver bra and panty set that had us *sh-bopping* like the Shirelles.

"Oh, mama!" Tara said.

"This one's headed for the bedroom floor," Lesley announced, all cocky confidence.

The rest of us clucked around the racks while the two of them ducked in to change again, speaking through the curtains as the lace flew. They kept Maria, the assistant manager of the store, hopping, sending her to the stockroom for more sizes. She had opened early to give us the run of the place and won our hearts by admitting she had a complex about her thighs.

"Is this what you expected from a group of widows?" I asked her.

She put down a box of panties. "I get it," she said. "I lost my mother. It's not the same, but when you lose someone you love, you have to put on a face every day for your work, for your kids. Beautiful lingerie is another kind of mask. It's a mask that says I feel sexy, I feel beautiful."

Meanwhile, Dawn was saying, "I'm going to want way too much stuff." She whipped aside the curtain to show us a clingy champagne-colored nightgown trimmed with a suggestion of lace. "I need a little piece of lingerie for when I go on a trip."

"You're going on a trip? A trip where you need lingerie?" I asked.

Dawn let loose one of her throaty laughs. "I don't have one planned. I'm trying to project one."

In fact, she had scheduled a getaway with Adam, the widower

she'd been seeing, in conjunction with taking their sons to camp. But once again the relationship had hit turbulence, and they were planning to drop the boys and turn right back. The drive alone could make or break the situation.

This lingerie wasn't for him, she said; it was for her, a reward for getting in the best shape she'd achieved in years. Denise had inspired her to commit herself fully to yoga, Dawn said. "I realized how good I'd feel if I got stronger."

She turned this way and that in front of the mirror to evaluate the nightie that Adam was destined not to see. If this was what strength looked like, I made a note to spend the summer strapped to a cross-trainer.

The second anniversary of Andries's death had just passed, and in some ways, to Dawn, it was worse than the first. It was especially hard on the kids, and it made her suspect that they had been putting on a brave front for her sake up to now. She imagined they associated the time of year—school concerts, the last weeks of classes, the onset of summer weather—with his death, and her daughter had become moody and withdrawn. The other day, out of the blue, she shouted and pounded her fists: "I want my daddy back! I want him here *now*."

Dawn gave a last twirl in front of the mirror. "Ooh, it would be nice to wear this for someone," she said. "But this is for me. If I can grab five minutes of feeling good for myself, I'll take it." She slipped back into the changing room.

"You should be the official La Perla spokesmodel," I said.

Tara looked after her fondly. "I was describing Dawn to a friend the other day," she told me. "I said she's like every man's fantasy . . . and seemingly every woman's nightmare competition. But she isn't, because she's so sisterly."

I couldn't help but notice that after pushing us to schedule this fling for months, Tara was hanging back, lingering by the dressing rooms, unable to focus. Yet there was a radiance about her that was impossible to ignore. She grabbed me by the arm to explain. It seemed that everything was changing for her just in the few weeks since our spa weekend. The curtain that had been blocking her had opened, and she was stepping out. She had sold her family's house and bought a new one, a smaller one—happily, a few blocks from where Lesley lived.

"Hooray," Lesley called out from the room. "We can hula-hoop together."

Tara smiled. More requests were coming in for voice-over work, she added. And the guy Tara had just met when we visited the spa, the guy who sent all the text messages—she could barely contain her astonishment at how their dates had evolved.

"You're getting along?" I asked.

She widened her eyes in amazement. "Yeah." She paused to collect her thoughts, but they scattered like mercury. "Really, out of nowhere," she began, barely audible. "Like a bolt out of the blue. There are connections and feelings there . . . and equally on his part." She looked off to the side, unable to meet my eyes. "I don't know whether it's because I'm feeling better and I'm embracing life and it's coming through to others, but . . . all this stuff is coming my way. I'm sort of overwhelmed by this guy." She turned back to me, genuinely flustered. "Not sort of overwhelmed. *I am overwhelmed.*"

Boy, could I relate. After all but giving up hope of finding passion again, to feel a connection with someone—someone *male*—was a shock. I saw it all in her face, the thrill and the trepidation over what might unfold. This man was coaxing feelings to life in Tara that she had nearly forgotten, that she thought she might never feel again.

Lesley returned to the mirror in a cream-colored gown, form-fitting but not transparent. It came with a matching robe, the better to wear with Craig's son in the house. "This is kind of virginal," Lesley said, pulling a face. She was distracted by Tara's flustered demeanor. "Tara, what's *with* you? What happened after the sexting?"

"It wasn't sexting. It was flirting via text."

"Did it get better? Did you go on a date? And?"

Tara didn't speak for so long that I thought she wasn't going to answer. Finally, she said, "He is ... an amazing man. Lovely."

"She's been so quiet about it," Marcia said.

"Her socks have been knocked off, girls," said Dawn. She peeked out from behind the curtain.

Will was going through a divorce, Tara told us when we pressed for details. He was fifty-eight, almost four years older than Tara. "He's very ... we both love words. He's got a great brain. He's an amazing father. His daughter is seven."

"Seven!" Lesley exclaimed. "I thought I was mad with a thirteen-year-old boy."

Tara hadn't met the girl yet. "We're taking it slow. He's very respectful. I didn't see it coming. I feel completely giddy." She waved us away and squeaked out a giggle, bordering on the hysterical. "All the things I didn't think I'd feel, I feel all of them. Unbelievable."

Tara's good news gave us a helium lift, and we returned to our flighty mission. Marcia corralled Maria and disappeared to a dressing room in the back. Denise and I turned to helping Tara. Her daughters had been urging her to "get out of those microfiber, flesh-colored whatevers," so she sought one special piece, a piece that would make a statement and give a boost of confidence, something subtly seductive, "not too tarty . . . because I am not a tart." We hit upon it, and I laced her in: a black silk bustier with corset stays up the back. Tara planned to wear it under a black tuxedo. It was classic. It was smoldering. It was Tara all over. No one understood better than Tara that elegance is refusal.

"Go, baby, go," Dawn said. "Lady, this looks beautiful on you."

"It's a fortune," Tara said. "I have never, ever splurged on myself on something like this." She closed her eyes and handed a credit card over to Maria.

I breathed deep to savor the vicarious shopping high. It pleased me to think how different we were from the pitiful widows in a Dickens novel or even from a real-life widow of fifty years ago; how, within reason, we could spoil ourselves if we chose. We had made our own way and could spend our own money however we wanted, and who was to tell us otherwise? For the most part, we modern women hadn't been financially dependent on husbands. Some in the group had been the big earners in their families. No one, I thought with pride, was lost without a man.

Tara still looked guilt-stricken, whether over the expense or something else, I wasn't sure. I thought of a theory Camille Wortman, the grief researcher, had put forward when I pressed her to think harder about why my group wanted to perpetrate this spree together. "Maybe it helps a widow overcome inhibitions," she said. "Maybe going with a group makes it less like she's buying something intended for someone who is not her husband. It's more acceptable, because she's doing it for the group."

Imagine my surprise when Marcia headed toward the cash register with a little cache of unmentionables.

"Talk about being out of your comfort zone," she said with her suppressed smile. "This is it for me."

"Marcia, you're blushing!" Dawn said.

Marcia's cheeks burned deep red. "I have to do this gradually," she said. She stuffed her purchases quickly in a bag.

"This was something I would never have done if I hadn't been with this group," she confessed to me while we waited for the others. "But now that I've been here, I would probably come back. It's another thing to learn. I'm changing, partially because I have to. And partially just for the hell of it."

Marcia became positively talkative. During her marriage, she said, she had become set in her ways. "You develop a lifestyle, perspectives, likes and dislikes. I got into a pattern. When everything got pulled out from under me, I thought, here's an opportunity to change some things."

In her wildest dreams, I doubt Marcia would have chosen to spend a couple of hours in this saucy shop. All her life, she said, people were drawn to her for her personality and intelligence, certainly not her bona fides as a girly-girl. It was hard to envision young Marcia at a slumber party, mooning over David Cassidy and the latest colors of lip gloss. "The girly-girls weren't the ones I was friends with. But this group is giving me another dimension."

Marcia had another motivation as well. A new boss had entered her workplace, a woman, a very capable one, for the first time ever. She was assigning Marcia more responsibility, giving a reason unheard of when Marcia got her start: to offer the female perspective. It was a tidal change in an office where Marcia's ability to talk sports with the guys had always been an asset. "I can start to show more femininity."

She gave a crisp nod around the store. "It's easy to re-evaluate with this group. They're not like anybody I've ever been friends with before, but they're very accepting and open. Otherwise, you get stuck, and your life continues just as before, only without your spouse instead of with him."

She was right. So much had changed for me since Bernie's death, but that didn't mean I couldn't still shake myself up. I asked our guide, Maria, to strip the mannequin of the one item in the store that was least likely to be worn by somebody like me. It was a corsetlike novelty straight out of a Feydeau farce, with a tiny skirt attached, barely enough to cover *le derrière*. The Aphrodite Skirted Bustier, according to the tag. It took some advanced work in spatial relations, but I tucked myself into it, hoisted everything into place, and stepped out to applause and wolf whistles. Then I took a good long look in the mirror. I will be honest: I thought I looked ridiculous. I also thought I looked great.

And not just because my friends said so. Although that helped. I had gained back the weight I lost when Bernie died, but I still had a pert little waist, a nice curvy tush. Not much going on up top, but not sagging up there, either. No way was I going to buy the Aphrodite Bustier, but it had done its work.

Then I took a good long look at my crazy, carefree companions, passing around their selections while making final choices. None of them were kids anymore, but they still looked smokin'. Lesley chose a black mesh negligee with peekaboo bubbles all over it; Dawn an abundance of flamboyant feminine froth; Tara a sultry, sophisticated masterpiece of simplicity. Marcia kept her choices pretty much to herself. Denise, well, Denise didn't need enhancement. These women were supple, fit, healthy, and in the prime of their lives.

Lesley might say, "Try having sex with someone new, thirty

years or twenty years or even one year after someone else." But, take it from me, this crowd had the figures for it.

Walking into the store that day, I had assumed I knew the underlying reason why a bunch of widows would band together to try on underwear. They were uncomfortable with their bodies, I presumed. They needed reassurance that they still had the requisite allure. Women are always hearing about how insecure they are supposed to feel about their physiques, and I had bought into the line. In fact, everyone looked fabulous, better than most men our ages. I didn't know what the others were thinking, but if anyone was concerned about body issues, she shouldn't be. No, I thought, it wasn't our bodies we were most concerned about. The insecurity was over what to do with them.

We had spent a morning of intimacy with trusted friends. But if anyone wanted sex, and it seemed most everyone did, she would have to plunge into the unknown, the emotional unknown. It would take more than some sassy posturing in a negligee to make the leap.

chapter

NINETEEN

*h*ere we were, twenty-first-century women with healthy libidos and post-sexual-revolution attitudes. Yet when some of us started seeing men, we conducted chaste, old-fashioned courtships. If you caught sight of me or Tara out to dinner on a first date, you'd think you were witnessing the comeback of Doris Day, any suggestion of sex more forbidden than deep-fried carbs. I invariably deployed the frumpiest of outfits, right down to underpinnings that would be perfectly appropriate in the presence of Dr. Vogel, my dermatologist. My attire was armor against the intimacy I feared. What exactly were we afraid of?

"You worry about what you're going to look like naked," Lesley announced. We were seated at brunch, bags of new va-va-voom lingerie tucked safely beneath the seats. Maybe I shouldn't have been surprised, but there were hearty nods all around. Lesley looked perfectly shapely to me, yet all she could think about was how much thinner she had been when she met Kevin, her husband, at seventeen.

"You know, it's not true that only size-two women get laid," I argued. "Men past a certain age don't look perfect either. And most of them have lost a fair amount of their near vision anyway. Give them naked, and they're happy. That can't be all that bothered you."

Lesley considered the question again. Now that she had five months of living with Craig under her belt, she felt more responsible than ever for guiding the others through tricky terrain. Sex with a relative stranger was a conundrum that called for her expertise, and she took it seriously. "You're right," she said. "You also think, 'Am I going to be able to separate myself from my husband?' How can you close off that part of your mind?" The rest of us leaned in. "Sex has many different meanings to people. I was so young when I met Kevin, I never had a lot of casual sex. I need to be committed in a certain way emotionally. It doesn't have to mean I'm in love, but it might have to be heading in that direction."

Everyone listened intently, each with her own perspective. Denise and Marcia, who had yet to meet the right man. Tara, who might have just met him and had to decide how far to take him. Dawn, who had met someone but couldn't seem to make it work. And, of course, me. I remembered all too well my struggles over how deeply to engage myself in the messiness of recoupling.

Tara agreed with Lesley. "For me," she said, "it's not enough to have a physical attraction. I'd have to have a mental and emotional attraction."

"That's the way I felt," I said. "I had no moral objection to casual sex. But when I was married to Bernie, I was making love with the man who was my closest friend, my most intimate confidant. Sex and comfort went together. Believe me, I had the urge for sex after he died, but the idea of a one-night stand was just too depressing. I'd had the whole package, and I wanted it again."

"And there's also the fear—am I picking the wrong guy?" Dawn added. "There's this danger that you might latch onto somebody because you think you may never find anybody else."

I could feel the anxiety ratcheting up. Everybody started reaching for Lesley's side dish of fries. She pushed it to the center of the table.

"I tore an article out of the newspaper about a scientific study," I said. "They put a woman in an MRI machine and gave her little electric shocks. They could see parts of her brain light up with anxiety. Then they asked the woman's husband to hold her hand, and they could see the anxiety go down. When a stranger held the hand, it didn't have the same effect. There's something about affection from someone you trust—it's soothing."

"After Martin died," said Marcia, "someone asked me if I relied on my husband. Did I depend on him? At first I thought no, because I'm very independent. But when I stopped and thought about it, I realized how much I leaned on him. It was emotional. I trusted him completely. I could say anything to him. He had my best interests at heart."

"He had your back," said Lesley.

That was it. No one wanted to get on her back with somebody who didn't have her back.

Lesley, we knew, had met Craig on Match.com. On a number of dates, they laughed themselves silly, conducted some serious talks about their families, and gingerly held hands, but it took a while for them to get seriously physical. "You feel guilt," she said, "not about sex itself, but about allowing yourself pleasure with someone else.

Because you still essentially feel married. You're thinking, I'm about to make love to a man who is not my husband. *What am I doing?*"

Not to mention the practical issue: does my body still work? Everyone in our group had gone through a long hiatus, and everyone had heard the admonition: use it or lose it. We shifted uncomfortably. Lesley said she had been worried, too. She had felt no sexual desire for almost two years. "I was dead inside. My daughter offered to buy me a vibrator. I didn't even have the desire for that."

It wasn't only sex. Lesley had stopped doing everything she'd loved when Kevin was alive—gardening, listening to music, taking walks, cooking. She couldn't bear to enjoy any of it without him. It was only after she began to find pleasure again in everything else that the desire to make love reasserted itself.

Lesley painstakingly planned her first sleepover with Craig. "I tell you, the first time I thought I was going to get naked in front of somebody else, I thought it would be devastating," she said. A friend took her to buy new lingerie, and she was so addled that she didn't realize until she saw the bill that she had paid fifty dollars for one pair of little black panties. She had a daughter living at home during a break from college, and Craig had his son, so they booked a hotel room. It was the night of her oldest daughter's engagement party, and the panties showed through her dress, so Lesley switched to something else and threw the panties in her purse. She also made sure to have a drink to calm her nerves. "I was still carrying too much weight," she said.

"Now we know how you lost it," interjected Dawn.

"When it was time to get busy," Lesley said, she changed in the bathroom and came out holding the fifty-dollar underpants in front of her chest, breaking the tension with a laugh. "I told him I spent fifty dollars for these, so he'd better appreciate them. So that's how I spent fifty dollars for panties I never wore. Worth every penny."

As it turned out, Lesley needn't have worried. Emotions counted for more than physical perfection. "You know, you think, next time around I'm going to get the hottest guy. He's going to have a twenty-four-pack, never mind a six-pack. But Craig's got this little tummy. He needs to lose some weight, but when you meet a person and you fall for him, none of that matters."

"All those details, all those lists you make go out the window," Dawn said.

"The companionship," Lesley said, "just sharing your life with someone—you thought you'd never feel it again. It's something to be grateful for."

Even so, it took courage. Perhaps that was hard for anyone to understand outside our circle, but we recognized that Lesley had taken a risk, a risk with her heart. Our hearts were like eggshells. Lesley had removed hers from lockdown, and we respected her for that. We wondered how she'd found the nerve.

She answered us without having to think, echoing something she'd said the first time we met. "Because the thing that I was most afraid of had already happened."

———

KNOWING LESLEY SOONER after Bernie died would have given me a much-needed shot of courage. And to think I had nearly excluded her from our group. I'd been talking to a woman who ran an adventure travel company, and she suggested I meet Lesley, everyone's favorite traveling companion on a trip to India the year before. I agreed to see her mostly to be polite. Lesley had already been widowed nearly two and a half years, longer than anyone else who was joining me. She was already dating Craig, whereas none of the others were seeing anyone then. And she was so randy and resolutely cheerful that I couldn't imagine what she had to gain by dredging up issues of grieving that she would probably rather forget. Yet once I heard her story over lunch at a restaurant near her home, I realized how much the rest of us could learn from Lesley about tenacity and resilience, even as she kept us in stitches.

Kevin's death hadn't been her only misfortune. Back in South Africa, she grew up in a tumultuous household. "My father beat the crap out of my mother," she said with the resignation of long forbearance. He left the family when Lesley was eighteen, and it was a relief, but her mother contracted ovarian cancer five years later, and Lesley watched her die over the course of a year. She still had her brother, who was fourteen months older. Everyone loved and admired him, but no one took the diminutive Lesley seriously or thought she would become successful, and she pretty much believed them. After high school, she found work as a secretary.

"People would ask me how I did it," she said, speaking of the loss of both her parents. "What was the choice?"

When she was seventeen, a friend fixed her up with a twenty-two-year-old guy who needed a date for a wedding while his steady girlfriend was out of town. When he turned a corner to meet Lesley, all she could say was, "Okay, this is cool." Kevin was breathtaking, absurdly handsome, tall, dark, with a forthright jaw and level eyes. They had such a good time that she was sure after one evening that she wanted to marry him. First she had to persuade him to drop the girlfriend, a quiet fellow student at his law school, a polar opposite from the boisterous, less-educated Lesley.

The tall lawyer and the pixie-sized dynamo married three years later, when Lesley was twenty, and they had three daughters while he launched a career in securities trading. Then tragedy found her again. Lesley's brother was killed in a car crash when she was twenty-eight. Kevin spared her by identifying the body—she could depend on him that way. All of her original family gone, she devoted herself to her children and her traditional marriage. Her job was to run the household and orchestrate a busy social life, while Kevin was the breadwinner and a weekend athlete who cycled, climbed mountains, and rowed for a national team. Lesley had to cut more roots when they left South Africa and moved to the United States for Kevin to set up an office. Lonely and friendless, only thirty years old, she gradually adjusted.

"We became even closer here in the States," she said. "We had just each other and our kids. We were great friends, and we had great passion. I swear I became crazier about my husband as we got older."

The last person anyone would expect to take his own life, Kevin was successful, active, a rock for his family. Lesley thought something must have gone amiss in his brain chemistry around the time he turned fifty and she forty-five. He couldn't sleep. He quit his job without discussing it with her first. He lost twenty pounds. "Suddenly, he dwindled away, and I had to keep it together, which was so different. I'd always been the precious one, you see. I didn't even know how to pay a bill online." Lesley discovered him organizing matters of family business, laying it all out clearly.

"Why are you doing this?" she asked him.

"You never know," he said. "I'm under a lot of stress. I could have a heart attack."

On the September morning when he killed himself, the house

was quiet. Their youngest had only recently started her freshman year away at college. Kevin knew Lesley was leaving for her facial appointment, and he put in his request for her to pick up a sandwich. Right before she left, she was standing at the top of the stairs, and he said, "Do you want to come down for a little bit and talk to me?"

"I'm running late," she said. "We'll talk when I get back."

Lesley always kissed Kevin good-bye, and he would make fun of her for it, but she explained by saying, "You never know. I could get knocked over by a bus." That morning, in her hurry, she forgot the kiss. When she arrived home, she passed his study, a dark-paneled room lined with photos of Kevin scaling mountains and winning races. He wasn't there, but she spotted his wristwatch, which he never removed, propped on the desk. There was something about the way it rested there that made Lesley think something horrible had occurred. She ran to the basement and found him, his pulse still faint.

Lesley didn't reveal how Kevin killed himself, and I didn't ask. My research experts had told me it was best not to force painful disclosures. Why prod Lesley to summon the most horrific memory of her life? I found it interesting that later, when our group first convened, instinctively, no one else asked her, either. A sign—Do Not Go There—was plain for all to see. All Lesley told me the first time I met her was that he chose a method that wasn't violent, knowing she would be the one to find him.

She tried mouth to mouth and called an ambulance, but he couldn't be saved. In a three-page note, he said he loved Lesley unconditionally, and he said he would like her to marry again one day. That was a kindness.

Eventually, the note helped her to understand. For the longest time, she wondered, "Was I not enough for him?" It wasn't possible, at first, to grasp his emotional torment. "Mental illness can be as serious as cancer," Lesley said. Over time, she and her daughters involved themselves in a suicide awareness organization, but that was a long way off. In the early days, they alternated between shock, numbness, and unimaginable despair.

"I felt a pain in my heart, like someone had stuck a knife in there and twisted it," she said. "I remember thinking, 'I can't get through another day.'"

Lesley had never thought of herself as smart or accomplished outside her realm at home. Now she would have to manage everything Kevin had overseen as a matter of course. She had to attend meetings at his firm to negotiate the sale of his shares in the company. "People offered to handle things for me, but I didn't want to be a little old lady who doesn't know what's cooking. I went to every meeting and pretended I knew what they were talking about. I read Suze Orman books so I'd have buzzwords to throw around."

But otherwise, she sank into an utter funk. "I felt that if a day went by without me crying, I was disappointing him." She took pills to sleep. She was haunted by the vision of how she'd found him, afraid to close her eyes for fear of seeing it again. For months, she wore the same pair of brown Bermuda shorts with a brown-and-white top until her daughters threw them away. She heard them talking about her. "She didn't comb her hair today."

"It took me a long time to acknowledge and accept that, as much as I loved him, he really did abandon me in a way," she said. One day, after about a year, the third finger on her left hand started to itch, and she took off the wedding ring. She and her girls began to make jokes, like about how much money they'd save on Father's Day. She thought about joining a support group but didn't, not wanting to talk about the suicide and fearing that others would judge her about it. It was hard enough venturing out in her small town, wondering what everyone was thinking, fielding questions at the supermarket about whether she had seen it coming. She and her daughters took a trip to Arizona, where a Native American shaman told her that whenever images of the suicide flooded her thoughts, she should conjure a vision from a happier time to replace it. She made a conscious effort to do that, and it helped.

Taking over Kevin's role as well as her own, Lesley began to realize that she was smarter than she'd given herself credit for. "I'd been given my pink slip; my job as a stay-at-home mother was done. But, like you, Becky, I'd been given a second chance at life. Now the challenge was doing it on my own."

Kevin had been a champion rower, and for the first time, Lesley signed up for lessons. She begged her coach to let her take a scull out into the choppy waves of the open bay before she was ready. The coach agreed, and predictably, Lesley tipped over the boat. Another rower asked why the coach had allowed it. "Because Lesley wants it so badly," the coach said. "Because she's fearless to the point where she doesn't care if she fails."

Given all that had happened to Lesley, it must have taken all her fearlessness to venture her heart with another man. She knew she was making the right decision on one of her early dates with Craig, when they were sitting on a park bench, talking about their children and holding hands. She placed her head on his chest—he was tall, like Kevin—and she listened to him breathe. She thought, *This. This is what I've missed.*

AT THIS STAGE in life, people come complicated. Lesley and Craig woke up every morning laughing and went to sleep at night still laughing. But by the time our group made its lingerie outing, their living conditions were turbulent and getting more so. His youngest boy, living with Craig and Lesley in her new house, alternated between resisting and craving a mother's touch. Then Craig's eighteen-year-old, out of school and looking for work, moved in, too. Lesley hadn't sold her old house yet, so her youngest daughter still bunked there when she was home from school, and the oldest was staying there until her wedding, only two weeks after our lingerie outing. Two homes, two families in flux, one young widow trying to steer them all to port. A perfect storm was gathering over both households, a collision of adolescent and postadolescent emotional fronts, with Lesley sailing right into the eye.

"The really hard thing is going to be the wedding," Tara said at our post-shopping lunch. "You know . . . when the dad should give the bride away."

"I'm going to do it, which is going to be tough." Other traditions from the standard playbook would also be cast aside. No veil over the bride's face, because the father usually lifts it; no first dance with Dad.

"It's one of those things you don't think about until it comes up," said Tara, considering her own daughters. "Every little princess thinks about that dance."

"I have to give the toast, too." Lesley rolled her eyes. On top of everything else, public speaking! "I'm going to be a wreck."

Marcia called for the check. I seized the lull to address another touchy topic, the trip I envisioned for the fall. Our utter failure to reach a consensus at the last gathering made me pessimistic about wrangling anyone as far as the state line, so I had scrapped all the options I'd proposed to such a clamor of dissent and cast around in search of a compromise. There was another itinerary through Morocco, with hikes through cedar forests in the Atlas Mountains, strolls through ancient souks and casbahs, and only two days riding camels in the Sahara instead of four. Best of all, there would be only one night in the dreaded desert camp. I spoke to a guy in charge of the trip.

"I know this sounds finicky," I said to him, "but just how rustic are the facilities at the camp? I'm traveling with women who seem rather...particular."

"You sleep in tents made out of Berber carpets," he said. "And believe it or not, there are two Kohler flush toilets, permanently installed."

"Stop right there," I said. "You're hired."

Pending approval from the group, of course. Cautiously, I presented my findings, and the atmosphere turned prickly but resigned. Marcia expressed more reluctance over tents and camels. Dawn looked dubious. Tara shrugged her assent. Denise was still and quiet. I shot a hopeful look at Lesley.

"This sounds like the perfect trip for all the princesses we are," she said.

I can't say anyone was thrilled, but they were willing to do this for me, for the group, and that was all I could ask. If the camels went on a rampage, if the toilets didn't flush, if no one spoke by the time we dragged our dusty asses back to the permanent dissolution of our friendship, I knew who'd be to blame. But everyone agreed

to go, and I was determined to draw my courage from Lesley. I'd
have to be fearless to the point where I didn't care if we failed.

────────────────

WE'D BEEN TALKING all day about taking risks, so I decided
to end our gathering by telling the women about a dream I'd had
shortly after I met Bob at the public fix-up with the Glamazons.
In the dream, I was visiting a foreign city, a city of palazzos that
spoke of a storied past. Instead of streets, all the passageways were
canals filled with water as clear as Evian—tinted the color of hazel,
actually—and incongruously enough, I was swimming in them. As
in others of my dreams, I was alone, searching for Bernie and unable to find him, except that this time I wasn't alarmed—no one
was drowning. I was swimming the way I'd swum in the Galápagos, assured and fast.

Soon I hoisted myself from the water and walked in my skimpy
bathing suit to the farthest edge of the city, at the top of a cliff,
so high it made me dizzy. It opened onto a bright vista. I inched
forward and craned over the edge. Below was more water, a whole
vast sweep of ocean. It shifted with swells like sighs and stretched
toward a limitless horizon. I had reached the demarcation between
the known and the unknown, the jumping-off point for a fresh
journey, if I chose. The sea was so clear that below the surface I
could see enormous fish, the size of catamarans, in fantastic iridescent colors, like parrots. I wanted to dive into the water. I wanted
to swim with those fantastic fish, but I was afraid—the cliff must
have been a thousand feet high. I felt the way I had when I dove off
the boat to chase the skipjacks, tantalized, exhilarated but scared to

my bones. Something in me wanted this adventure. Something in me wanted to back the hell away from the edge of the cliff.

I looked farther out to sea and saw a splendid whale, a captivating creature, also beautifully colored, the size of an ocean liner. It was spouting a long plume of water. The phallic symbolism was too preposterous, yet what can I say? I wanted to swim with that whale even more than I did with the fish, to abandon myself to a discovery beyond my imagination. I awoke still on the precipice, poised between fear and desire.

chapter

TWENTY

i just want you to know," he said in a reassuring tone, "nothing is going to happen here tonight."

Of all the lines spoken at all the candlelight dinners in all the world, I had to walk into that one. I took a sip of champagne and tried to figure out where this evening was headed. I didn't have much time, either, before a whole lot of something started to happen.

I was standing maybe a foot away from an attractive, available man, a man giving me the once-over with clear, empathetic hazel eyes, who at that very moment was stirring risotto—yes, risotto, with saffron and scallops, and oh-so-tenderly, as Dr. Spock might stir some baby formula—on the stovetop. A man who actually knew how to make risotto without having to look at a recipe. A man who was making it for me.

Bob and I had worked our way through a number of hands-off but increasingly steamy dinners at restaurants in the city, where I amused him with my ardent appetite. "I want to cook for you," he invariably said, with appreciable relish, before we parted.

I couldn't be sure whether he meant something more. It was a couple months since we'd met, and that evening I'd taken the train to his small town in Connecticut on the strength of a dinner invitation that promised to stretch late into the night. Afterward, he said, he could put me back on the train, or I could crash in his daughter's room. I'd already seen it on a tour of the house, a confection of pink and lavender bedding heaped with stuffed animals. She was spending the night, perhaps too conveniently, at her mother's in a nearby town.

If I had been twenty years old, I had no doubt how the evening would end, and I can tell you it wouldn't have been in a window seat on the New Haven line or bedded down with a menagerie of bunnies and bears. I mean, let's be real. This man and I were both unattached, he had those eyes, and he knew how to make risotto.

And that would be only the first course. In a burst of what may or may not have been romantic overkill, he had also whipped up osso buco, an arugula salad with roasted beets and pears, the kind of French cheese platter that required a map of the Dordogne, and a decadent fallen chocolate soufflé cake with thyme-scented vanilla ice cream that he'd churned by hand that afternoon. He was Renaissance Man on steroids, in case I had any doubts. We'd wash it all down with an array of wines, also French. Almost any home-cooked meal might have done the trick. Little did he know, this over-the-top feast was like heroin to me.

On the other hand, I was no longer twenty years old. Sometime in between my salad days and tonight's salad, my policy of fear-tinged abstinence had taken hold, and I clung to it despite ample evidence that if there was anyone with whom to dispatch this just-say-no nonsense, this man could be it.

I'd known it from the night of the Glamazon dinner, when I profited from one of the payoffs of decades of social experience, which is that it doesn't take a lot of vetting to recognize a like-minded soul. Was it love at first sight? No, not really. But I knew in the most rational way that this man was a worthy companion. I called some friends the next day to tell them, "I met him. I met the guy."

By six that morning there was an e-mail from Bob asking me to accompany him the following week to MoMA, apparently the first-date location of choice, to see a Brice Marden exhibit and dine afterward at the museum's super-hot restaurant. As it happened, I'd been trying without success to finagle someone into joining me for exactly that. I wrote to Fred to root out more about his friend. "I would say, and I mean this in the best way," Fred answered, "that he is a person of temperament. I believe Bernie was, too. If you have recently met men who are sort of wishy-washy, Bob certainly isn't that."

Temperament? As Scooby Doo would put it: Ruh-roh!

I had a nicely fitted little sleeveless dress picked out for the occasion, but at the last minute went with a full-coverage black top and a dirndl skirt by an avant-garde designer. Yes, a dirndl. I cringe at what it telegraphed.

Bob threw himself into the exhibit with the enthusiasm I'd witnessed when we first met, freely proclaiming his opinions, teasing out mine. He brought the same curiosity to dinner, where he puzzled over ingredients and plotted how he could riff on them at home. His exuberance was palpable, if a bit unsettling. I learned that if Bob heard a song he liked on the radio, he'd grab his guitar and play along. Like me, he had become a writer in part to partake of unfiltered, high-octane experience, taking on an assignment so he could cook with a great chef in Europe, play sideman to a rock musician, fly on a company jet with the plutocrat of the moment, or go on location with a movie director. Once he talked a magazine into letting him spend a month learning to tango in Argentina. His take on all of it was original, full, I suppose, of temperament. He reminded me of my best self, the bold one, the explorer, the one with the active, original point of view, before I got all closed and timid.

I'd been worried that men in my age bracket would be stuck in a rut, but Bob was fifty-six, and he was going full blast. He was all in. Which raised the question: was I? There was no denying that this was the sort of man I'd been seeking. For the first time since I'd started dating, for the first time since Bernie died, I had no excuse to avoid the hardest question of all. Could I conceive, ever again, of letting one person matter to me as much as the one I'd lost?

────────────────

P*UTTING ALL THAT ASIDE*, and I did as much as I could, I recognized that this was someone I could have fun with. The next few weeks were a montage from the modern rom-com story line. Casual dinners turned into four-hour restaurant marathons where we actually closed the joint. Our phone calls sent Verizon stock soaring. If we'd been paid by the word for our e-mails, we would have doubled our incomes. An adroit conversationalist, Bob brought out the same in me. I told him about my sheltered past in western Pennsylvania, of trying to strike a balance along the

way between daring moves (moving to New York, becoming a journalist) and prudent choices—progressing from yearbook editor,
honor roll habitué, and grad school wonk to responsible holder of
full-time jobs and regular contributor to the 401(k) plan. Bob had
grown up in eastern Pennsylvania and put himself through college
playing in rock bands. After he graduated, he jumped off the professional track for a stint in the music business. He had followed his
enthusiasms ever since.

"There doesn't seem to be an uptight bone in your body," I said,
forgetting for a moment that the subject of bodies was on my re-
stricted list. We had met in a little pasta place in the Village that
got a write-up in the paper the day before for its orecchiette with
sausage and broccoli rabe. The dining room was fully booked, but
Bob talked our way into seats at the bar.

"You don't fool me with that Hitchcock-blonde façade," he said,
shifting back in his stool to get a better look. By now, I had switched
up my datewear to some flattering jeans and a tailored jacket. "I get
the feeling there's nothing uptight about you, either."

"Once, that might have been true. But for the last few years I'd
have made a first-class nun."

Like most couples in the flush of infatuation, we were dancing around the subject of where this might be headed, conducting
discussions, purely hypothetical of course, about our views on Relationships, our thoughts on Commitment, our beliefs about the
ideal arrangement for Intimate Companionship.

"My philosophy since Bernie died," I explained, purely hypothetically, you understand, "is that I need to construct a system that
allows me to be happy living by myself. I have my friends, lots of
them, in fact. I have my interests, lots of those, too. I've reached the

point where I have something going on almost every night of the week. It's not the same as marriage, and it's not what I expected at this point in my life, but it's very full, very satisfying. And I don't need to worry about losing one person who means everything to me. What if I become attached to someone and we break up? I can't handle any more loss right now."

Bob looked at me as if I'd become a vegan. "First of all," he said, I assume hypothetically, "nobody's going to break up with you."

I opened my mouth to object, but he silenced me.

"And as for your philosophy, if I thought I'd have to live that way, I'd have to join a castrato boys choir, or maybe a religious retreat. All right, maybe not—the food would suck. But seriously, sure, I was blindsided by my divorce. It made me question whether men and women were meant to inhabit the same planet—make that the same universe. But one nightmare implosion shouldn't put a person off soufflés. I could never accept the possibility of a life without love. It's like food, it's like sleep, like breathing. People are meant to make love, and they're meant to be in love."

"I like soufflés, but they fall," I countered. "And they're not the only source of food. It's okay to like soup, too. And it's valid to find satisfaction in a variety of friendships instead of one overarching, all-consuming romance that might blow up in my face."

He gave me a long appraising glance. "No offense, but soup is soufflé without the air. There's magic in soufflés. Settling for soup when you want soufflé is the act of a coward."

"Maybe I *am* a coward," I said, purely hypothetically. "But cowards are safe."

FOR ALL HIS hypothetical talk, I noticed Bob wasn't rushing into anything, either, perhaps out of respect for my caution, perhaps to protect himself. Or perhaps he wasn't as interested as he seemed. It had been five years since his divorce, but the toll was still visible. Most of the time, he had an unforced ease and assurance, overridden, at key moments, by a skittish look I'd learned to recognize. It had turned up at the end of all our assignations up to now. We'd find ourselves getting all goofy-eyed on the street at a moment when a kiss might be appropriate. Suddenly, that look would cloud Bob's eyes and his head did one of those *Exorcist* 360s.

"Look, a cab!" he'd blurt out. He'd dash into traffic like a running back and stuff me inside, alone, before I could say . . . well, not much. I didn't have the nerve, either. From the safety of the backseat, I'd watch him recede into the streetscape as the cab pulled away.

And I'd think, what if this man got sick? Let's be honest, what if he died?

========

I DIDN'T WANT to make a mistake. Neither did Bob. What do you get when you have two people who are setting off enough sparks to start a forest fire but don't want to make a mistake? An awkward standoff in a Connecticut kitchen.

That afternoon when he'd picked me up at the picturesque little train station in his picturesque little town, the sparks were flying again. He drove me on a brief tour: sailboats in a former fishing harbor, a thumbnail beach, Nantucket-style saltbox houses. Everyone on the street had a Labrador retriever on a leash. Very quiet. The kind of quiet that gives New Yorkers the heebie-jeebies.

What do people *do* in Connecticut, I wondered? I'd read Rick Moody and John Cheever. Mostly dinner parties and wife swapping. I wasn't much of a cook, and I was nobody's wife anymore. The thought still stung. I felt in my pocket for the return train schedule. 4:43, 5:43, 6:43. I could make any of 'em.

Stepping out at the beach, we ran into a woman Bob seemed to know. "Yikes, let's go," Bob said. He backtracked like a trapped animal as she picked up his scent. Too late. She zeroed in on him, bursting into noisy tears.

"This isn't a good time, Cindy," Bob said. Who was this woman? Ex-girlfriend? Ex-wife? *Current* girlfriend? *Current wife?* Her dog hurled itself up my leg, spackling me with sandy footprints.

"Uh, your . . . uh, dog . . ." I started to say. Cindy didn't bat an eye my way, and neither did Bob. Whoever she was, she seemed to have more emotional claim on him than I did. I walked ahead while they spoke in addled stage whispers.

He caught up with me a minute later. "I'm so sorry about that," he said, looking mortified. "She's just a friend, going through a hard time. We used to walk our dogs together."

Couldn't he come up with a better excuse than that? I felt again for the schedule and cursed myself for not wearing a watch.

So I was really on edge when we finally crossed the threshold of his place, where the turf would be studded with quicksand and land mines. Rented in a rush during the divorce, the house was a knock-kneed former summer cottage, built in the 1920s, overlooking a sparkling stream. Inside, it was all white wainscoting and tilted pine floors, charming and cozy, with logs ablaze in a sandstone fireplace. There were fresh white roses in a vase on the coffee table and the luxurious scent of long-simmering veal wafting from the kitchen. Either it was the osso buco or Just-a-Friend had made it there ahead of us and boiled a bunny.

"This is Wink," Bob said proudly, indicating an immobile mound of brown fur on the living room rug. Dog, I presumed. Asleep, or taxidermy project? I wasn't much good with animals. I hesitated. Was I supposed to pet it? Was it rude to wake it up?

"What kind of dog is it?" I asked. Midsize, I guessed, taking in a long snout, arcing tail, and dainty white paws.

"We call him mixed breed to his face."

A mutt, then. I felt a tug of sympathy.

Bob and I soon fell into the easy conversation we'd always enjoyed, and he popped a champagne cork, sheepishly licking the spillover off his knuckles. We worked our way into a pocket-sized kitchen as darkness fell outside. I supposed there were stars out there, so far from streetlit Brooklyn. Bob placed some votive candles on an antique farmhouse table, throwing a veil of intimacy over the room. It took on a golden glow that illuminated the weathered cabinets and floorboards. The setting should have put me at ease, but ease didn't come easily to me anymore. Strange place, strange man, strange sensation. Strange.

There was no choice in that tiny space but to stand phone-booth close as he set to work on the risotto. I leaned against a counter next to the stove. The windows started steaming up, and his eyes turned guarded and edgy. Poor Bob. No cab to hail out here. It hit me that this situation might be even stranger for him than it was for me. Bob's divorce had been followed by a three-year relationship with a woman who broke up with him by e-mail, then a lonely year or so after that. The woman on the beach probably fit in there somewhere. Divorce, misguided love affairs, and death. Between the two of us, I figured, we had the full range of romantic cataclysms pretty well covered.

All that trauma was very much there in the room, palpable as the scent of saffron and fennel, but I'd be lying if I didn't tell you that the most immediate thought in my head was more mundane: I hadn't kissed another man in twenty-five years. I did the math while I was standing there.

Bob interrupted my calculations. "I'm sorry if I seem nervous tonight," he said. "It's just that I want everything to go well between us."

The look again, and he said, "I just want you to know. Nothing is going to happen here tonight."

I wanted to reassure him, and I spoke without thinking. "What I think about us," I said in a hurried, level voice, "is that it's just going to work." I believed it, too, even as it burst from my mouth like a New Year's Eve popper. I could almost hear the faint discharge, followed by the cascade of words as they fell to the ground like so much confetti.

Bob stopped stirring and put down the wooden spoon.

"Is it hard to make risotto?" I asked quickly. Very dopey question.

"It's actually very simple," Bob replied. "Like a soufflé. You just stir the ingredients, and it all comes together perfectly."

Then without any fuss, he reached over, cupped my face in his hand, and kissed me. It was an admirably straightforward kiss, direct, right on the mouth, and not too long, without any accompanying fumbling or groping, but still somehow warm, very warm.

I'd like to say that everything fell into place afterward, as it does in a Trollope novel, when the lovers' hands meet for the first time and their future together is settled. This wasn't so simple. We lived far apart, he rooted by his daughter, I by work, friends, my life as I'd envisioned it. None of this was what we'd been led to expect; none of it felt at all familiar. None of it felt safe. Nevertheless, in the reverberations from that kiss, everything else drifted to the periphery. I opened my eyes and saw him clearly, and I thought, *Ah... there you are.*

chapter

TWENTY-ONE

just inside the front door of Tara's place we nearly tripped over a good-sized cardboard box with red letters stamped on top: *HANDLE WITH CARE*.

"What's in there?" Marcia demanded.

The withering look on Tara's face revealed that the box was loaded with meaning, meaning she wasn't willing to share, not before a high-octane cup of coffee. She elbowed away the question and led us toward the kitchen. It was six days before movers would cart everything out of the house, a graceful, tan-shingled beauty built in 1895 and restored to a magnificent polish by Tara over two decades. Her new home in Connecticut would save her a bundle, and it would also be cozier, more inviting, with the feel of a seaside cottage, whereas this house in suburban New York was substantial, a home for proper entertaining, for raising a proper family. I gawked at stately antiques as we passed through a formal dining room and parlor. We had come to help sort through things and pack, but the July day was too damn glorious, and Tara had told us to bring bathing suits for a side trip to the beach.

Alas, I saw, the house was neater than mine on my best day. Aside from the mystery box, everything remained in place. Couches, tables, rugs, pictures, even the smallest lamps and vases, stood impervious to the coming upheaval aside from a little round sticker on each. Red for the new house, yellow for a tag sale, blue for storage, and so on, with stickers for her daughters, for donations, on and on. Everywhere we turned, there was a colored label, except on that box in the entrance hall. It may have been the only possession the fate of which had yet to be sealed.

Tara limped ahead of us in flip-flops. She'd broken two toes on her left foot when she tried to move a dresser by herself and it fell on her. She broke one toe on the other foot when she tripped over a suitcase she'd left inside a bedroom door. Yet improbably, Tara was at her most glowing that morning, casual in a tunic and white linen capris, her eyes gleaming under dishabille, sun-streaked hair.

We reached the kitchen, and... *What's this?* A man. And quite a nice-looking man at that.

We stopped short, and I bumped into Denise from behind. Tara turned to see our reaction, looking like a cat that had managed to swallow a handsome canary, despite three broken toes and a lifetime's worth of stuff to pack.

"This is Will," she said, entertained by our surprise. He stood up from a stool at the end of the kitchen island, facing one of the most dangerous hurdles in any new relationship: friends, and the meeting thereof.

"You're a brave man, Will," said Dawn.

He shrugged nonchalantly. "I hear about all of you all the time. There isn't much I don't already know."

Having just returned from the bakery with a breakfast stash, he gestured for us to join him as he sat back down and broke a blue-berry muffin in two. Dude, Tara's black Pekingese, scrambled greedily under his feet. The rest of us exchanged looks of approval. Here was a man who was comfortable nibbling gourmet baked goods in the company of his new girlfriend and her posse, whatever fevered speculation he might be setting off.

"Will is in touch with his feminine side," Tara explained, gliding around us and pouring from a coffeepot, reading our thoughts. She leaned against his shoulder, and he wrapped a long arm comfortably around her waist. He's in touch with a lot more than *his* feminine side, I thought.

Lesley was the only one missing that day, vacationing with one of her daughters, but I knew she'd be hungry for every detail. An imposing man, Will stood over six feet tall, tanned and clearly fit, his light hair mostly gray, a pleasing combination with the kind of blue-gray eyes you see on a Siamese cat. Barefoot, dressed in rumpled white linen shorts and a green-and-white striped shirt with the sleeves rolled up, he drew out each of us with the ease of Charlie Rose. Marcia, he discovered, would be moving into her new apartment in September; Denise was editing a novel set in a yoga studio; Dawn was worn out from a long drive with Adam to pick up their sons from camp. Most intriguing of all, Will commiserated with me about how Bob and I had managed to date while living a couple of hours apart, just about the distance that separated Will from Tara.

This man might as well have been marked with one of Tara's red stickers—he was a keeper. The two of them obviously shared the same relaxed sociability. Their rapport was easy and fond. You know how you can tell when a couple is clicking—you see that they admire, not so much the beauty or the intelligence or the wit of each other, but the everyday quirks that make someone real and distinct, that might even annoy someone not in love. I could tell that Will felt that way about Tara. He never looked fonder than when she described her rigid color-coding system. "What can I say, I'm a control freak," she said.

"I'm *so* pleased to hear you say that."

We liked him immediately. We liked that Tara looked so happy, that the two of them had that *Cupid and Psyche* thing going on. Despite all the lifting she'd been up to, this was not the Tara we'd seen at our first meeting, the one who seemed to be carrying a heavy load. This Tara was lighthearted and loaded for fun.

"I'm not going to make you ladies pack," she said. "I'm up for a day off, chilling at the beach with my friends." But with Marcia moving soon and the rest of us anticipating dislocations of our own someday, she knew we'd want her wisdom on how to manage it. New lives, new places, fewer things.

Will padded behind with a coffee cup as Tara started a tour in the family room next to the kitchen.

"This is *my* room, the one I redid after David died," Tara said, although it was evident without her saying a word. Whereas the rest of the house was elegant, with those formidable antiques, this space had the signature black cashmere touch, casual and simple, yet luxe and chic. I wanted to curl up in that room and luxuriate in the sunshine that poured through two walls of windows. The arrangement was offhand, mixing styles and periods and functions with careless zest.

"You put the table and the desk and the couch all in one room?" Marcia asked.

"Sure, why not?"

Before, Tara said, everything was darker. Now the color scheme played off shades of eggshell touched by a few bold, graphic accents of black. The new couch was a modern piece with a nod to Empire style, in white linen, with black and white pillows tossed along the length. That entire tableau had earned a red sticker, heading to the new home. The same with a bleached wood trestle dining table, surrounded by Parsons chairs slipcovered in linen the color of unbleached muslin. She had also red-stickered a filigreed antique birdcage and two Art Deco coffee tables made from mirrored glass. For Tara, clearly, a home wasn't merely a place to live but a means of self-expression. She loved nothing more, she said, than finding a broken antique in a junk shop, spiffing it up, and making it her own.

"This was the room that held the most memories," Tara said. "It was the one I . . . really needed to change."

Since Tara had filed for divorce before David's death, we knew there were heartbreaking associations in the house as well as treasured ones. We could only guess how they complicated the process of making that change. After all that had happened—the separation, the grown daughters moving out, and then David dying—Tara was left in the emptiest possible nest. The formal, family-sized house was all wrong for her now.

"You know, the process of transformation has happened much more here." Tara touched a hand to her heart. "The house hadn't caught up. It feels disjointed, suburban . . . weird."

I recognized that this was true, but I was also sure that wrenching herself out of the family home had to be giving her fierce pangs, pangs that Tara wasn't about to let us see. She steered us onto a south-facing porch that looked out onto a sloping lawn. Beyond a bank was a leafy wooded area, left in a natural state. Will shifted to the side and sat on the ground gazing into the trees, granting us some space as we circled Tara and she drew on a well of memories.

"I used to take out the saplings on this bank every spring. Then I would blanket it with wildflowers. I didn't do it this year . . . I didn't see the point." She shrugged. She smiled, but we felt the force of her nostalgia. "Down below here is an old root cellar. It was the girls' secret place." She gestured farther out, toward the trees. "My youngest used to go on hunts down there . . . sometimes with her dad. She would come back with a checklist. Mommy, I saw one hippopotamus, two giraffes . . ."

The subject of children broke the reverie and led her to tell us about the buyers of the house, a young family of five. Tara had invited them over, gone over old blueprints with the parents, and toured the bedrooms with the kids. The little boy decided to place his stuffed animals on the same shelf Tara's daughter had, a shelf built by Tara's father.

"Holy shit, look!" I said. I had just spotted an animal sauntering through the woods below. It was a coyote, and a big one, practically, to my urban eye, the size of a Subaru. "*Shit!*" several of us yelped in unison.

Tara told us that a large coyote had attacked two children in town a week before. They weren't seriously injured, but the community was on the alert. Now here was the possible culprit.

"This is too symbolic," Denise said. "Danger lurking in the suburbs."

Tara ran to call the police as the coyote slunk behind some heavy bushes and Will kept an eye on it. In a flash, a patrol car arrived, and a sharpshooter strode into the yard carrying a shiny rifle with a long scope. "We need to let them know that we are not a part of their food chain," he said ominously.

Faced with this menacing man and his more menacing rifle, I found myself rooting for the coyote. But Tara had raised children there and felt no such hesitation. She pointed out the coyote's last location and left Will to help the sniper with his mission. They didn't find the coyote, but Tara learned that it met its fate a week later.

Meanwhile, back in her decorous parlor, she showed us that the only items marked to move with her were a zebra rug and some framed family photographs of David on a beach with the girls. "I will absolutely have a place for these in the new house," Tara said. "All the happy memories."

"Do you feel awkward about Will seeing them?" I asked.

"I never talked to him about it. But he thinks it's healthy that we . . . talk about David. It's part of who my girls are . . . it's part of who *I* am."

Most everything else in the parlor was for sale, lots of dark wood end tables and stout upholstered chairs. "That's not me anymore," Tara said. "None of these things would look right in the new house." Her attitude was brisk, unsentimental. This new Tara was shedding an old skin, becoming looser, freer, unmoored from the strictures applied to the wife of a more conservative man, but the transformation had demanded a series of tough decisions over the last two months. She had uncovered everything she owned from long-forgotten drawers and backs of closets, and every bit of it, from salad forks to scrapbooks, had been examined, appraised, and rated for its importance and its worth, every object a repository of memory, happy or sad, significant or banal. A whole life summed up in its things, each of them put into perspective and accorded its place in a new life.

Some decisions were easy. We came to a tiny study where a chintz sofa faced a fireplace. She chuckled. "This is the room where David would always say, 'Let's go have a drink in front of the fire,'" Tara said. "It really meant, let's go discuss how Tara is spending too much money." The recollection at this remove seemed to amuse more than rankle her. Most of the stickers in this room seemed to be yellow—sell.

Some decisions were more complex. David's desk, in an office with hunter green walls, was a ponderous mahogany beast from the nineteenth century. I could imagine generations of owl-eyed men poring over ledgers at this desk. Practical? Hardly, but her daughters laid claim to it.

Finally, she took us to a corner of the basement behind the furnace. I wondered why, until Tara made a sweep of her arm around racks of clothing and plastic storage boxes. "This is the last of David's stuff," she said. "Clothes, sweaters, sports equipment. I asked the girls what they wanted." One took his hunting jacket to remember their backyard safaris. Otherwise, they wanted some T-shirts and a couple of sweaters.

"The same thing happened with my kids," Dawn said. "They only wanted Andries's T-shirts."

All of us confessed that we had saved some odd piece of well-worn leisure wear, still infused with memories of touch and smell. Tara had given away David's good suits, and now everything left of value was here behind the furnace, an ignominious location, I suppose. But that's what happens with the stuff of the missing. What else would we do with it—put it on some kind of permanent museum display, a diorama of the useless?

Getting rid of the husband's things—all of us had pushed ourselves through the onerous task, Denise with the help of friends in the first month, Marcia over several months with her nephews. Dawn pointed out that Adam still hadn't faced up to the disposal of his wife's possessions, after years. "I think it's a classic case of not dealing with your past, not dealing with your loss—not dealing!"

"It's a matter of forcing yourself," I said. People tend to think of transformation as organic, I thought: baby birds flex their wings and leave the nest; caterpillars transfigure into butterflies; plant shoots unfurl from tiny seeds; maple leaves wither and fall. In the natural world, reinvention may be driven by the tides or the seasons. But for women in our position, rethinking our way of living, the process was more deliberate, a series of hard choices—what to leave behind, what to keep. That included possessions, of course, but also all that they represented: patterns, habits, actions, traits of personality.

Sometimes those decisions felt brutal. Upstairs, we had seen Tara's ornate Scottish sideboard, the first antique she ever bought, a beautiful piece and loaded with memories. Now it wore an ignoble sell sticker: it wouldn't suit the new house. I thought about photographs of homes in magazines, where rooms are edited of any objects that don't fit the scheme. The owners must possess a savage lack of sentiment in order to create a space that looks forward rather than back. Here in the flux of Tara's place, we saw the process in action. She was trying to balance sentiment and brutality to bring about the transformation she sought. It took the cool resolve of a sniper.

Pulling her aside, I asked if she had any final words of advice.

She performed one of her trademark theatrical pauses and said, "Let's go to the beach."

We followed her back upstairs, but there it was again, the unmarked cardboard box, the one decision yet unmade. Tara regarded it as if it were the coyote.

"Yesterday, I was up in the attic," she said, "and I found this."

We stood still for a moment, staring down the box. It held its ground, like a live thing. For the first time that day, Tara became a bit overcome.

"What is it?" asked Denise, voice lowered to a reverent hush.

Tara looked at her hard, and then spoke in her slowest, clearest voice. "My . . . wedding dress. I didn't open it."

We circled the box, according it a respectful distance.

"What will you do with it?" I wondered.

Tara didn't answer. She looked at me through pooling eyes that signaled this decision was beyond her. In a houseful of memories, here was a package too sensitive to open.

chapter

TWENTY-TWO

*t*ara and David had been the golden couple. Everyone said so. She was a prize catch, a college student, a classic beauty with a Garbo voice, when they met on a blind date. He was a find himself, handsome, whip-smart, halfway through an MBA at Harvard. I heard the whole saga the first time Tara and I met, over lunch in her family room, more somber back then, before the makeover. A real estate agent had told me about a young widow who was house-hunting, and Tara agreed to speak with some reluctance.

She seemed tense and listless eight months after David's death, engaged in a standoff with gloom and unsure what to do with herself. "I'm putting one foot in front of the other," she said, rebuffing me at first. "I don't need anything else in my life right now." Nevertheless, she had pulled herself together in jeans and a twinset, black cashmere of course, and served a ladies' lunch—zucchini bisque, chicken panini with pesto and red peppers, and a chocolate brownie.

Tara and David had it all before it went wrong. She was a bit of a bohemian who loved to dance and write, a senior at a women's college that emphasized the arts, the daughter of a civil engineer. David was more conventional, old-school, with courtly manners and a penchant for business. "It wasn't love on the first date," she admitted. "He was buttoned up and well dressed, and I was into self-expression and . . . a bit dramatic."

After she graduated, Tara took an advertising job in New York, and David had a summer internship at an investment firm. They continued to date long-distance during his last year at school.

It was a heady time for Tara. She felt lucky to land a spot on Madison Avenue in its heyday, when the ads were well written and the art direction flawless. It was glamorous, fizzy fun, and Tara looked the part, thanks to a sister in the fashion business who out-fitted her in free-spirited samples at wholesale prices from Giorgio Sant'Angelo and Calvin Klein. Tara had taste even then. Money was always short, so the sisters shared a closet-size Upper East Side apartment that they carved up with room dividers.

When David graduated and started full-time at his firm, mar-riage followed, when he was twenty-seven and she twenty-four. They squeezed into a charmless one-bedroom walk-up awkwardly split between two floors. He jokingly called it "a top-floor duplex penthouse." They had no furniture to speak of, just a table from her mother and a chest of drawers from his. "It was our first place, and the happiest," Tara recalled. "Really happy times."

She gladly followed him to London when his employer asked him to relocate. "I looked forward to the adventure of living some-where else," she said. When the firm offered a shipping container for their things, they had to laugh. The entire household fit into a few suitcases.

Tara discovered soon enough that women execs were scarce in British advertising. Finding a spot comparable to the one she'd held in New York was next to impossible. In the meantime, she proceeded to walk everywhere in the city and snag cheap flights all over Europe, often meeting David on his business trips. Eventually, she landed a job. She wrote the agency's maternity leave policy when she had her first child, and the golden couple continued to shine. "My God, David was so handsome," she said. "So stunning and elegant in his suits. We had ... so much fun. I threw wonderful dinners with his mover-and-shaker friends and my creative friends." Tara rose through the ranks to become the agency's first female head of new business and board director.

When they moved back to New York after nine years, they bought the house. He launched his own firm while she headed a foundation that awarded grants to college students. Throughout it all, working and raising two daughters, Tara clung to her bohemian identity. When she met me at the train, I grinned at the big green peace symbol on the side of her car.

About five years before he died, David began to withdraw from family and friends. Tara knew that he was under unspoken strain from work and the death of his mother, but she also recognized a snowballing depression, and soon she noticed that he began to drink more frequently and furtively. "Substances became a way to dull the sadness," she said. "It was a slow, insidious change."

Over the next four years, the drinking surged out of control, and Tara struggled to protect her family from the toxic fallout. One daughter had left for college when the troubles began, but the other was still finishing high school. Life at home became unmanageable. "We sought help from treatment programs, therapists, doctors ...

with little success," Tara said. Prescription drugs only magnified the effects of alcohol.

David was fifty-six when his heart failed; Tara was fifty-three. She grieved for what could have been, a golden existence squandered, and for her daughters, suddenly fatherless as they entered young adulthood. Tara, alone among our group, had watched her marriage dissolve during the course of her husband's illness. Any grief is layered with regrets, remorse, and contradictions, I thought, Tara's possibly more than most.

She was in a tight, dark spot when we first met, out of place in her home, out of place in her town, out of place in her social circle, where nuclear families prevailed. More than once, at the hair salon on a Saturday afternoon, someone would ask, "Are you going to so-and-so's tonight?" Tara would have to explain that she hadn't been invited. Even at the first meeting of our group, Tara told me afterward, she worried that the others wouldn't think her worthy to join because of the divorce proceedings. "I loved David as much as the others loved their husbands," she said. "I just lost him sooner than death took him."

In some ways, Tara seemed to be the saddest one at the outset of our group. Over time, however, I saw that she possessed a flexibility, a willingness to make the hard choices it takes to start over, and the backbone to call in a sharpshooter if necessary. By the time our group met at her house, she had succeeded in finding new work doing voice-overs, a new man, and a breezy new house near the sea where she could breathe. I recalled, from our first meeting, how she said, "You can't go backward. You're never going to have what you had. You need to create your own life." Now, somehow, she was pulling it off.

Tara didn't look that day like someone who had spent the last several years in chaos, with the chaos of the move still to come. She looked impossibly assured. She had a color-coded system for it all; she had control. For the first time since—when? her youth?—she alone was in charge. She alone—the casual one, the one who had fulfilled her formal obligations and could live now as she pleased.

At the beach a mile away, we changed into swimsuits—bright bikinis for Dawn, Denise, and me; a sturdy black one-piece for Marcia, and a more modish one for Tara, with black net edging that resembled chiffon, the nylon-Lycra equivalent of black cashmere. We ate lunch on a shaded deck overlooking Long Island Sound. Will joined us after a quick swim and submitted to questions about his family. He had introduced his seven-year-old daughter to Tara the week before.

"She's a little sweetheart," Tara said, smitten.

Later, after Will wandered back to the beach, Tara got a chance to dish about him. "In some ways, he's more like me than David was," she said. "He's scrappy, a free spirit." We the jury murmured our approval. "I was dubious that something like this could even exist. If I had written the script myself, I'd have thought, well... maybe after I get settled in my new house ... maybe I could go back to the kind of work I used to do, put my heart and soul into it. After all that, I thought, *maybe* it would be nice, if it exists at all, to find ... this kind of relationship. And maybe I never would. The funny thing is, this started the weekend we were all at the spa, when I least expected it."

After lunch, Dawn napped on the beach while the rest of us talked and read. Distracted, I swam a few laps in a pool that over-looked the sound. When I came up for air, I saw an affectionate tableau: Tara and Will leaning against the railing, looking out to sea, their arms around each other, wrapped in matching red-and-white striped towels. They looked just like a couple to me. How quickly that had happened. Problem solved.

Then I checked myself. I remembered how irritated I got when people assured me that finding Mr. Right would put a happy cap on my own story of widowhood, as if that alone would erase all that had happened before. The ol' man trap: thinking a man was a cure-all. Will alone wasn't making Tara happy, I was certain. He was a reward she'd earned for making herself happy.

Anyway, I knew from experience that there were any number of trip wires not visible in that tableau—children, geography, stubborn patterns of behavior developed over decades of adulthood. Not to cast doubts on their prospects, but blending two lives at our age was a project to rival the subprime mortgage bailout. I knew that it took more to seal a midlife romance than a kiss and a set of matching towels. Or a kiss and a plate of risotto, for that matter.

chapter

TWENTY-THREE

a truly exceptional cook, Bob fed me the scallop risotto the night he invited me to his house, the first of many delights over the next few months. He fed me his signature pasta bolognese. He fed me butterflied leg of lamb stuffed with olives and rosemary that he rolled and hogtied like a rodeo star. He fed me chocolate chip cookies with a double dose of chips. He pulled off showstopping feats in the kitchen, his and mine, and I ate like a starving person. I had dreaded the thought of anyone needing me again. It had never occurred to me that someone might feed me rather than need me, and that he'd take such pleasure in it himself.

Bob stirred other appetites in me, of course, deep, nearly forgotten cravings, long suppressed and ready to ripen. Later, he liked to kid me about my hopeless effort to sleep in the wee hours of that first night. He'd glance over and see my eyes fixed on the ceiling with a zombie stare. I'm no prude, but the realization that I was lying there next to a man who wasn't my husband was too freaky to allow me rest. Besides, I think sleep implied a level of surrender I wasn't yet ready to embrace. But the other embraces that night were remarkably easy, and I'm not an easy girl, as you know.

After I formed my group of widows, we often found ourselves talking about how, once we took the plunge, we felt scandalously free about our sexuality. There was something about being wounded... it had made us vulnerable, but it was profoundly freeing, too. Having lived through the worst, we found it was hard to take mere inhibitions and insecurities seriously. Having been without pleasure, we reveled in it now. The sex, it turned out, was even better than the food.

Bob and I zipped past all the other milestones of a new relationship. I learned that, left unchecked, he'd slather piri-piri sauce on just about anything. He learned that I read the Sunday Styles section first. I discovered that six in the morning was doggy wake-up time, when persistent white paws tugged at any blankets trailing off the bed. Bob learned that I got my best ideas in the shower. I met his parents; he met my mom. "I guess this makes you the official boyfriend now," I said. We were the talk of gatherings where we got to know each other's friends. Everyone who'd seen me through the last few years of pitiful circumstances was thrilled for me now, as if I were one of those Hollywood stars up for an Oscar after a spell in rehab.

We established a staccato existence. Since Bob's daughter, Lily, stayed with him half the time, I'd see him alternate weeks. During off weeks, I had my autonomy and my social life with my friends. The perfect setup—my previous full plate, with a satisfying dollop of love, in handy portion-controlled servings. Aside from the sensation of defenses falling (maybe crashing?), something felt extraordinarily right.

After a couple months of this, it was time to meet Lily. Call me

naive, call me inexperienced with children, but I expected this passage to be as easy as all the others with Bob. I'd never had children,
to my regret, and as a result, they seemed a bit alien to me, but man-
ageable, kind of like Wink. When the dog first graced my apartment with his presence, I repeatedly started at sudden encounters
with a wild animal as he brazenly made himself at home around
the place, but I soon learned to regard myself as his humble servant,
fixing his dinner or scratching his ears on request. Besides, he was
Bob's responsibility, not mine. So was Lily. By the only account that
mattered—Bob's—she was a father's dream: sweet, loving, never a
spot of worry to her dad.

Bob invited me to dinner in Connecticut one night when Lily
was there. An inveterate researcher, I had studied up on this—in
contrast to younger children, teenagers were the most averse to
new love interests of their parents. Lily had just turned fourteen.
Atoms were about to collide.

Petite, with luxurious dark hair, Lily was a perfect lady that evening, polite and agreeable, displaying a zany sense of humor. I was
utterly charmed. The three of us were in stitches through much of
the meal. She tactfully didn't say a word when Bob nervously over-
cooked the steak, and after I left, chastely, on a late-night train, she
gave him a thumbs-up on his choice of me. This was too easy! But
over the next weeks and months, when I showed up for a weekend,
I never knew which version of Lily would meet me there. Sometimes we'd review geometry homework or play a lightning round
of Monopoly; other times that quaint little house felt like a particle
accelerator for all the moody collisions going on. There were entire
weekends when Lily wouldn't look at me and referred to me only
when necessary as "She" and "Her," as in, "When is She going to

leave?" or "Are we eating dinner with Her?" Bob and I were careful
not to show affection in front of her, but still she wedged herself
between us when the three of us walked anywhere and plunked
down in the middle if we nestled on the couch. When we went to a
restaurant or a movie, she sat as far from me as if I were the source
of West Nile virus.

I couldn't blame her. She had witnessed the disintegration of her
family in a divorce, and any change in the dynamics with her dad
now would likely set off new distress. She felt threatened, of course.
What if her dad ran off to New York with this vixen; what would
become of her? I knew Bob's devotion was too fierce to allow for
that, but divorced parents do such things, everyone knows. I found
her mood swings poignant. I was the adult here; I understood what
was going on; and she was, after all, Bob's responsibility, not mine.

At the same time, where did that leave me? Genuinely intimi-
dated by a ninety-pound schoolgirl. It was possible that I had come
this far in a quest for love only to fall short because I couldn't finesse somebody who still watched cartoons in happy-face pajamas.
I was the adult here, but the adult wasn't in control.

Once Bob tried to discuss the situation with Lily when I wasn't
around. "Someday you will grow up and have your own life, and
I'll be here by myself," he said. "Do you want me to be alone for the
rest of my life?"

"Yes."

Bob wasn't easily deterred. He asked me to join him for a
five-day getaway to Paris eight months after we met. Paris had
been one of those zingers, a place where Bernie and I had enjoyed
such dreamy escapes that I hadn't been able to consider returning
without him. On the first afternoon there with Bob, we shook off

jet lag to stroll arm-in-arm across the Pont des Arts, our tummies filled with buttery croques monsieurs. It was a warm June day, and sun sparkled off the fast-rushing waters of the Seine below and the limestone edifice of the Louvre across the way. I leaned close to him and breathed in my incredible good luck. I could have lived out my remaining decades alone, a proper widow nursing memories of love until my fading years, but this marvelous man had somehow appeared and opened my heart again. I had defied expectations, my own and everyone else's. I had pulled myself up from the depths of grief, surrounded myself with caring friends, continued my work—not ideal work, mind you, but a paying job at a newspaper when such a thing was hard to come by—and I had held out for a man who made me truly happy. Now I was in Paris again.

I gave an approving once-over to Bob, who was taking in the Parisian spectacle with similar contentment. He returned my admiring gaze, and his expression shifted. It was the skittish look again, the one I hadn't seen since our first days together, but there was tenderness as well.

"Get a look at this view," he said. "I'm inspired." He draped an arm across my shoulders as we turned upriver toward Notre Dame and the Île Saint-Louis, and he spoke into my ear. "What do you think about getting married?"

That's what he said—*What do you think about getting married?*—but it sounded more like static until the words reconfigured in my mind as I turned to see that he'd meant them. Still, I didn't respond, and I could tell it unnerved him.

"Aren't you going to say anything?"

It was everything I'd hoped for, everything I feared. I struggled to compose an answer.

"I don't see how we can," I finally said. "Where would we live?"

"We'll figure it out." He was incorrigible—that temperament again. It fell to me to be the cautious one. Where to start?

"You can't move out of Connecticut," I began gently. "I know you wouldn't leave Lily—I wouldn't love you if you could. But *I* don't want to leave New York, for all kinds of reasons. I couldn't get to my job from Connecticut, for one. And I don't *want* to live in Connecticut. My life is elsewhere." A rush of feeling pulled me toward the dream of permanence that marriage would provide, but an opposing current spun me another way. If I'd gained any wisdom from the last few years, it was that friends and work and autonomy mattered, too. I'd be sacrificing all that if I uprooted myself for him, but it made me heartsick to not say yes, a blind, unthinking yes, the way they do in the movies.

"We'll figure it out," Bob urged, maddeningly, again. For the rest of our stay, Paris served as the backdrop of an ongoing game of Rubik's cube, as we puzzled for a configuration that allowed all the pieces to fit, but they never did. We weighed the possibility of Bob moving to the city, where Lily could visit on weekends and holidays.

"That won't work. We have to be realistic," I said in despair. "She's a teenager, and she'll want to spend weekends with her friends. I hate to say it, but we can't get married, we can't even live together. You really have to stay put until Lily is finished with school. She has to come first."

Where did that come from? This was a curious twist—Lily had become my responsibility, too. And what was best for her, I knew, was for me and her father to live apart, to remain single, to continue our herky-jerky back-and-forth. It wasn't the full enchilada, but it would have to be enough for me, and I hoped it would be enough for Bob.

———

DAWN'S CHILDREN had a blast at a camp for kids who'd experienced the death of someone close, a bit like our adult group without the lingerie and champagne. On a bright, clear August Saturday, we volunteered to work there behind the scenes. While the Blossoms, as even I was beginning to call us, set out glue, glitter, and crepe paper for arts and crafts in the dining hall, we didn't have much chance to catch up with each other, but that no longer mattered. By now, we stayed in touch between meetings, as friends do, and that month there was much to tell.

Tara had updated me on her last moments in the old house when we met for lunch a week after she left it. Once the movers hoisted everything out, Tara, all alone, had picked her way through the detritus left behind—broken reading glasses, shoes without mates, coffee-stained napkins scrunched up by customers of the furniture sale. "Nothing was left in that house but dirt and crap," she said. She herself was filthy as a chimneysweep, crud encrusted under her nails, her white linen pants imprinted with grime. She wished she could collapse in the shower, but there wasn't a single towel in the house.

She gulped. What now? Two boxes stranded on the floor of the family room, boxes she didn't recognize, somehow left without color codes. *Fuck.* She tentatively peeked inside. Gingerly opening folders with dirty fingers, she saw files she had forgotten to categorize, letters the girls had sent to their father from summer camp.

Any nuclear family would have chucked them right out. But to Tara they were evidence of normalcy, before everything split apart. Her daughters would need this stuff, she thought, something to cherish.

Tara crumpled onto the dirty floor, done in. Her attention drifted outside, to her once-beautiful lawn, crisped brown by the dull July heat. She flashed on the Easter egg hunts she and David had staged for the girls when the lawn was lush, green, and edged with flowers. It slowly registered that she was sobbing, huge, full-throated sobs. Tears streamed down her dusty face from her eyes and her nose. "It was a big ugly cry," she told me. She let it rip, sobbing for forty-five minutes without stopping. After weeks, months, of parceling out colored stickers and putting one broken-toed foot in front of the other, she let herself go. "It felt great," she confided through a lopsided smile, "cleansing, cathartic."

That night, bunking at a friend's, she slept the deepest, longest sleep she'd had in years. For a few hours, for now, everything had found a place.

———————————

I MET MARCIA the evening after she closed on her new apartment. She turned the key and let us in to the empty, echoing living room, and there it was, the city twinkling at our feet through banks of windows, all the way down to Lower Manhattan and the harbor. If you squinted, you could see the Statue of Liberty. Not a bad reward for a lifetime of hard work. I startled Marcia with an impulsive squeeze. She edged away and cracked one of her twisting half smiles, hashing out where she would place the large-screen TV. Not an idle consideration—she was increasingly concerned about losing touch with her godsons, her husband's nephews, and she hoped they'd join her for marathon sports blowouts. She had also snagged season tickets to the Giants, on the forty-five-yard line, with them in mind.

At work, Marcia was lapping up even more responsibility, thanks to the new female boss, who hoped to promote Marcia even higher. In her spare time she was reading a book called *Taming Your Gremlin.*

Informative? Yes, Marcia said in her flat, blunt voice. "I'm learning that people like people who are pleasant."

———

FOR DENISE, the month of August solved the mystery of her husband's sudden death. She'd waited an entire year for the results of the autopsy, her imagination conjuring ghastly possibilities the longer the determination was delayed. On the anniversary of the sorrowful day, she tromped down to the city department of health. She wanted an answer, *damn it.* Everyone seeking birth or death certificates crowded around her, clasping numbers like customers in a deli. After an hour, she was summoned to plead her case to a functionary behind a glass cage.

The woman heard her out, then turned on a microphone and blasted over a public address system: *"Can the death unit come forward?"*

More waiting, more paperwork, and an assurance: the certificate had been lost in the bureaucracy; it would arrive shortly in the mail. It did, with the simplest explanation. Steve had died of a heart attack. That was it. The final resolution of his fate, and the passage of the anniversary, lifted a cloud for Denise. Encouraged by the Blossoms, she went on her first date, a museum fix-up, *another* museum fix-up. It was a Volvo date, Denise said: steady, safe, reliable, but with no acceleration.

———

IT WAS JUST the right speed for a widow still on her learner's permit. Dawn, on the other hand, was ready to turn in her license. For months now, she had been wrestling with the question of whether to settle. Settling—I'd often pondered it myself. Was it better to shack up with an acceptable guy, an OK Joe, rather than slog along alone? Ever since the night when our group went to the museum, Dawn had been telling us that Adam was what she called *good on paper*, a widower with two kids she had grown to love, who meshed with her two kids, a ready-made nuclear family. But Adam's former wife still practically haunted the house, so filled was it with her belongings and his wistfulness for her.

"It could have been such a happy ending for two pretty crummy situations," Dawn told me when I reached her on speakerphone as she was driving home from work. "But everyone's got to want the happy ending. I don't think he does happy well. And I don't do sad. So there we are." She laughed, and I knew this was serious. Dawn always looked for the humor when things were at their worst. She and Adam had decided to split.

"I debated, is it worth it because it's fun once in a while?" Her voice quivered. "But at a certain point it stopped being fun. His kids were getting closer to me. And I can't, I can't, *I can't*. It just rips me apart." She pulled to the side of the road to compose herself.

She expelled a blast of frustration a few seconds later. "I was stuck with a man who was stuck." She couldn't help contrasting him with the women in our group, all upbeat people, she felt, going through shattering times but determined to come out whole. "I'm not saying we don't have our bad moments," she said. "I have my moments, and they're *bad*. But it's not who we are at the *core*."

"What about his children?" I asked. "Will you ever get to see them?"

"I don't know." The day after the breakup, Dawn kept a commitment to take his son with hers to a dinosaur exhibit in the city. "Stay close to me," she told them on the street. "I don't want to lose you guys."

Adam's boy looked up at her and said, "Dawn, how could we ever lose you? You're a beacon of light."

"I could have cried right there in the street," Dawn told me. "How sweet is that, how painful is that?" She laughed again. It was her heartiest laugh, for when she hurt the most.

———

THE MORNING OF her daughter Lyndsey's wedding, Lesley and her three girls wore Kevin's old blue dress shirts to have their hair and makeup done, so he'd be with them in some way. Later, at the ceremony, there would be a big mashup. Craig and his three boys would attend, their first encounter with a lifetime's worth of friends and relatives. The pressure was on the mother of the bride to hold herself together while she steered a course between past and future.

Denise and I passed around wedding pictures in the car when

Lesley gave us a ride to our volunteer day at the camp. The bride looked tremulous in an ivory strapless dress and long lace veil, Lesley a bit sober in iridescent taupe silk with a portrait neckline. "You can see I didn't smile a lot," she told us while we sat in traffic. "I was trying too hard not to cry."

Her nerves, she said, were tighter than harp strings as she waited to escort Lyndsey down the aisle in the garden of a country inn. The procession took forever—eight bridesmaids, including Lesley's other daughters, Robyn and Nikki, along with ring bearers and flower girls, enough to populate the Rose Bowl Parade. Lesley held her face in a rigid mask; the bride began to hyperventilate.

"Calm down, Lynds," Lesley urged. "Take deep breaths." It was their turn to walk, and the bride had clenched like a vise. She couldn't move.

Throughout the flotilla of bridesmaids, an uninvited blue jay had refused to cooperate, its persistent chirping cutting right through Pachelbel's *Canon*. Someone sitting in a row behind Craig let out a stage whisper: "Oh God, that's Kev." In any case, the bird stopped right on cue.

Lesley saw gooseflesh rise on her daughter's bare shoulders. Her breathing evened. "Okay, I'm ready," she sighed. "Dad is here."

At the reception, Lesley displayed two photographs of Kevin next to a lighted candle. He had given her, she said in the toast, her most precious gifts, her girls, and then, to lighten the mood, she added that he would be proud of Lyndsey for coming in under budget. Otherwise, Lesley kept the focus on the bride and groom. After that, she could relax. She and Craig outdanced the kids as the party extended late into the night. The only glitch occurred when an old friend was miffed about her table assignment. "You've lost yourself," the friend accused Lesley. "You're not the same person you were."

Deeply hurt, Lesley struggled to shake it off. "Afterward, I decided, of course I've changed," she told me and Denise. "And you know what? I *like* the person I've become."

In fact, Lesley was exultant about her new life with Craig. He was different from the serious, dark-eyed, driven Kevin. "Craig feels like an old pair of slippers," she said. He made her laugh as never before, and he was every bit as affectionate as Lesley. She had found herself relishing the same physical abandon that I did in a new relationship.

Even so, the complications with his family and her family and his friends and her friends reminded me of what had scared me about getting involved with other people: the other people. I had to contend with only Bob and Lily, whereas Lesley had a whole unruly contingent of interested parties. Her daughters thought Craig wasn't sophisticated enough for their mother, and they weren't fans of his sons' table manners. The girls still declined to stay at Lesley's new place with the boys there and urged her to visit one of the girls' homes for Thanksgiving and Christmas, leaving Craig and his sons to celebrate at Lesley's alone.

"I feel like I don't have a home anymore," one of her daughters said to Lesley.

"They're old enough," said Denise. "They're on their own anyway."

"I know," Lesley said distractedly. "But the mother in me, the nurturing side of me . . . their home is their security."

Meanwhile, Lesley's new house was hardly a sanctuary for her. Craig's youngest son had seemed fond enough of her when he first moved in, but once his brother arrived, they formed a sullen solidarity that boxed her out. All Lesley could do over screeching licks of an electric guitar was bite her tongue while Craig, caught in the middle, tried to impose civility.

Lesley and I commiserated for the rest of the ride about the difficulty of forming new households out of the shards of splintered ones. Lesley and Craig had chosen each other, and Bob and I had, too, but the children hadn't asked for new adults to butt into their lives, and vice versa. We all had to make room for each other, and none of us quite knew how.

There were plenty of complications to go around. All of us—Denise, Dawn, Marcia, Lesley, Tara, me—had set out on a path to reinvent our lives with no idea of the scope and variety of the complications that awaited us. Aside from maybe the blessedly remote and empty dunes of Morocco, it was anybody's guess where each of us was headed next.

chapter

TWENTY-FOUR

i didn't know which was more distracting, the view or the guests. It was the last gathering before we took off for Morocco, and the vista from the roof of Marcia's new apartment building was a knockout. Someone swam lazy laps in the atrium pool as the Manhattan skyline shimmered in the final rays of the October sun. In the distance, the Empire State Building rose like a silver spear.

Marcia made our visitors feel instantly at home with chitchat about cars and football. "I'm glad you guys are here," she said to them. "I'm usually the odd one out with this gang."

The rest of us didn't take offense. We were proud of Marcia for her successful real estate coup, pleased with ourselves for whatever role we'd played in her decision to pull it off. By now it was clear that we all gained from our connection to one another, providing companionship, listening, trading points of view. But one point of view had been consistently absent so far, and it came from a source of particular fascination: men.

And here men were, four of 'em, a lot like us, widowers around our ages, a couple of them graying around the temples, but mostly not much worse for the wear. They had already made themselves useful by carrying platters of food to the roof and hefting patio chairs around a big picnic table as we shrugged off the first nip of fall. One had brought chocolates, another wine, yet another a box of bakery butter cookies tied with a ribbon. Glasses clinked, and hands reached politely for empanadas and crudités. We out-numbered the men by one. Tara had begged off that night for a birthday celebration for Will, but the rest of us saw this as a rare opportunity for insight into the masculine mind-set.

My attempts at research on the subject had gotten me nowhere so far. There are a lot of clichés about how widows and widowers differ, perhaps the most common being "women mourn, men re-place." Men are less burdened by guilt, so the conventional wisdom goes. They jump onto the Internet a few weeks after their wives die to hook up with fondly remembered high school sweethearts. While we make do with Lean Cuisine at home, widowers supposedly live the high life, beneficiaries of limitless fix-ups, recipients of unsolic-ited covered dishes, winners of sought-after roles as extra men at dinner parties. If the stereotypes are to be believed, then perhaps men are better equipped than we are to overcome grief and achieve happiness *à la minute*. Perhaps, we thought, they possessed coping mechanisms we could co-opt for ourselves. With a little luck, we could ply these specimens with enough wine and finger foods to extract their secrets.

I had already determined that there'd been little actual study on gender and grieving, with the few citations I uncovered finding little difference between the sexes. It was up to us to reach some highly invalid and unscientific conclusions based on four random guys we corralled by asking around.

Was I hoping for more? I'm only human. These were men, eligible men, and I just happened to know some eligible women. Dawn was free again, and Denise and Marcia hadn't become involved with anyone yet. I noticed Denise decked out in a smart dress and Lesley a showy blouse. Marcia dressed for comfort in pants and a polo shirt, and most of the guys wore pressed cotton shirts and khakis. A take-out place provided the empanadas, their fillings identified with offbeat labels.

"I see you're having the Viagra." Toby, a forty-nine-year-old lawyer with salt-and-pepper hair, leaned toward Denise conspiratorially. "Is that because of the name or . . . ?"

"It's because I like seafood."

It seemed like a good time to address the stereotypes.

"After you were widowed," I interjected, "how long was it before you started seeing other women?" Might as well get right to the juicy stuff.

Toby, our most ingratiating guest, was quick to answer. "My wife died of cancer just a year and two months ago," he said with visible sorrow. He balanced a cocktail plate on his lap and dipped an empanada into a puddle of tomatillo sauce. The first time someone suggested fixing him up, he continued, was on the porch of his house after the funeral, but he declined. "I'd say I've dated six to ten women since then."

I was afraid to give away my thoughts by glancing at my crew. Six to ten women in a little over a year—none of us approached that level of industriousness. Chalk one up for the conventional wisdom.

"Has it been weird for you to see other people?" Lesley asked.

"I wasn't nervous about it," Toby said. A father of three, he'd been married twenty-five years, longer than some of us, and yet he admitted to kissing every one of those women on the first date. When he moved his first relationship into the bedroom, he claimed he did so without reserve. "She was actually thrilled at how easily I doffed my clothes. Her reaction that first time helped me with the other times."

Other times? Toby, the cheerful doffer, made us look like pikers. "You didn't find it awkward at all?" I asked.

"No."

Another guy weighed in. "For me, it wasn't any more awkward than the first time with anybody," said Mitchell, a fifty-seven-year-old journalist with a full face, wire-rimmed glasses, and a complexion that betrayed a lifetime of desk work. Mitchell hadn't remarried, even though he'd been a widower for fifteen years. "I had my first encounter six months after my wife died, with somebody I'd known for a long time," he said. "My wife was dying of cancer for six or eight months, so it wasn't like I wasn't used to the idea."

I had been expecting cocktail party repartee in this cosmopolitan setting, but the men were getting right down to it, seizing a rare opportunity to discuss their private lives. For once, our group didn't say much, content to fire the questions and hear what ricocheted back. Toby refilled Denise's wine with a headwaiter's finesse and offered more to Dawn. She placed a hand over her glass to decline.

"What about you, Bryan?" I asked our youngest guest.

Bryan, not yet forty, was a former lawyer turned sommelier with a lean physique and intense expression. More fashion-forward than the others, in pegged jeans and an open-collar black shirt, he had first found himself in bed with a woman four months after the sudden death of his wife, he said. "The woman and I had already had a relationship before my marriage. She was also a good friend, so there was a high level of comfort. It was no weirder than when I was just dating people."

"I think women feel more pressure than we do to have their bodies look a certain way," Mitchell said matter-of-factly, straightening his glasses.

Bryan set down his plate, his intense appearance growing more earnest. "There *is* something I've been reflecting on. It's been two years since my wife died. The relationships I've been having have been less emotional, more physical. The bar is set really high after you've had the kind of relationship I had with my wife. It makes it hard to put my heart in it now."

This was the first reference to emotion, and Lesley, touched by his vulnerability, made a comforting sound. The other men stopped eating and nodded in agreement. It clarified my thinking about what they were saying. I had to admit I'd been listening with a judgmental bent, surmising that these guys might be cold customers, that they might not have loved their wives much if they could hop back into the sack with such dispatch. But Bryan's comment reminded me of something Professor Bonanno had told me, how studies had shown that widows and widowers who jumped into new affairs loved their spouses no less than those who didn't.

"You're so young," Lesley said to Bryan with solicitude. "What happened to your wife?"

She had died suddenly, as Denise's husband did, of an undiscovered heart condition, collapsing in a restaurant as the couple paid for lunch. They had married only three months earlier, and she was seven months pregnant. By the time an ambulance arrived, Bryan said, it was too late to save her or the baby. Marriage, pregnancy, the loss of a wife and child—the sequence of events was almost unimaginable. Bryan had been so grief-stricken that he stayed at his mother's for six weeks before he could bear to go home, and when he did, for months he couldn't bring himself to put away one of his wife's bras that was dangling on a bathroom doorknob. Yet he was also capable of initiating new romances in the face of grief, and he saw no contradiction. This evening was going to be more revealing than I thought.

The other men observed Bryan with a been-there commiseration. I could tell that all of them missed their wives desperately, still mourned them with heartfelt surrender, as we missed our husbands. Nevertheless, they seemed capable of holding opposing emotions in heedful balance, both grieving and plainly enjoying the perks of being the new bachelor on the block.

"I often have one foot in the past and one foot forward," Toby was saying when I turned back to the conversation. The others seemed to have mastered that same duality, something we women had struggled to achieve.

By now the sun had dipped lower in the hazy sky, and bright shards of the Hudson River winked and dodged between skyscrapers. I was curious about the one guest who had been silent so far. Glenn was a youthful-looking fifty-two, with a smooth face and balding head. He was a friend of Dawn's whose wife had died in the north tower of the World Trade Center almost ten years earlier. He'd been following the conversation at a polite remove.

"Have you been dating, Glenn?" I asked.

"I'm not ready to consider the idea," he said, looking toward the other men with some chagrin. "People have offered to fix me up. I pretty much tell them I don't do that."

So not all widowers strive to replace. Behind Glenn's obliging expression, I observed a skittish sorrow. Whatever we all had suffered, he seemed to be in deeper. I flashed again on the Twin Towers, resisting the memory, aware that Glenn had to visit it every day. The conversation stalled, so I posed another question. How did they think the experience differed for widows and widowers? Did they hate their label as much as we hated ours?

"*Widower*—it's a strange word, but I don't mind being identified with it," said Toby, who had test-driven it on so many dates. "It's generally a positive when I meet women. It means I'm not a divorced guy."

The others signaled their agreement. "For us it's a plus." Mitchell, the journalist, warmed to the sociological nuances of the issue. "I think for a woman, being called a widow is kind of a negative. It's a stereotype that makes you sound a little older, sort of *used*, to be crude."

Used. Say what? I recoiled, and I couldn't help taking in the other women's expressions. Where was a coyote when you needed one? My first impulse was to challenge him to a duel, but somehow all of us managed to hold our tongues. As Marcia once observed, this was an accepting and open group. It was old news to us that *widow* suffered from dreadful PR.

"Your perception is . . . interesting," Marcia said with uncharacteristic diplomacy.

"If a man is divorced, women think, *oh God, all the baggage*," Mitchell elaborated. "And if he's never been married, they think he's gay, or just weird. But if you're a widower, it signals that you are marriage material, and you get sympathy, which I don't think is true for a woman."

It had never occurred to me that this man would be considered a hot commodity while I was perceived as damaged goods, yet none of our guests stepped forward to disagree. The word *used*—it called to mind primitive notions that an available woman with sexual experience was somehow tarnished, whereas a man was not. I took in the dark circles under Toby's eyes and Mitchell's khaki pants, which looked as if they'd been left too long in the dryer. I couldn't help thinking that these guys were simply beneficiaries of a favorable ratio, their value enhanced and their egos massaged by their relative scarcity in comparison to us. Supply and demand.

Then I thought about all the negative variations on the word *widow*—black widow, widow's weeds, the widow-maker. Even at my newspaper, *widow* was a copyediting term for an extraneous word at the end of a paragraph, marked to be deleted to save space for more valuable material.

"I just hate the word *widow*," Marcia said to Mitchell. "I've never analyzed it the way you did. To me it means that I lost my husband."

"But with us," Mitchell said, "there's no stigma."

"Then why do you say there is with us?" I pressed.

"Maybe because there are more older widows, the word just reads as *old*."

A big coyote, I thought, one that hasn't eaten in weeks.

"Yes, with us it's a positive," Toby weighed in. "We are way up on the hierarchy of singles." He gestured, one hand several inches above the other.

From my slot at the bottom of the hierarchy, I felt my hopes of any love matches arising from the evening deflate. You had to respect the men for their ... um, candor, but it wasn't weaving any magic on our women. Their expressions ranged from bemusement to distaste.

"So many of the women I meet cry when I tell them," Toby continued, with a touch of sheepish gratification. "Years ago, when I was single, they didn't cry."

"When I tell my story to women I've dated, they become very emotional," said Bryan. "I always feel a little guilty. I had a woman straight out ask me once, 'How much sympathy sex have you had?'"

Mitchell and Toby laughed, and Mitchell said, "Never enough."

"Sympathy sex—I'm not familiar with the term," I said. "Women offer you sympathy sex?"

"Yeah, okay, there were a couple." Bryan had the grace to appear embarrassed, and Toby shrugged his assent.

This was a new one on us. We'd fielded many reactions from men to the news that we were widows, from "I'm sorry" to "Creepy" to "You don't look that sad," but none of us had received an offer of a charitable dip in the sack.

Then Lesley posed a question that had haunted many of us. "With all this pressing the flesh, do you ever feel guilty?"

"No," the men answered, like a Greek chorus, all of them except Glenn.

The women eyed each other, a fleeting pantomime that expressed equal parts "It figures" and "Why couldn't *we* pull that off?"

Toby hedged a bit. "I don't feel guilty," he said, "but there are echoes that make me think: how would my wife feel about this?"

Just then—you couldn't make this up—a flash of lightning streaked across the sky, accompanied by a sonic boom. Gathering clouds, unnoticed, had blocked the sunset, and now we realized they'd converged into towering thunderheads. The air crackled. We scrambled to gather up the remaining food and dash for the elevator.

Back in her apartment, Marcia assembled chairs around the couch and we claimed new places. Toby slid in next to Denise, launching a private conversation. The skies let loose, and rain mixed with hailstones battered the windows.

"Wow, my first storm here," Marcia said as torrents obliterated the view. "Cool."

We turned away from the deluge, and Mitchell reflexively hiked his glasses higher on his nose. "I want to say more about guilt," he addressed the group. "It has to do with a fundamental question, which is whether you believe that you can only love one person. And of course there are myriad people out in the world who you could fall in love with. If you believe that, which to me is a given, then one love is not any better than another love."

Marcia stood to stack plates on the kitchen counter while we pondered what I had to admit was a wise philosophy. Toby passed around the chocolates he'd brought. The theatrical storm outside threw us into a cocoon of greater intimacy, and Mitchell spoke again in a wistful tone.

After fifteen years, he said, he still hoarded an odd assortment of keepsakes, like dozens of tiny perfume samples that his wife collected at department stores. He wished he still had his wife's wedding ring, now in the possession of her sister. "I just feel that it's a talisman," he said, straining for words. "My wife is fading into the past. And things get fuzzy. The date she died, our anniversary... I used to know them. Now I have to look them up That's why I wish I had the ring back. To remind me that I was married, to *this* woman, and that it was real."

We all looked at each other, unspeaking, surprised at the power of that thought.

"Would you like to marry again?" Lesley asked him gently.

"No," Mitchell said with stoicism. "What I long for, which is something I can't have, is a relationship with someone I've already known for twelve years. That's gone. That's the sad thing."

The rest of us listened in perfect sympathy as thunder swallowed his words. At first, with all their talk about easy fix-ups and seemingly zipless fucks, some of these guys had sounded more resistant to grief than we had, but now my heart went out to Mitchell, to all of them. For all their romantic conquests, they were suffering, uncertain how to proceed, reluctant to sever ties. For all the sympathy sex that they received and we did not, for all their reveling in the sudden availability of fresh conquests, they were missing the same intimacy that we missed.

Toby must have been thinking along the same lines. "It strikes me that you women are lucky to have each other," he said.

"Yes," said Mitchell, regarding everyone in the room. "I can't in a million years imagine men getting together once a month to talk about this stuff. I think women are more serious about their emotional lives."

"Women overanalyze," said Bryan, striving to provoke, and we repaid him with hisses.

"We treasure the fact that we can talk about intimate things," I said.

"Honestly, I have no one for that," Mitchell admitted.

The other men nodded and agreed, more or less.

"I have friends," said Bryan, "but I lost the one person I unconditionally could say anything to." At parties, he often found himself nursing a glass of wine while others talked about having children and passed around sonogram pictures, avoiding his gaze. "I am their worst fear realized."

Lesley was moved to comfort him again. "You have to come back here once a month to talk to us," she said.

I felt the men were looking at me, as if for permission. "What about Morocco?" Toby asked, kidding, I assumed. "I've always wanted to be the guy who sweeps in out of the desert, unshaven and armed with a sense of humor, to rescue damsels in minor distress."

"You've been watching too many movies," I said, laughing him off. "Sorry guys, women only."

The party began to fracture into individual conversations. Toby worked the room and managed to cadge phone numbers and e-mail addresses from Dawn and Denise. He told Lesley he liked her accent and gave me a frankly appraising up-and-down look before saying, "If you were available, I would *definitely* date you."

"Toby's a mover," Dawn said to me with a shake of her head. "The guy's enjoying himself, and I suppose you can't fault him for that."

After the men left, we women clustered in the kitchen, loading glasses into the dishwasher. The men, we agreed, were not so different from us, aside from some gentlemen's-club attitudes about sex, and, if some of them were to be believed, the abundant availability of partners for it. The guys had their sympathy sex, but we had friends, we had each other. And soon enough, we'd be far from home, testing the strength of that bond.

chapter

TWENTY-FIVE

*i*t was Dawn who pointed out that people would tell us ad nauseam that time would make all the difference, and that hearing this would make us want to smack them. But people, I learned, are right. Time might not make *all* the difference, but it was definitely on our side.

I had wanted to retreat in the aftermath of Bernie's death. I had wanted to take care of myself, *by myself*. I didn't want commitment. I didn't want responsibility. I didn't want a husband, a one-eyed dog, a stepdaughter who didn't want me around. I didn't want a hot mess of a life split between New York and Connecticut. I didn't have the desire; I didn't have the strength.

Six months after our trip to Paris, Bob and I took another trip, a long weekend in a shack on a beach in Tulum. We ate tacos filled with habañeros and snapper delivered off a wooden boat, vegetated on a hammock, reevaluated from afar. Not much had changed since our trip to Paris, when we considered and abandoned thoughts of marriage.

Lily still wasn't wild about sharing her dad with me, but time was working its healing powers between us. One weekend my newspaper, pleading budget cuts, declined to send a photographer for a story I was reporting on teenage parties. Lily, it occurred to me, was a crack shot at functions with her friends, so I enlisted her. She kept a level head and snapped a vivid series of pictures of kids dancing around a pool. The photo editor published them with pleasure. I didn't mention that Lily was fourteen. A few weeks later, a photographer was canceled again, and Lily volunteered this time, coolly capturing close-ups and scenic views aboard a boat for an article on cultivating oysters. Lily became intrigued by my job and asked me countless questions. She started to find other aspects of my presence acceptable as well. Without thinking, she might sit next to me instead of Bob, sculpt demented creations with my hair, or ask my advice on social dilemmas with her friends. Bob teased me, as we burrowed our feet in the warm Mexican sand, that the day might dawn when Lily would call me by my name.

My job wasn't progressing as well. The latest owner of *Newsday* wanted even shorter and less ambitious stories, and I was bored. More and more, as I immersed myself in research on widows, I wanted to write about that—write what you care about, write what you know—but I needed space and time to do the subject justice. I kicked around with Bob the possibility of leaving my job and pursuing the topic on my own. From a lazy beach in Mexico, the project seemed less daunting than I knew it would be.

And suddenly, so did marriage. We scribbled notes in the back pages of a paperback. Becky, Bob, Lily, Wink, New York, Connecticut—there had to be a way to make the pieces fit. Lily's custody arrangement—every other week—must have been as

discombobulating for her as it was for us. We considered changing
it so she would spend school nights at her mom's, and weekends,
holidays, and summers with us. Bob and I thought we could keep
both our places, living and working in New York during the week
and shifting the whole show to Connecticut on weekends. Maybe
Lily would consent to summers in the city.

I'd already noticed that remaking a life at midstride was more
complicated than brokering the subprime mortgage bailout. Make
that the subprime bailout combined with a renegotiated divorce
settlement. This treaty would demand compromises from all of us.
Were they compromises I was willing to make?

From the perspective of a restful Mexican beach, the logistics
didn't seem as cockamamie as they no doubt would prove. And the
expense of keeping both households afloat didn't seem as formidable. From a clarifying distance, the dream of being together seemed
more important than mere matters of where to live and when and
how, not to mention what it would cost. Time had worked its magic.
I felt solid enough to do this, solid enough to want this.

When we arrived back home, fate dealt us an opportunity. *Newsday* planned more cutbacks and offered the staff a voluntary buy-
out. If I took it, I would sever my ties to my once-beloved job and
devote myself, as Bernie had, to writing about what mattered to
me. A few weeks later, the landlord of Bob's ramshackle house in
Connecticut said he was putting it up for sale. If we took the buy-
out money to make a down payment, we could cut the costs of our
convoluted two-home marriage plan. Everything was conspiring to
force my hand.

Back in my apartment, alone, I deciphered all the hieroglyphics
we'd made in the paperback on the beach. They took up the back

pages, the inside covers, and the margins of several chapters. For all of this to work, I had to quit the job I once loved, buy a house I didn't love, and marry a man I did. I had to change everything, and I had to do it all at once. I felt the way I had on my voyage to the Galápagos, where unknown creatures and undiscovered sights beckoned from shore and sea. If I wanted an adventure, I had to abandon the safety of the boat.

━━━━━━━━━━

OUR FRIENDS WERE expecting a simple, casual backyard cocktail party on a sultry June afternoon. And so it appeared, until Bob gathered them under a canopy of trees by the stream behind the house—*our* house, for all of four days. Then he cranked up a creaky recording of the Dixie Cups singing "Going to the chapel," the only clue that we were launching this party with the ultimate happy ending—a wedding.

After surviving our share of heartache, finding someone new had been a fortunate surprise, so it seemed only fitting to hold a surprise wedding to celebrate. We ditched the usual accoutrements: no ballroom at the Acme Wedding Mill, no Sheetrock cake, no unwanted gifts, no wedding gown that looked like a holdover from the Miss America pageant. Even my first marriage when I was in my twenties had been pretty simple—I wasn't going to go all ostentatious at this point in my life. This wedding would be Bob's and mine alone, informed by experience only we could know.

Throwing out the rulebook, we recognized, could have invited trouble. The ring bearer would be Wink, one of the great failures in the history of obedience training. We took a calculated risk making all the food for sixty people ourselves, with help from Lily and two of our best friends. Thunderstorms in the forecast threatened to turn the yard into the La Brea Tar Pits. Whatever happened, we would have to roll with it. We reminded ourselves before everyone arrived: falling in love is a happy accident, too.

I made my entrance floating out the back door in a weightless white cocktail dress inset with shimmering patches of silver, like clouds. All my nearest and dearest were there, everyone who had worked to pull me through. Bob waited, in jeans and a jacket, by the stream, following me with an expression I can only describe as adoring. I'm pretty sure I was looking at him the same way. Lily took her place beside us, wavering between smiles and tears, glad for our happiness, I was convinced, but all too aware that the dream of a child of divorce, her original family reunited, was dashed for good. Wink stood protective watch next to her, in black bow tie, his single eye overseeing the ceremony with appropriate dignity.

The serendipity of the moment didn't escape me. Bob and I had known each other for only a year and a half, but we had decided to do this, to marry in the face of uncertainties we knew too well. I couldn't help but recall the path of my first marriage, but the aware-ness that nothing is certain to last, rather than overwhelming my happiness, served to heighten it, stoking the urgency to reach for this now, to hold nothing back. I took Bob's hand without reserva-tion, looked into those hazel eyes, and thought, *I'm really marrying this guy!* How lucky can I be?

When the final "I dos" were out of our mouths, the celebration began, and the thunking bass of "Some Kind of Wonderful" by the Soul Brothers Six carried us into the crowd for congratulations. I might have chosen something from Verdi, but marriage is about compromise, after all. Everyone professed joy at our element of surprise, and not only because it took them off the hook from buying us toaster ovens and place settings.

The last guests hit the road by midnight. Bob and I took shelter in the house, said good night to Lily, and talked over the party, as couples do, the first shared memory of our married life. Everything, we concluded, had veered in the direction we least expected. The dog performed like a veteran of the Royal Shakespeare Company. My girlfriends cried on cue. Lily declared the food "insanely delicious." Torrents of rain fell on every nearby town, but not a drop landed on us. Everything unfurled perfectly, exactly as we'd hoped. I knew too well that all endings aren't happy ones. But after half a lifetime of facing up to the unforeseen, the most surprising element of our surprise wedding was this: sometimes things turn out exactly right.

chapter

TWENTY-SIX

*f*ès beckoned like a thousand-piece puzzle. I'd never seen a place so ancient, so foreign, so strange. The city was a jumble of labyrinthine walkways and dwellings the color of sun-dried mud, seemingly unchanged since the ninth century. A corona of dust levitated above. In the distance, the Middle Atlas Mountains loomed. This much I could see as I leaned against the railing on the balcony of my hotel room, situated on a hill overlooking the medina. I'd been warned not to venture into the maze without a guide. I would surely be lost. I must wait for the Blossoms to traverse it with me.

The twilight call to prayer swelled over the city. Fès is that rare place where the call is performed live by the muezzins, not piped in by a recording. A mournful undulating voice wafted from a distant minaret, and then another joined from elsewhere, and another, weaving together in a pleasing dissonance of devotion. The sound was hypnotic, somewhere between music and chanting and a babel of nagging uncles. The call surrounded me, mystical, like the city, profoundly strange, profoundly foreign to my ears.

I had achieved my goal: I wasn't in Kansas anymore. The other women were supposed to join me as they arrived, on various routes, through Paris or London or Casablanca, depending on their stash of frequent flyer miles or tolerance for discomfort—higher for me and Denise, who schlepped overland by car through Rabat and Meknès; lower for Marcia, who flew first-class through Paris, with an overnight at the Ritz. We were scheduled to rendezvous on my terrace after sunset, when the prayer call faded. A slice of moon rose over the medina, and I felt a shiver of delicious anticipation, followed by another when I thought, *How cool is it to say, "The moon rose over the medina"?* I listened impatiently for that knock on the door. Once again, with the clarity of distance, I felt what I could not feel back home, when I was in the middle of it, and I realized with a start: I missed them.

When I inaugurated our group, I had expected that I would remain at a bit of a remove from the others. I was further along in widowhood, after all, remarried for more than a year, in fact, by the time we met. But a funny thing happened on the way to Morocco. Here it was November, eleven months in, and we had come to count on each other, to learn from each other's choices. Even though I was a wife again, I recognized that of everyone I knew, only these women, having lost what I had lost, understood what that meant to me, the joy and dislocation of starting again. Only they understood that I could be happy with one man while still pining for another who was gone. These women were the role models I'd been seeking. Widowhood—it was better to explore it with a guide. Now I had five.

I gave thanks for the fellowship they provided as the last notes of the muezzins dissolved into vapor. Each woman had singular expertise to offer. The mothers and I spoke often about strategies for stepparenting. Don't push it, we agreed; don't play the pseudo-parent. It was working for me and Lily; we were reaching a rapport. Before I left home, I'd helped with her search for a college, and they advised me on that, too. Dawn bucked me up with positive Dawn-isms when I was whipsawed by weekly travel between Brooklyn and Connecticut. Denise, with her editing chops, soothed my concerns about my work, and Marcia chortled at my stories about sharing an office with Bob.

My marriage was a constant source of happiness, but the circumstances strayed far from the unencumbered life I once envisioned for myself. Despite being in possession of two places to live, Bob and I couldn't manage one where we each had our own room to work. There were moments, when he conducted business on the phone while I tried to write and Wink whimpered for a walk and Lily asked to use the car ... and ... and ... when our workplace resembled the floor of the stock exchange at a quarter to four. Sometimes it seemed as if we had set out to see how many obstacles we could pile in the way of our new union, how many pressures we could withstand. Had I ditched a model that was too simple for one that was too cluttered? This trip with the group would offer new perspective and a welcome break. My posse offered me release; it had my back.

Which made me all the more apprehensive about the next ten days. Traveling together can strain the best friendships, and I was only just coming to understand how much I wanted ours to last. To say that this was a gang of forceful personalities was an understatement. If we could survive Marcia's vociferous objections to camels and camping and Dawn's preference for mojitos on a beach, Denise's cool tranquillity and Lesley's irrepressible humor, Tara's urge to shop and mine to undertake a crazy-ass desert adventure, this journey would be an achievement to rival the first walk on the moon.

Like a pot on a boil, everyone arrived at once. Tired from travel but jazzed with excitement, they squealed at the darkening view of mountains and city as stars began to pop overhead. Marcia had scooped up a complimentary bottle of champagne from the Ritz, so Dawn led a toast: "To a fabulous trip."

We each raised a glass. "To our dead husbands," Lesley added. "We wouldn't be here if they hadn't died."

Scandalous! But we knew each other well enough to laugh. I filled everyone in about plans worked out by our guide. Many stalls in the medina would be closed the next afternoon for *Jumu'ah*, the Friday prayers, so we would slot in a mountain hike, freeing up time for a longer shopping spree in the souks on Saturday.

"Becky," said Tara, "that's the best thing you possibly could have said."

Somehow, Tara had overlooked instructions to pack hiking boots, so she would have to trek through craggy terrain in suede loafers. This was a sure tipoff, I thought, to her reluctance to undertake the more vigorous portions of our itinerary. And Marcia was already fussing about the desert camp. "Bathrooms in tents—how can they keep them clean?" At least everyone seemed mollified by this first hotel. A converted old palace just outside the walled city, it would be the most luxurious of the trip. I couldn't worry about the rest of it now. I had to give everyone points for making this journey at all.

Whatever unknowns we were about to encounter, news from back home came first. I couldn't help noticing that Dawn was fidgeting with excitement, and not at the prospect of a mountain hike. She was an eyeful on her worst days, and tonight her radiance rivaled the moon. Tara, who had traveled with her, explained. "I arrived at the airport, and I saw this woman with her phone out, texting like mad, and I said, 'That looks familiar.'" Yes, love had struck again, with technology playing Cupid.

Feverish texting had been going on for more than a week, and the person at the other end was a guy she'd met at a racetrack. He had actually been driving one of the racecars, which made him sound to me like the very definition of a dangerous fling. But he was not a professional driver, I was relieved to learn—it was a hobby that diverted him from running his own company. "He's an entrepreneur, like me," Dawn told us. "We have *so* much in common."

Unfortunately, this didn't include a place of residence. Collins lived more than three hours away, so they had rendezvoused a week ago in Manhattan, taking rooms in separate hotels. Dawn took it as an omen when they wound up across the street from each other on the same floor, able to wave from window to window. Within hours, she knew this was serious.

"When he looked at me, I felt the same way I felt when I first met Andries."

"On the first date?" Marcia asked.

"Collins said it wasn't really one date. Lunch, dinner, breakfast, lunch—he counted it as four. But whatever it was, it worked, let me tell you." She fanned her face against an inner heat and told us that, unlike Adam, Collins wasn't stingy with his feelings. "You know how a guy looks at you, and it goes beyond what you look like?" She made an approximation of a smitten face. "That's how he looked at me. But I haven't been able to see him since. I had to get ready for this trip. This didn't come at the best time, girls."

"Sorry, girl," I said.

"I'm telling you, I cried tears of joy." Dawn wasn't stingy with feelings, either. "It had been so long since I'd cried any other kind of tears."

We linked arms and looked out over the city, now hushed and ghostly in the moonlight. Lesley tentatively broke the silence.

"I have to ask you all something, and . . . I'm going to cry." Her face flushed, and the tears came fast, the first time I had seen Lesley come apart. We waited, braced for the worst, until she could speak. "What do you do," she said, still struggling, "when you're so in love, so happy . . . but it's breaking apart, not because there's anything wrong with it, but because of external forces?" She looked at us plaintively, expecting an answer. "How do you fix it?"

"Oh, babe," I said, pulling her closer.

"How do you fix it?"

Craig had seen her off from home, she said, but he wouldn't be there when she returned. She conveyed her quandary in spurts, through tears. They weren't breaking up, not entirely, but tensions over children had reached a point where they decided they couldn't live together anymore. "I told my girls, 'Suck it up. This is the man I love.' But I don't know if Craig is willing to do that with his boys."

More and more often, she and Craig had been shutting each other out of decisions when it came to their respective kids. It reached a head when one of Lesley's daughters injured her leg in a car accident a couple of weeks before. Lesley rushed to the hospital, calling her other daughters, not thinking to phone Craig until she had some news. It was a pattern that ran deep since Kevin's death, she and her girls circling the wagons in the face of trouble, a pattern that didn't leave room for Craig. He felt shut out, hurt.

He sent her a text: *I can't do this anymore.* He needed to attend to his own kids, he said. "So we're going to try just dating again," she said miserably.

"This may save the relationship," said Marcia, but we all knew Lesley wanted more. Family was the center of her life, and she lived to make a home for someone and partake in the ready affection that arose from living together. She continued to weep, while the rest of us traded grim expressions.

"How do you *fix* it?" she asked again.

"Look," said Dawn, "not to say anything about the relationship with Craig, but this pain has to do with the other loss, too."

Lesley nodded fervently, swallowing and crying harder.

"It's another loss," Dawn said. "Losing *again* is very hard."

"That's why it was so brave of you to enter a new relationship," I said. This was what I had dreaded for myself—losing someone again when I'd already lost more than I thought I could bear.

"You can throw yourself into something to erase the pain," Dawn continued, "but when it doesn't work, it's very hard."

Lesley apologized for crying. "You are the only ones I can talk to about this," she said.

"Someone was asking me the other day about what we do," said Tara, "and I answered, 'We lift each other up.'" Looking at Lesley, I wondered if that was enough.

———

WHEN I ARRIVED for breakfast on the sun-washed hotel terrace, Dawn was entertaining the troops, reaching into the past. She pulled out photographs of her children and Andries, who was as handsome as advertised.

"Look at him. So young, so gorgeous. He'll always be young, the bastard."

Lesley's merry laugh returned. Grief, we knew, comes in waves. She was eating fried flatbread studded with olives, figs, and the fleshiest dates I'd ever seen. It was impossible to feel low under the spell of the sapphire blue sky, the cubist canvas of Fès stretched out below, and the clay-colored mountains beyond.

Lesley had been discussing her situation again, this time with the rubbery resilience I had come to know in her. "I realize I underestimated. I had thought if it didn't work, I could just walk away. But I can't"—her voice wavered—"because I'm crazy about him."

"Keep an open mind," Dawn cautioned. "You may be better apart. But if it doesn't work, bear in mind that you give much more credence to the first guy you meet—you know, *after.*"

———————

AMID TOURISTS in Western dress in the lobby, one woman stood out. An elegant figure in a lime green djellaba, the floor-length hooded robe worn by Moroccan men and women alike, she had almond eyes and long, thick, coffee-colored hair.

"I am your guide, Saida," she said. She extended her hand.

We repeated slowly: "Sigh-EE-dah."

"Yes," she said. "In Arabic, it means *happy.*"

We had managed to engage one of the rare Moroccan women who worked as a guide, and I felt an immediate kinship. Modestly covered, she looked much like other local women I had seen so far, but the color of her robe had more punch, her manner less self-effacement. Her quick eyes darted over us, seemingly as eager to learn from these strangers as we were from her. Saida appeared amused rather than annoyed that we were running late—the scourge of group travel—after our chatty breakfast. She hustled us onto a van that would take us to the countryside and introduced our driver, Laarbi.

Marcia held up her BlackBerry. "Can I get Wi-Fi on the hike?"

"*No,*" we cried.

Luckily, Marcia became engrossed when we peppered Saida with questions. She held a university degree in English, we learned. Married, a devout Muslim, a resident of Fès, she was the mother of two daughters. Her background was Berber, one of two main ethnic groups in Morocco, along with Arabs. Saida watched the road from the front seat of the van, but she kept an ear cocked when we fell into our usual gossip. "I didn't know what to think when I heard you are all widows," she observed at length. "You are a fun group of ladies, I think!"

We were soon bumping along a country road toward some verdant mountains, and we passed a woman carrying hay bales on her head. Eighty percent of the women in rural areas are illiterate, Saida told us with scholarly precision. Some of them marry as young as twelve. Men, she said, are allowed up to four wives.

"How many husbands do women get?" Dawn asked.

Saida laughed. "We are working on that!"

Released from the van into the fresh dry air of the Middle Atlas, we scrambled uphill toward white limestone peaks on a dry riverbed that was carpeted with loose rocks. Saida removed her djellaba, revealing army-green cargo pants, hiking boots, and a slim, athletic figure that could rock the casbah if she let it. A local Berber man who knew the trails joined us for the hike, and Tara, teetering but uncomplaining in her inadequate shoes, tried to communicate in French and Spanish. He taught her a few words of Berber, and they settled finally on a pastiche with a touch of sign language. He pointed out sage, thyme, quince, and pomegranate that grew under the shade of Aleppo pines and tall, majestic cedars. We sniffed and tasted. Marcia took photos with her fancy camera. We pushed on, upward, and no one talked about home. Saida took our picture from atop a rocky bluff with a valley behind.

"You are all so beautiful," she said.

"I'm keeping this picture," Dawn said, "to remind me what I looked like *before* I had four husbands."

chapter

TWENTY-SEVEN

*a*fter the twilight call to prayer, Saida guided us through medieval gates into the heart of Fès, where our footsteps echoed in narrow, deserted stone passages barely illuminated by dusky lamps. We reached a tapered pool of light at the entrance to a *riad*, a traditional Moroccan home. The exterior wall of mud brick gave no hint of the welcome we found on the other side—a courtyard of multicolored tiles with a babbling fountain at the center. The air was tart with the scent of lemons that hung on trees within the walls. Rooms opened off the patio and several balconies above, circulating light and air from within the house rather than through windows opening onto the street. The design deflected heat, Saida explained, and guaranteed privacy, especially for women.

This *riad* housed a restaurant, booked exclusively for us that night. Saida motioned for us to follow her. We passed under an archway into an open-air dining room with ornately carved wood ceilings. Three women in djellabas sat gravely at a long table, on banquettes buttressed by mirrored pillows. In the impossible dim light, I strained to see their faces, but their heads were wrapped in scarves, their eyes cast downward. Saida had invited them to be our guests for dinner.

"They are like you, widows," she said, and the word hit me hard.

Widows—months of hijinks with our group had demystified the label by now. We saw ourselves as normal American women, and although we'd taken our lumps, we were moving along—relocating, traveling, dating, remarrying—all of it conveniently possible in our go-go American culture. I couldn't imagine, wasn't even sure I *wanted* to imagine, the life of a widow here in Morocco, where women in the best of circumstances were so constrained. They enjoyed a few more freedoms than those in some Middle Eastern countries—free to drive, work, vote, and dress as they chose, within limits approved by their families—but men dominated those families. I knew nothing about how a woman here would cope if suddenly left to fend for herself. I'd become so close to the Blossoms that I saw widowhood through our relatively privileged circumstances.

"How will we communicate?" I asked Saida. My voice sounded sharp and rattled.

"Don't worry, I will translate. It will be fine."

I was less concerned with language than the cultural divide. Our guests appeared modest, solemn, their hands folded on laps like novitiates at an abbey, and they sat very still, except for flitting glances at our Western clothes and hair. Tara took a seat next to me and leaned in close. "I hope you don't think I'm a coward," she whispered, "but I don't want to say how my husband died . . . considering how Muslims disapprove of alcohol."

For a few minutes I watched with unease, trying to figure how this would play out. The Moroccan women spoke to each other haltingly in Arabic. Apparently, they had never met before, either. Saida's penetrating eyes followed the conversation, deciding what to translate. How selective was she going to be? "They are saying you all look much younger than your age," she said. Very selective indeed. "I will ask them to tell about themselves."

Seated next to Tara, Rashida, a plump woman with a broad flat face, declined to speak at all. She was afraid to tell her story, said Saida, who explained that Rashida was fifty-five, the mother of five children, all of whom lived in one room in the medina. She had cleaned in the courts before the work became too hard and now relied on support from friends. It is one of the pillars of Islam, Saida said, to help the poor, especially widows.

We have so little in common, I thought, despairing. Wait till they get an earful about Marcia's suite of corporate offices and Tara's house with bedrooms for every child. I glanced over at Rashida and saw that she was following Saida impassively, like a stone Buddha in a brown patterned robe and black headscarf.

Waiters distracted us with a clattering of plates. They dropped a bowl of *harira* in front of me, a thick porridge of chickpeas, lentils, and tomatoes with a heady bouquet of Moroccan spices. We passed the customary accompaniment of dates and cookies made with sesame and anise, displayed prettily on an inlaid plate.

"We have a similar cookie that comes from Italy," Dawn asked Saida to translate, trying hard to connect.

A young woman next to Dawn watched her with a sweet, timid smile. Magda was forty with pale skin and heavy caterpillar brows that gave her an air of dark gravity. Her husband died of cancer seven years ago, she explained to Saida in a barely audible voice, and she was raising a fifteen-year-old son by working at a clothing store in the new part of town. "She is educated," Saida said. But she had left it to her son to decide whether she could come tonight, a strange-sounding power balance to our ears. "He decided it was okay, since she will only be with women."

Were all Moroccan women so subservient? I couldn't imagine anyone in our group summoning the meekness required to conform to this society. I felt Tara next to me, stirring in frustration. But I was also interested in the woman on the other side of Magda. Outwardly, to my eyes, she didn't appear as docile as the rest. She was more brightly dressed in a vivid turquoise djellaba and red head-scarf, which gave her a modern, almost fashionable look. Her arresting face was considerably darker, her stout body sturdier, and she spoke with the harsh accent of a country woman. Her name was Naima, we learned, and at forty-seven, she had been married three times, twice widowed and once divorced. Naima worked on a farm outside the city to support five daughters and a son. It was rare for widows to remarry, Saida said. "She is lucky woman."

"Tell her she is our hero," said Marcia.

Saida translated, and Naima laughed, a firm, barking laugh, the first break in our guests' restraint.

Silence descended again as the next course appeared. According to Saida, it was called *b'stilla*, a dense creation of seafood, vermicelli, and black trumpet mushrooms infused with lemon, saffron, and cinnamon and wrapped like a present in sheets of flaky phyllo dough. While we picked through the crust to vent a fragrant steam, I noticed the Moroccans studying Tara's embellished silver top and dangling earrings with sidelong fascination. The rest of us had introduced ourselves. Tara was the only one who hadn't yet shared any particulars.

As if on cue, she cleared her throat in a manner meant to attract an audience. "My husband died almost two years ago," she began. I thought she'd leave it at that, but her smile was fixed and so was her mind, as if accessing a memory bank. "Um ... he died of, um ... heart failure, but it was due to ... to an illness." She sighed audibly and shot me a what-the-hell look, barreling ahead. "He was addicted to alcohol," she said decidedly.

Naima, our guest from the country, following a moment later in Arabic, reacted as if jolted by an electric shock. She interrupted in a staccato, guttural dialect.

"Her husband was also very sick," said Saida with surprise, "and it was almost the same problem."

Naima and Tara locked eyes, and a whole new dynamic took over. We all began to talk at once, a riot of conversation, in whatever language. Even Rashida, the silent one, broke her affectless composure. She still did not speak, but she was newly alert to the heightened exchange.

"But I am dating a lovely man now," Tara assured everyone over the din.

"Becky is married again," Lesley tossed in. "And I also want to say I'm dating somebody."

Our Moroccan guests perked up at this hint of gossip and congratulated our seeming good fortune. "They ask you, Lesley, are you going to marry him?" Saida asked.

"I don't know. He has children who are difficult."

"Because for us, if you are dating somebody or know somebody, you *have* to marry," Saida said. "It is not acceptable to be dating. In

Morocco, you should not be with your husband before you marry. You should not even have coffee with him. His family will come to your family, and you can see him then and decide. My husband saw me at university, but this is what he did before we could speak."

Of course we knew this was the custom in some countries, but it was so far outside our ken, to our Western ears, it sounded barbaric. Dawn wore her disbelief like a billboard. "But what if someone who wants to marry you is totally wrong?" she stammered.

"How can you know this person? How?" Saida answered. "It is, as we say, like a pomegranate." She cupped her hands to illustrate. "You take the pomegranate, open it." She turned her palms upward and lifted first one, then the other. "It could be red. It could be white. It could be sour. It could be sweet. It is up to fate how lucky you will be."

"If you date someone, that's it? You're *done*?" Dawn was still incredulous.

Saida and the other Moroccans nodded in unison. "This is what we do as Muslims."

The soft-spoken Magda directed a remark to Saida, then turned her grave, shy smile toward Dawn.

"She says she feels so sorry she cannot communicate with you."

Dawn looked at the childlike Magda, conscious of her youth. "Ask her whether she wants to marry again."

"Yes, she would love to, but her son forbids. Someone introduced her to a man who wanted to marry her, but her son cried."

"See? More problems with children," Tara said, exasperated. "Why does a fifteen-year-old have so much power?"

The Arab speakers held a vigorous discussion, and Saida cut through it. "She is sure that if she marries, the husband will not treat him like a son. All women who are divorced or widowed find it hard if they have children. And when they are grown, when a woman is more than forty, she becomes too old."

I saw Magda's options shrinking before my eyes. All the obstacles we faced in starting over paled beside what she had to contend with. Saida explained what was considered the correct attitude toward the loss of a spouse: "God gives you this person but takes this person. When we are born, we know we all will die at a certain time. So we should not be sad. We should accept our fate."

"How does Naima keep finding husbands, if it's so difficult?" I asked, indicating our guest in the brilliant blue robe.

"Some things are changing. She is very strong, like a *rebellion* woman. And now a friend has sent her *another* proposal. This man has a house he will give to her."

So Naima was a Moroccan *widow provocateur*, in opposition to strictures that imposed a circumscribed destiny. Men, we learned without surprise, had few such concerns. They often selected a new bride from the crowd that came for mourning. Sounded familiar, I thought—sympathy marriage instead of sympathy sex. "He can marry as soon as the first night, the following day," Saida said. "Usually he marries a young woman. My father is seventy. His wife is younger than me, thirty-seven years old."

"But she will be a widow!" Dawn cried over our general objections.

"She'd rather be a widow *with a house*."

I considered how far our romantic visions differed from the transactional nature of marriage in this poor country, and from the look on Lesley's face, she must have been thinking the same. "Did they love their husbands?" she asked.

Magda nodded, and Naima looked impatient to answer, but she checked herself abruptly as waiters arrived to pour mint tea. As soon as they left, she spoke in a straightforward way. "With her last husband," Saida said, "she wished it was she who passed away and not him, because he treated her well. She loved him a lot. The first one, too. She is lucky woman." Then Naima's words turned rapid and harsh, and she shot sideways looks toward Tara. "But the second one, the one she divorced," Saida continued, "because of the drinking, he did not treat her well."

We could barely hear Saida finish, because a wild clamor of Arabic erupted. The previously silent Rashida, initially afraid to speak, was galvanized to do it now, and whatever she said lobbed a grenade into the dialogue. If we had assumed she was a timid creature, her full, strident voice set us straight, and the others' reactions matched her in vehemence. The Americans, uncomprehending, turned to Saida for guidance.

"You have to hear this," she finally said. "Rashida did *not* love her husband. She felt so happy when he passed away."

Now that Rashida had found her voice, it would not be stopped, and Saida translated in tandem with diplomatic efficiency. Rashida was turned not toward Saida, but to a disconcerted Tara, as if willing her to understand, and smacked her open palm against the table for emphasis, over and over, until the teacups clattered.

"Her husband used to drink a lot," Saida said intently, "and he would come home, where she had kids. He would tell her, take your clothes off now. He would tell her, have sex now. In front of the kids, it doesn't matter. He will make her do this like she is an animal, you know?"

Tara held Rashida's furious gaze.

"When she says no, he beat her. The kids are seeing this. They are suffering. Eventually, she says she has no feeling toward him, because she *hates* him. Now finally, she is happy. She is safe." Tara reached toward Rashida's stout arm. Inwardly, I rejoiced that the creep would trouble her no more.

Dawn didn't hold back. "Thank God he's gone," she said. "Wasn't there someone who could help her?"

"That is what family is for in our culture," said Saida with resignation.

Lesley began to say something, but the Moroccan women's words grew more vehement as Rashida continued slapping the table and Naima, the strong one, the rebellious one, raised her voice to match.

She explained that she too had been abused, by her second husband, before she divorced him. "He drank, he beat her, and he broke her nose. He had a big knife, and he put it here"—Saida stretched her neck and bared her throat—"and she cannot move; he holds her like she is a puppet. When the kids come home from school, they saw her face was red and there was blood and everything. She divorced him, and now she is safe."

Everyone around the table, Moroccan and American, was fired by anger beyond speech. I wanted to express everything I was feeling, but I didn't have the words, even in English. Our troubles, however slight in comparison to those of the Moroccan widows, had made them believe that they could trust their stories to us and that we would understand. I wanted to tell them that I couldn't know what they had suffered, but I appreciated the grit it took for them to survive. I wanted to tell them that they had made me appreciate that sometimes a woman is better off being a widow than subjecting herself to degradation and abuse. Even Magda—I recognized the boldness in her refusal to seek the support of another man who might be cruel to her son. These women were anything but meek. How could I have thought otherwise? I hoped that my face projected all that I was feeling. I looked to the other Americans and saw it on their faces, too. The voices of Rashida and Naima grew even bolder, fiercer, seeming to draw power from the unity all of us felt.

"They should do what we have done," Lesley said. "It's good to know other women. It's good to talk."

Saida translated, and the others exuded assent. "Yes, we do this, too," Saida said. "In Morocco we have women who are suffering, who are not happy, but they have fun sometimes together. Women organize parties with their friends. We contribute money for tea and hire musicians, only women. And all the bad things inside come out. Sometimes the women dance and turn until they fall on the ground, and they lose consciousness until we spray orange water on them. Then—how do you say it?—all the genies come out of you. The bad spirits."

"You find release," Tara said, nodding with slow comprehension.

"Yes. You are with other women, away from your other life. And the genies are gone."

I saw relief on the face of the once-silent Rashida, even a hint of triumph. She had survived her brutal marriage, and she had found the strength to tell the tale to strangers from a world away and make them understand.

She asked Saida to translate another thought. "This lady," said Saida, "she asks me to tell you, it is international. It is good to talk."

Rashida stood, beaming broadly, and clasped a startled Tara to her sizable frame. "Do they mind if we embrace them, too?" I asked.

"Of course not," said Saida. We stood and embraced, and walked out into the night together. At last we had hit on common ground, the one remedy we shared—the company of like-minded women as a balm against trouble, a force for good in the battle with genies.

———————

WE MADE OUR WAY through the cat's cradle of the medina, passing through medieval ramparts to a square where we said good-bye.

"We'll likely never see them again," Tara said in her theatrical way. The words hung in the sudden hush when a van pulled away to deliver the widows home. I was aware how much history had transpired on this spot, how little changed was this place, this people. "But we formed a bond in a moment, don't you think?" Tara turned pensive eyes on our dazed and sobered group. "We all love. We all hurt, no matter where we come from. I felt they were our sisters, our friends in shared tragedy."

"But they were so different," Marcia demurred. "For us, it's a matter of emotions, psychology, doing what we need to do to motivate ourselves. But they have this additional layer of difficulty because of their society. They don't control their destiny, whereas we do."

Like a pomegranate, I thought. It is up to fate how lucky you will be.

"Yes," Tara agreed. "How much lighter we are. How scared they were ... lonely ... ostracized. We have already decided to lead rich, full lives. It was a stark reminder that we have a choice."

"It was depressing," said Dawn, still haunted by the genies we'd unleashed.

Tara shook her head. "No, I feel we lifted their spirits, and they lifted us ... to keep going." She looked at each of us with firm resolve. "Because we can."

chapter

TWENTY-EIGHT

*W*hat is this, rush hour or something?" Marcia flattened herself against the wall of a narrow passage, tucking her camera under her arm like the game ball at the Super Bowl. It was bad enough that so many people were packed into this constricted alley, but then a man shouted, *"Balek!"*—Look out!—and a mule nudged its way through bearing bolts of shimmering silk on its back. A donkey lugging a crate of Coca-Cola brought up the rear. Marcia twisted to avoid them. "Oh God, will the camels smell like this?"

Saida had led us again into the heart of the medina, this time by daylight, when the eerie emptiness of the night before had given way to this maelstrom. We were swirled through crowds that bore us along like rapids or pooled in eddies. Smells of dung and smoke and bubbling kettles of soup and rotting flesh from leather tanneries wafted in every direction. I sidestepped a donkey that muscled Lesley into a stall selling teapots. "Wouldn't you know it?" she said. "I'm attractive to jackasses."

She'd had a rocky night of sleep after our dinner with the

Moroccan widows. Too many thoughts closed in around her. "Yesterday was so meaningful, I wanted so much to talk to someone about it. I was so grateful to Craig for not being like those men. I just wanted to talk to him, and I couldn't reach him. He didn't answer his phone." At home, she said, they would lie in bed for hours at night and talk and talk before they went to sleep. "Now I don't have that, and I'm so insecure."

"You should take him at his word," I said. "He says he loves you, and he wants time to sort things out with his kids. You have to assume he means it. You can't get reassurance now because you're here."

"I know," she said. "But today is the day he's moving out."

"Yallah!"—Let's go!—Saida called.

Lesley collected herself and plunged back into the crush, determined to lose herself in the day.

A crying child toddling by was startled into silence at the sight of Dawn's platinum hair. His mother turned and mimed a thank-you as she passed. After our evening with the Moroccan widows, I felt kinship with the women surging around us who otherwise would have struck me as picturesque in their exotic coverings, like theme park employees at Colonial Williamsburg. Many stopped to make kiss-kiss greetings with Saida so she could introduce us. There were strong communities within the medina that gave order to the seeming chaos. Each neighborhood, Saida said, was defined by its own mosque, school, fountain, grocer, and *fondouk*, or way station, for travelers and their beasts of burden. There was also a communal bakery, easily spotted because women bore rounds of dough there each morning and returned later in the day for fully baked loaves of bread. Environmentally, it's genius—one oven for the whole street! And it does double duty heating water for the *hammam*, Saida told us.

We'd read before the trip about *hammams*—the public steam rooms and bathhouses. "Actually, they are much more," said Saida. "The *hammam* is the place where the women meet and talk. It is not respectable for women to sit in cafés." But while a husband might object to a wife going out with friends, no one can stop her from taking a bath, so the *hammam* is where the real social action is, gossip exchanged, problems worked through, marriages arranged. "A mother looking for a bride for her son can see if a woman has a beautiful body, so she will tell him she has found the most beautiful woman for him."

"But women dress so modestly in the street," I said. "They let it all hang out at the *hammam*?"

"That is where we get to know *everything*. We will go together. You will see."

Marcia looked dubious, but the rest of us approved. "I want to try at least one new experience every day while we're here," said Lesley.

But there was no time for the *hammam* that day, thanks to another tantalizing component of the medina, the souks, where artisans make and sell everything under the sun. There was a henna souk and a slipper souk, a fabric souk and a leather souk. Make up the psychedelic shopping list of your dreams, and it's likely we passed a closet-sized shop that sold something on it: tropical fish, severed goat's heads, live chickens, fava beans, aphrodisiacs, breast enlargement cream, clay masks for hair, kohl for eyes. We saw baby shoes, tombstones, and filigreed silver belts that brides knot around caftans on their wedding days. The souks had us covered from cradle to grave. There was a guy on the floor of a cubbyhole using a Bunsen burner and a few primitive tools to make combs and brace-lets out of sheeps' horns. We passed men in an alley dunking skeins of silk thread into steaming basins of vegetable dye while kittens darted underfoot.

"I grew up in this souk," Saida said. "My father was a tailor, and my mother was an embroiderer."

Normally, I'm cynical about shopping on a trip. Globalization has led to homogenization—you can get the same swag every-where, I thought. But the decorative arts of Fès put Prada and Gucci to shame, and our varsity shoppers took one look and flashed: the mall! Marcia scored first, snagging a geometric rug hand-knotted by a collective of women weavers, destined for her modern new liv-ing room. Lesley bought one with a primitive design so she could do over a space that Craig had been using as an office, and then snapped up a djellaba the color of olive leaves to keep her warm at night. Tara found an antique mirror appliquéd with amber and bone for the front hall of her new house. Even I, the shopping cur-mudgeon, succumbed to spices for Bob and dangling Berber ear-rings that Tara assured me would appeal to Lily. Each transaction, a protracted game of offers and counteroffers, ended with a benedic-tion when we reached a price: *"Bessahah wa toulaamr."* Or roughly, "Long and healthy life."

We heard music—drums and lutes and tambourines—and Saida urged us to step inside a *riad*. It was just as we'd been told, a party for women, all in their finest jewels and silks, the colors of indigo and saffron and poppy, dyed right there in the fabric souk, I sup-posed. They were celebrating the birth of a baby, and as strangers, we were welcome to stay—there would be dancing later. But we would be making an early night. In the morning, the desert called. It was time to push on.

———

HEADING SOUTHEAST TOWARD the mountains at first light, we began a process of stripping away, beginning with the sensory overload of Fès. A hike in a cedar forest of the Middle Atlas cleared the smoke and fumes from our lungs. Saida taught us how to ululate, making a high-pitched, wavering sound with her throat and tongue that sounded musical coming from her but like a pack of harbor seals from us. We let loose anyway—who was to hear? "Only women ululate, only when they are happy," she said. "And never by themselves. Only groups of women—it is shared happiness."

"I have such a girl crush on Saida," Lesley whispered.

I had been dreading these couple days of the trip, mostly motoring through increasingly barren countryside in the van, breaking for lunches or walks. But as more and more was stripped away, we carried on the most intimate conversations of our acquaintance. Towns yielded to scattered villages, where women washed rugs in streams, preparing their homes for feast days. We passed into the High Atlas Mountains, where even settlements gave way, and green forests faded into scrubby patches of dormant lavender. Marcia took scads of pictures, smiling her crooked half smile.

At first our conversations focused on matters from home. Collins had been sending Dawn enraptured text messages since we'd arrived, inviting her and the kids for Thanksgiving, even making plans to redo a guest room to their taste, all this after a single two-day date. *Just when I think this is going too fast,* he wrote to

Dawn's delight, *then I think it's not going fast enough*. Dawn kept asking me what I thought of love at first sight, wanting details of how
I had taken to Bob right away.

"I didn't love him at first sight," I said, "but I knew that he was
someone I *could* love and probably *would* love, if that makes sense."

But Collins's messages stopped abruptly, and within a day Dawn
plunged into despair. "He's an attractive single guy. He must have
other things going on."

"Maybe something came up," I said.

"Oh, *something* came up all right."

Marcia turned to Lesley and said, "Thanks to you, even *I* get that
innuendo."

"Maybe I shouldn't do Thanksgiving with him." Dawn turned
to address us from a seat near the front. "Because my kids will love
him and then . . ." She moaned. "Oh . . . before I met Andries, I had
the world by the balls. If some guy wanted to date me, he had to
work at it."

"So he's a jerk," said Marcia. "That doesn't mean he doesn't
like you."

"Give him a break, everybody," I interjected. "It's only been
twenty-four hours. We were all better off without this technology."

"I know, I know. It's just that I want my life to be settled! No
more uncertainty! I just want to know that this is *it*, that I can
relax."

We pondered this for a moment. All of us knew the bitter truth,
that nothing—marriage, love, life itself—could be counted on to
last, that certainty was a mirage, if an enticing one.

"When I was little, I used to consider being a nun," Dawn said.
That broke the mood with a laugh. "When things went wrong

with guys, I used to think I was being punished for not following through. When Andries died, I thought that, too."

"Dawn, honey, you need to relax," said Tara. "You need to enjoy this moment, *now*, and stop worrying about the future. Let things percolate. The percolation is half the fun."

From the distance afforded by these vast, unfamiliar mountains, Tara considered her own attitude toward uncertainty. "Will is the real deal," she said, but she resisted thoughts of permanence or marriage. The two of them kept their separate homes, they dated, they saw each other on weekends, they were bound by love. She didn't want the responsibility of being a stepmother and didn't see the need for constant companionship. "This is it," she said. "I've raised my family. I'm done. I'm enjoying this for what it is."

I remembered something she had said at our very first meeting: "I'm trying to come to appreciate the not knowing."

My instinct was to take Tara's side. After everything we'd gone through, we knew who we were. We shouldn't need the sanction of the state or even a shared home to feel complete. I admired Tara's backbone for resisting the illusory security of marriage. Yet I'd been drawn to marriage myself. Was I weak for trying to wrap myself in certainty, even knowing it to be stitched in gossamer, or was I strong for taking the risk?

I looked out the window, my stomach turning at the sight of precipitous cliffs, and Tara interrupted my thoughts. "When you've lost a husband, it forces you to think about how to live . . . maybe to come up with what is a better way to live. You depend on yourself. And if you happen to be fortunate enough to meet a Bob or a Will or a Craig or somebody else, so much the better."

"Kevin used to say, 'I can't make your happiness for you,'" Lesley said. "You have to be happy for yourself." She sighed. "But I still want marriage. I told Craig before I left, I'm not here only for the good times. I'm here for the bad times, too. I *know* what that is."

We waited in attentive silence as she turned away, toward the view, stung by the memory of Kevin. "I deserve a man who will fight for me," she said at last with a note of finality. "I deserve better."

───────

OUR VAN SWOOPED and pivoted around hairpin turns as we reached the highest peaks. By now the colors had grown even fainter, dwindling from warm clay to taupe to mocha, just dry earth with a few rocks strewn about. We stopped for lunch on a terrace with a magnificent craggy view. Marcia tortured herself by grilling Saida for details about our desert camp, each new detail eliciting more anticipatory horror. The tents were woven from camel or goat hair, Saida wasn't sure which. We'd be riding camels in the dark, returning home after sunset. We'd wash from copper jugs, heated over a flame. We wouldn't be able to carry a change of clothes.

"I can't wear the same clothes twice!" Marcia said.

"Marcia, haven't you ever done a walk of shame?" I asked.

"No!"

We had to explain to Saida what that was, the first step in a tutorial on American sexual mores. It seemed that we were scandalizing her with explanations of condoms, oral sex, menopausal sex, you name it, but when Saida had to step away to make a request to the kitchen, she cried out: "Don't talk more until I get back!"

"Saida, we've ruined you," Tara said.

What did Saida think of us? I asked when she returned.

"I won't deny that I have learned a lot from you," she said after a moment's careful thought, "and I appreciate how you treat me like one of you. You are a brave group of ladies who continue their life in a beautiful way. You are optimists, very chic, having fun, and hoping to meet a nice man in the future." We basked in her generous description until she continued. "Women in our culture are different. They will say: 'This is the end of our life.' They are dead in life."

Back in the van, we began a slow descent from the mountains. Saida told us that in this remote countryside, there were still a few elderly Berber widows who had followed a nearly forgotten custom. When their husbands died and others tried to take away their land, these women tattooed blue beards on their faces. "It tells everyone, I am powerful. I do not need a man. *I* am the man of the house. It works!"

Self-reliance versus attachment. Independence versus love. How best to be powerful. We considered the choices we faced back home. The road ahead flattened out and a landscape the color of gravel blunted the perspective to either side. In the course of this journey, we had stripped away civilization, vegetation, life, color—complications. Now even the mountains were behind us. We were heading to an empty place.

chapter twenty-nine

Y*allah,*" Saida said. "Come. Everyone. You must go to the *hammam.*"

We had stopped at a hotel, a renovated old casbah in a grove of swaying date palms. Creaky and tired after hours in the van, I had zero interest in the *hammam*. The girly-girls in our group had tried the one in our posh Westernized hotel in Fès. They had warmed up wrapped in towels in a steam bath, and then an attendant escorted them each to a private room, applied some clay to their skin, and rinsed it off, treacly music playing all the while. It sounded like a reprise of our spa visit months ago.

So I was late showing up at this *hammam*, wrapped in nothing but a terrycloth robe, as instructed by Saida. Marcia hadn't made it yet, either. We had all seized an opportunity to contact people back home, our last chance for several days, and she had been browbeating someone on her phone when last I saw her, something about business that was cooking in Australia. Did I say browbeating? Browbeating would be gentle for what Marcia was doing. She was giving somebody holy hell. Dawn at least got some relief by making a call. Collins said that he'd been out of touch because he left his phone at the office, a story she didn't buy entirely but couldn't dismiss entirely either. I had received a welcome e-mail from Bob: "I love you indecently," he wrote. That would see me through.

Steam blinded me when I stepped inside the *hammam* door. I began to make out a kaleidoscope of green and blue tiles on the floor and walls, and a large basin of running water, like a public well, when an indistinct shape appeared in the mist, gradually coming into focus as a Moroccan woman, her black hair tied in a loose topknot.

"Off!" she ordered, rapping the sleeve of my robe like the head nun at a Catholic school, only she was disconcertingly naked except for a pair of red cotton bikini underpants. Hysterical laughter broke out all around me, and through the fog I made out human forms, some of them sprawled on stone slabs, some on the floor, each one naked as the day she was born.

"Nobody here but us rotisserie chickens," said Dawn.

"When in Rome . . ." I whipped off my robe and tossed it outside the door. I know women are supposed to aspire to utmost thinness, but I was relieved that Bob's cooking had put a little flesh on me by now. I hoped I looked less pinched, more like one of Matisse's Moroccan odalisques.

"Down!" the headmistress commanded.

I dropped to my knees, arms in the air, in the international posture of "Don't shoot!" but she wasn't satisfied. "Down," she repeated, her breasts dangling in front of my face, so I stretched out on the floor.

Next thing I knew, her hands were all over me, and I mean *all* over me, under my arms, behind my ears and—"Open!"—between my legs, rubbing in some kind of black soap that smelled of eucalyptus and olives. She let me sit up and marinate while she rushed from one to another of the Blossoms, scrubbing and polishing like the employee of the month at a car wash, while we got more and more raucous in turn. This was nothing like the sissy spa experience my girly-girls were used to. It was a bachelorette party without the booze, not an event for anyone who took herself, or her friends, too seriously.

"What is going on here?" I asked. But before anyone could answer, the headmistress advanced on me with a bucket of water and dumped it right over my head. I was still sputtering when she refilled it and smacked me with gallons of water in the face, from the side, the back, while the Blossoms howled. "Down," she ordered again, and this time she spread a scratchy paste all over me, leaving it to form a crust.

Saida had headed off alone to some kind of whirlpool bath in another room, but before she left she had told the others fond memories of the *hammam* from her childhood, when friends would spend the day ululating and turning buckets upside down to beat them like drums, a ritual of pleasure and escape. The mud I was steeping in right now, made of clay and roses and chamomile and lavender, was the same brew she remembered from those halcyon days.

The others left to take a breather from the steam, and the attendant zeroed in on me again, scrubbing the mud with a glove that felt like a Brillo pad, as sheets of outer skin peeled off me. Unable to communicate in Arabic, I begged for mercy in rudimentary French. *"Pas trop fort?"*

It was then, through the fog, that I saw a stunning sight. It was

Marcia, pale and shiny, squinting through the steam as she crept into the *hammam* like a bond trader balancing on a ledge on Black Friday, her face still glowering from the fight on the phone. The headmistress, arms akimbo, wasted no time. "Down!" she barked. I waited for Marcia to explode, to pull alpha-female rank on this martinet and say, "No, *you* get down!"

"Down!" the mistress ordered again. To my shock, and no doubt hers, Marcia hit the floor and submitted to the black soap treatment. I was sucking in my breath at the thought of the outraged objections this indignity would set off, when Marcia opened her mouth wide and emitted the most surprised and hysterical laughter I have heard in my life. I knew what was coming when I saw buckets being filled, but Marcia didn't until she took a shot full in the face. More water rained down on her head until the laughing stopped, and I grew concerned. Had a line finally been crossed? Would an enraged Marcia touch off a cross-cultural dispute with only me, clad in a layer of mud, to mediate? I heard nothing but the hissing of steam and the trickling of spigots.

Finally, I got up my nerve and asked: "Are you okay over there?"

Marcia spat out, "Of course I'm okay. I was laughing so hard I swallowed clay!"

It was my turn for another splashdown, and the two of us soared into new flights of laughter.

We met the others in their robes under the palms. After much recounting of our latest adventure and much comparison of our rosy, gleaming flesh, Lesley got serious. "How safe we feel with each other," she said. "It's sacred."

And how far we had come. Eleven months into our year together, all the masks were finally off. Venturing deeper and deeper into

Morocco, we had removed ourselves from familiarity of place. Now we'd stripped away something of our everyday selves, as well—modesty, privacy, a couple layers of skin. We would approach the end of our journey stripped and cleansed, with skin like newborn babies, everything washed away but each other.

"Do you ever feel when we're all together," Dawn posed, "that none of the bad stuff happened to us? Even though we gathered for that purpose, I forget it sometimes. It's not such a part of us as it was a year ago."

"We've seen it lift," I said.

"There are times when it feels like we're together," Dawn said, "just because we're together."

―――――――

"WELL, BECKY, you finally got what you wanted," Marcia said, not pleased, not pleased at all. "We're in the middle of *nowhere*."

And it wasn't promising. The van had dropped us off at the very edge of the Sahara, in the far east of Morocco near the Algerian border, where we waited for Range Rovers to pick us up and continue. The earth was flatter, the color paler, even more neutral than we'd seen before, the ground nothing but cracked, hard-packed clay, too dry even for dust. A lone man buzzed by on a motor scooter, balancing a goat on his lap. We'd left behind us the last oasis, Rissani, a stop on caravan routes since the seventh century, populated by women covered completely but for their eyes and tall men in turbans and robes the color of the sky.

"I was seeing an acupuncturist before we left," Denise said. He'd been helping to relieve some stress-related pains she'd been having.

"He told me that the most distinctive thing about the desert is that there is no smell."

"What about the camels?" said Marcia.

"Marcia, I'm trying to say something serious here. I was telling him about how I needed to get out of the past and get on with the rest of my life, how hard that is to do. He said the desert is the perfect place for me to be, because one of the main reasons people stay connected to the past is that they associate smells with people or places or events." We nodded, remembering how we had saved our husbands' worn T-shirts, how the scent of leaves burning in the fall or flowers budding in the spring reminded us of unwelcome anniversaries. "The desert is the perfect place to disconnect from the past and be in the present."

"I'd like to leave behind the feelings I don't want to have anymore," said Dawn. The rest of us agreed.

"We should have a ceremony when we get there," said Tara. We decided on a ritual we'd seen at the camp for grieving children where we'd volunteered. Each of us would write down what we'd like to say to our departed husbands, and we'd place our notes in the fire at the desert camp. "I'd better start now," Tara said. "I'll need five pages."

But two Range Rovers arrived, piloted by Blue Men, members of a nomadic tribe of Berbers who had traversed the Sahara in peacock-blue robes since the third century BC. They seemed unapproachable, nodding a quick greeting, their faces half obscured by scarves and mirrored sunglasses. We bumped farther east across the stony desert floor, lulled by monotony in the still heat. A shimmer to the north turned out to be a mirage. In the distance before us, mountains gradually appeared, but they were mountains unlike any I had ever seen, mountains the color of gold. "What are those?" I called to Saida in the backseat.

"Those are no mountains," she replied. "They are the famous dunes, the Erg Chebbi."

I'd seen sand dunes at the beach before, but nothing like these, majestic tidal waves sweeping toward us, dunes that rose eight or nine hundred feet in height. We gasped with astonishment as we drew closer, finally skidding to a stop at the base. This was the place we'd been searching for: a place unlike any other.

Saida showed us how to wrap scarves around our heads and faces to protect us from the sun, and it was time to go. After all the anxious buildup about camels, we took to them right away. There was a fair amount of squealing on our part when Ali, our Berber guide, helped us in turn with the awkward mounting, the camels whipping us forward, then back as they stood first on their back legs, then their front, but the camels themselves took our silliness in stride. Marcia squeezed her legs into the saddle to the point of bruising, but she stayed on board with teeth-gritting determination interspersed with laughter of the sort she'd unleashed in the *hammam*. Everyone felt the vertiginous rush of adventure.

The camels, tethered end to end, swayed silently beneath us into the dunes, and we patted them with unexpected affection. They were male, but their demeanor had a subversive feminine side, thanks to tender lips, big dreamy eyes, and long lashes, not to mention soft camel toes padding gently forward. The sky was huge, and the sun began to settle into scattered bands of wispy clouds, gilding the sand to a high burnish, highlighting every ripple. The camels' rocking gait made us feel like sailors on a patchy sea, where the dunes, seemingly permanent at first, were shifting imperceptibly around us.

Ali stopped us at the foot of an enormous peak and helped us dismount, indicating that we should shuck our boots and clamber barefoot to the summit in the yielding sand. Breathless, we perched at the lip of the towering wave, clasping each other for balance, although if we had tumbled no harm would come to us as we sank into the most forgiving of landings.

"It's like nothing . . . nothing I've ever experienced," said Lesley, and no one disagreed. We stretched our arms over our heads toward the sky. Ali spread blankets on the sand and gave us privacy by moving away.

"Sit, quickly," Saida said. "The sun will be setting soon."

Shafts of pink and orange pierced the clouds, lighting up the sky like the aurora borealis, as sand in every direction began to turn from gold to orange. The atmosphere itself took on a sudden wash of color, imparting the suggestion that we were suspended between earth and air, nothing but pure radiance above and below. I had wanted time and distance from our everyday world, and here it was, a place out of space, out of time, where the past and future couldn't touch us.

I thought of Bob, my new love, far away. I thought of Bernie, forever out of reach. Both would have loved this place. For the first time, I could imagine both of them present together, in this place where space and time had no meaning. I thought of everything I wanted Bernie to know, everything he had missed. How much I missed him. How much I loved him still. How sorry I was for what he had suffered. How happy I was with Bob, and how I treasured Lily. I felt the presence of them all in the absence of the desert. They filled this empty place.

Here in this place out of space and time, I realized that it was possible to love two men at once, one who was present and one who lived only in memory. They were both very much with me now, and I was the better for them both. I looked at the sweeping dunes, unconnected from everything familiar, and realized that I had failed at my misguided goal of a life detached, that my attachments surrounded me, even here. Yes, I still knew, attachment can be suffering. Attachment can be scary. Attachment can be messy. But attachment is life.

The pigment that surrounded us deepened into reds and purples, like a Rothko painting, seemingly spare, but practically vibrating with intense color and meaning. I remembered my other attachment, my newest attachment, to the Blossoms, and looked at them, all of them—transfixed. The desert silence didn't stifle our communion. I knew their thoughts. Tara, with her eyes shut, was seeking peace. Denise repeated *Here we are* in her head like a mantra. Dawn prayed to her God. Lesley vowed always to look ahead. Marcia seized the fleeting opportunity, calculating aperture settings and shutter speeds, greedily capturing pictures before the light was gone.

Denise touched her fingers to her throat, where Steve's wedding band dangled from a leather cord. I knew that Steve was here along with Bernie, and David and Andries and Kevin and Martin. They would never be gone entirely as long as they were here in memory, as long as we created new memories that included them. Bob and Will and even Collins were here, and children, too, and stepchildren, moms and dads. Quite a turnout.

After nearly a year during which the number of times any of the Blossoms cried when we were together could be counted on the fingers of a single hand, everyone cried now. Except perhaps Marcia—

I couldn't tell with the camera in front of her eyes. But I could see that she finally had ditched the crooked ambivalent grin and fully committed to a smile, spread clear across her face.

Finally, as twilight fell, we ran down the dune to our camels, who carried us to camp. Colorful kilims covered the sand between a cluster of tents made of rough fabrics in primitive patterns. A fire burned in the center to ward off a fast encroaching chill from the vastness on every side. We surveyed the layout.

"Well, Marcia, are you going to survive?" I asked.

"I have to say, this is one of the highlights of my life," she admitted. "I'd come back in a minute."

Everyone threw back their heads to ululate.

Once again, it was Saturday night. Our night, as it had been all year long. Three Blue Men picked up instruments—a lute, a castanet, and a drum made of goatskin—to play traditional music by the fire. The musicians earned their pay that night, if only for keeping straight faces while we improvised dorky dance moves, ejected any lingering genies, and let loose with our patented harbor-seal madrigals. The stars overhead? You can only imagine. After polishing off a rustic lamb tagine by lantern light, we retired to our tents and slept like babes. Denise dreamed that her camel tucked its head inside her tent to nuzzle her and make her feel safe.

Before sunrise, everyone mounted the camels in the dark, eager to go on one more trek. Atop another truly big kahuna, we nestled together under blankets for warmth until the sun shot up quickly, bathing our faces. The wordless exchange at sunset had given way to our usual clowning and talk. "I'd like to dream about something more than camels," Dawn said.

"Oh," Denise cried, "we forgot to put our notes in the fire!"

"It doesn't matter," Tara said. "I got the feeling we all took care of what we needed to do at sunset."

It was true. I caught Lesley watching me. "I tend to forget that this whole group started with you and your experience," she said. "I think you put a lot of things to rest here."

"Yes," I answered. "I feel far away from where I'd ever imagined, yet exactly where I should be."

"Sometimes," Lesley said, "all we need is a little perspective."

I waited at the pinnacle, reluctant to leave, while everyone dashed to the base of the dune, their light steps leaving footprints in the sand. A faint wind began to fill them in. Tomorrow, they would be gone. By the next week or the next month or certainly the next year, the dunes themselves would flow into new surging and receding shapes. Nothing lasts, except in memory. I ran down the dune, following the tracks. The tribe moves on.

chapter

THIRTY

*e*ndings are also beginnings. Nobody knew that better than the Blossoms, which may be why emotions were all over the map at our last official meeting.

I arrived at Marcia's bearing a covered dish and none of the trepidation I'd felt on a Saturday night in January exactly one year earlier. There wasn't any question that our utterly amateur widows' support group was a smash, that our theory of companionship without gloom had flowered into friendship, that everyone had thrived along with it.

"Becky, this guacamole is over the top," Dawn declared.

We clustered by the window, where the pulsing Manhattan vista was as changeable as the desert. Everyone, it turned out, was wearing black, our chicest black, and what Lesley would call kick-ass boots. We looked forward to an evening of fond reminiscence, all those shared memories we'd racked up while scrupulously ignoring the five bogus stages of grief. When suddenly: waterworks.

Tara read aloud a note she'd written to me just after we met, full of hope and anxiety about what was next for her. "My new life is taking shape ... rather like a hurricane ... after years of dark days," she read. "For some, the weight of unfilled hopes and accumulated responsibilities could be crushing. For others, thank goodness, this could be a moment to reconnect with an earlier, younger, less compromised self."

We all got weepy along with her. A release, a year's worth of emotions, several years, really. Tonight was an ending. Another ending.

"Look how far you've come since you wrote that," I said.

"How far we've all come," Tara said. "We all lost our footing for a time. But we found our footing together."

Denise and I put salad and chicken and couscous on the dining table. It was time to eat again, but as usual, the others were too caught up in conversation to take a seat.

"Marcia! Down!" I ordered. A year ago, she might have shot me a look like I was one of her lackeys, but her face cracked into laughter along with everyone else's. "Well, it worked in Morocco," I said.

"I never laughed my ass off like I did in that *hammam*," Dawn marveled.

"The amount of time we've spent laughing—it's ridiculous," Lesley said. "And the *stuff* we talk about."

"I talk about stuff with you guys that I have a hard time bringing up ... even to my family," said Tara.

We tucked into the meal. I looked at each woman individually, each face so intimidating a year ago, so familiar now. I knew that Tara didn't eat shellfish, that Lesley took her mint tea with sugar, that Marcia couldn't stand *The Sound of Music*. We plucked lint off each other's sweaters and fallen eyelashes off each other's cheeks.

I thought about my meeting with Professor Bonanno at the grief lab, about his theories on overcoming loss, the novel experiences he recommended, the fun, the ties with friends. He might have years of study under his belt, but tonight I wanted to hear from my own experts.

"Why do *you* think this has worked?" I asked.

"We're not best friends," Marcia began, "we're all *very* different, and yet there's a ..."

"...a bond," Tara and Lesley said simultaneously.

"Yes, a bond we've created."

"Tara said it once before," said Lesley. "We feel safe."

"We can say, 'That guy is cute' without feeling guilty," said Tara. "We can say 'I want to have sex again' without feeling guilty. We can say 'I feel like crying' without feeling like we're dragging in somebody who doesn't want to hear our story."

"I learned that grief is a process, and you can choose how to handle it," Dawn said. She inhaled a sharp breath. "I can't talk about it, because I'm so emotional, but I just want to say how grateful I am for each and every one of you."

"We're the blubberers on this side of the table," Lesley, seated next to her, apologized.

Dawn changed the subject, asking Denise for the recipe for her salad dressing, which she'd made with capers she'd brought from Morocco, and then admiring her ring. "My wedding ring," Denise said. Lesley had expressed interest in seeing it, so Denise wore it on her right hand that night, for the first time since the funeral.

"I'm a private person," Denise said, as if we didn't already know. "This group was so out there—it was freeing."

Marcia agreed. "Becky and I were the only ones of us who joined a typical bereavement group," she said, "but it was so depressing compared to this. Still, I think if we had been in a typical group, our personalities would have come out eventually."

Tara grimaced. "Sorry, but I wouldn't have lasted a week," she said. The rest of us laughed. She summoned all her powers of vocal drama to add, "I . . . want . . . to . . . live."

We passed around seconds. "But we *did* all talk about our losses," I said.

"Sometimes," Lesley said, "but nobody ever said, 'Let's talk about Kevin,' 'Let's talk about David.' It was never about how they died. I remember at our first meeting my heart was going like crazy, because I was going to have to say that my husband committed suicide. But it didn't matter. This was about us." She started to blubber again. "You are my soul mates. I love you all."

Others joined in, except, as usual, Marcia.

"Marcia," Lesley said, "do you ever cry?"

"I do. I just do it in private, that's all."

It was so unlike Marcia to concede that much, as unlike her as getting on a camel and trekking into a sea of sand with women she didn't know a year ago.

"We've influenced each other, don't you think?" I said.

"I like to think that I convinced you all that we should be having more sex," Lesley said, and we all agreed.

"I have a serious answer," Tara announced. "This group has made me braver. My journey would have been a lot more tentative without you. You convinced me to listen to myself, first and foremost . . . and stick with what I heard. You gave me courage when I needed it."

We recalled how full of fear Tara had appeared at our first meeting, how she found the nerve to raise the subject of alcoholism to the Moroccan widows, how her honesty gave them strength in turn to tell their stories, too.

"I wouldn't have been able to do it," she said, "without the courage I got from this group."

"All I can say is, thank God I made the cut!" Lesley said. "But what about you, Becky? What did you get?"

I busied myself pulling cookies out of the oven, the chocolate cookies with the molten centers that we had learned to bake at our cooking class, while I weighed many possible answers. "This recipe," I could have said, but I knew I owed them a thoughtful response.

"Even though I'm further along in this process," I said finally, setting down the tray and taking off the oven mitts, "my life had been knocked off course, just like yours, and I'm still reorienting, still making decisions every day about what to do next."

I placed the cookies on the table, a powerful temptation, but the group sat suspended as they cooled, waiting to hear what more I would say. I took my seat and thought again about Bernie's words when something needed to be done: *Let's put our heads down and go.*

"I think when anybody is reinventing herself, she's got a choice." I went on, feeling my way. "She can stay detached and look inside herself for answers. We've all heard that advice—finding yourself." I shook my head and threw them a dubious look. "Knowing you has shown me that, at least for me, finding myself wasn't a solitary task. The way for me to move forward was to get out there on Saturday night, to engage with other people, to engage with the world, to engage with *you*. Funny as it may sound, I've found myself by going *outside* myself. I've found myself through action, through action with you."

Dawn reached for dessert and offered a final Dawnism as a bene-diction: "To stay detached, Becky dear, is not my idea of living."

———————

OVER THE NEXT MONTHS, our little tribe kept moving. De-nise began to come into her own. After a year and a half of pushing through shock and toiling to make ends meet, a window opened. In February, she ran into someone she had dated briefly in the past. He was going through a divorce and needed a place to live. Denise needed another roommate so she could afford her cherished apart-ment. A few months later, the course of true romance and the vicis-situdes of real estate dovetailed nicely, and he moved in. Toby, one of the widowers she'd met at Marcia's, called after that to ask her out, but he was too late.

In the end, her new relationship didn't work out either. "But it got me six months closer to normal again," Denise said philosophi-cally. "Luckily the widow thing has made me tough." And deter-mined. The books she edited began to make their way to stores, and three of them made the bestseller list.

Dawn's love life continued to play out in the spirit of fortissimo. She turned out to be right about Collins. Their quick passion was destined to last, but not without its share of drama. They lived far apart, as Bob and I had, and like me, Collins had no experience with children. But she drew on lessons from the rest of us and worked through the logistics. Luckily, she said, "my daughter is a hugger—she's good at breaking down barriers." Both children warmed to spending time with Collins, hanging out in the garage while he tinkered with his car or darting outdoors with him when he did his best to compensate for Dawn's well-known deficit in sportiness. "It's all right to love someone else," she told the kids. "It doesn't mean you didn't love Daddy."

For his part, Collins began to appreciate that raising children might be one of life's more rewarding challenges. He and Dawn talked about a future together, maybe moving somewhere new to both of them, someplace warm. But Collins couldn't wait. He proposed marriage, and Dawn accepted. He plans to move into her home, commuting to manage his business, so the four of them can form the nuclear family that Dawn and the children yearned for.

Marcia sent us each a gift after the last meeting, a stunning coffee table book, bound and printed on the best paper, of photographs from our Morocco trip. At her next evaluation at work, she received highest marks for teamwork, and the parties she held for colleagues on her new roof became legendary.

Outside the office, she thrived as well. "Every time I walk into my new apartment, I feel glad," she told me. To stay in touch with her godsons, she organized a once-a-week project to explore new restaurants together, as well as a more ambitious expedition—a trip to Southeast Asia, no expense spared, selected because the centerpiece was an excursion on the backs of elephants. Whatever she paid, it was worth it if only for the resulting pictures of Marcia aboard a hulking pachyderm. This was Marcia, I had to remind myself, whose previous model for a daredevil vacation was a survey of Parisian restaurants that served the thickest, richest béarnaise. I teased her that close contact with large animals was her new obsession, which she confirmed by planning another excursion, this one to the Arctic, to photograph polar bears.

Lesley and Craig split up for good a week after our last official meeting. Friction between the two families finally overwhelmed them, but Lesley never let her daughters speak ill of Craig. "I'm grateful to him," she said. "He taught me to feel again." After the breakup, she didn't get out of bed for two days. In the loneliest hour of the second night, she was sure she felt someone tapping her back. "It's okay," she heard Kevin say to her. "I'm here looking after you." Lesley never told us exactly how Kevin died, and we never asked. At our last meeting, she hinted that he had killed himself as a character had in a movie, but none of us had seen it, and none of us tried.

Resolved to heal before taking on new romance, she devoted herself to volunteering on behalf of suicide prevention. But a friend spotted Craig on eHarmony.com, which gave Lesley the impetus to go on a few dates herself. By summer, a promising guy materialized on the Internet, and like Dawn, Lesley settled into a long-distance relationship. "It's a huge gamble," she said, "but I never for a minute considered that I wouldn't try again."

Tara was well satisfied with her new man, her new work, and her new home. "I love my life," she said more than convincingly. She still took voice-over jobs, but she also returned to philanthropy, serving on the board of a new venture to benefit outstanding underprivileged college students. Tara and Will remained a solid, committed couple, but they agreed they needn't be together ... all the time. He kept his home, and she kept hers, turning it into an eclectic showplace—wall-to-wall cashmere, just like Tara. The Moroccan mirror is the first object anyone sees in her front hall. In fact, Moroccan motifs repeat throughout the house, and pride of place in her living room goes to a photograph of the Blossoms on the crest of a dune.

There were more endings and beginnings, for Lily and Bob and me. She graduated from high school a few months after the last official Blossoms meeting, and we put Connecticut behind us when she headed to college. Lily never fails to call me Becky now, except when I visit her at school, where she presents me to friends with a higher honor: "This is my stepmom."

My husband and I have settled in the Brooklyn apartment that I shared with Bernie. Bob likes it as much as I do, and he insists we keep Bernie's photo on the mantel. "I feel close to him," Bob likes to say. "He looked after you for twenty years, and I look after you now." To make room for our new family, Lily organized a stoop sale of Bernie's jazz records, but Bob opted to keep most of them anyway, interspersing them with his rock-'n'-roll collection. It's crowded here—Bob and I still share an office every day, like partners in a mom-and-pop store. We comment on each other's work and revel in our good fortune. It's the life I dreamed of when I lost the one I'd made before.

And what of the Blossoms? I wondered that night at Marcia's, our year of blossoming complete, whether I would ever see them again. And if so, would it stay the same? Nothing does, as we know best, which is as it should be. Yet our group lives on, no need for organized activities, no need for the guides who ushered us through our many discoveries, no need for tears. *Especially* no need for tears. We gather often in twos or threes, and we always have plenty to say, because to share a story, as we now know, is to truly understand it. Dawn and Tara remain fast friends. Lesley steers her bicycle over to Tara's house when she wants a little perspective. Denise and I lounge around Marcia's rooftop pool on hot summer weekends. Marcia the lawyer and Lesley the housewife get a kick out of implausible dinners they plan together.

And when we gather all at once, steeped in our collective insight and wisdom, we still laugh until our insides hurt. Everyone stayed overnight at Tara's and Lesley's one weekend, and we agreed to rally at sunrise on the beach, where each of us would share one favorite memory from our year of Saturday nights. We got too busy talking, as usual, and missed the moment, which was just as it should be, too. If I had to come up with my own stages of grief, the last and the best would have to be friendship. Although love is pretty great, too.

They say that grief is a process of finding comfort. Together, with Denise and Dawn and Marcia and Lesley and Tara—and me— that is what we did. The worst had already happened. We were ready for anything.

acknowledgments

*d*enise Roy, Dawn Jiosi, Marcia Wallace, Lesley Jacobs, and Tara Nicholson Olson—after all the adventures we've been through together, what I feel most is gratitude. They generously shared with me their time, their thoughts, their high spirits, and ultimately their friendship, which I value most of all. I am grateful to them beyond measure for the courage it took to tell their stories and for tolerating my ever-present notebook and tape recorder. We documented dozens of hours of meetings, discussions, and often madcap exploits, which I have drawn upon to write this book, and I salute the women's resolve in putting practically nothing off limits.

Along the way, we enjoyed the wise counsel of many talented guides. They included Lauren Groveman, the cookbook author and cooking teacher whose chocolate cookie recipe, among other delicacies, still lures me into the kitchen; Katie Hanson, our knowledgeable and entertaining escort through the art museum; Maria Rendon, the sympathetic assistant manager of the La Perla shop;

and of course Saida Ezzahoui, our fearless leader in Morocco who for ten glorious days became one of us, a Blossom.

Others helped us set up our adventures, most notably Judith Walsh of Art Smart Adventures; Ginny Lopis from The Lodge at Woodloch, the spa in Pennsylvania; Brandon English from the Comfort Zone Camp, where we volunteered; and Edward Piegza, from Classic Journeys, who satisfied our demanding standards by setting up a mishap-free Moroccan trip, complete with fully functioning toilets.

For helping me to locate the women and men who participated in this yearlong adventure, as well as holding my hand through the writing, I have many to thank: Fred Plotkin, Liz Beinfield, Gail Pellet, Kathy Kukula, Rozanne Gold, Diane Terry of Private Journeys, Elizabeth Beier, Laura Schneider, Sue and Stanley Schneider, Elizabeth Sanger, Barbara Selvin, Mary Kuntz, Alexis Gelber, Rosalie Weider, Leslie Meredith, Myra Shendell, Margaret Polanesky, Betty White-Ross, Loyda Rivera, and Jackie Leopold.

Professor George A. Bonanno of Teachers College at Columbia University and the author of the fine book *The Other Side of Sadness*, was invaluable in guiding me through the research on grief, as was Professor Camille B. Wortman of Stony Brook University and Dr. David B. Goldenberg.

The Blossoms often discussed whether love at first sight exists. I learned that it does from the moment I met Joy Harris, my agent, champion, and honorary Blossom. I was fortunate to have as my editor and ardent cheerleader Vanessa Mobley of Crown, who not only offered me wise counsel but is one of the best lunch conversationalists going and also introduced me to the Alabama Shakes. And she is only one member of the talented and hard-working team at Crown, which, lucky for me includes Molly Stern, Miriam Chotiner-Gardner, Penny Simon, and Julie Cepler. Jaya Miceli created the lovely cover.

Lindsay Maracotta, my friend, weighed in with razor-sharp comments on the manuscript.

My sister, Nancy Martin, whose books have brought her legions of fans, offered me crucial support and advice on how to tell a story with grace and narrative coherence. My mom, Barbara Aikman, has given me a lifetime of unstinting love and guidance and can take credit for whatever good qualities I may possess. I thank Lily for welcoming me into her life, making helpful suggestions, and tiptoeing around while I wrote.

All the happiness the Blossoms found together is enriched by the memories of those dear ones no longer with us: Steve, Andries, Martin, Kevin, and David among them. My dad, John, remains in my heart, as does my departed husband, Bernie Lefkowitz, who inspired me throughout our life together and inspires me still.

No one contributed more to this book than my husband Bob Spitz. Working back-to-back in our little office as I wrote the manuscript and he completed his biography of Julia Child, I'm surprised the words *Bon appétit!* didn't slip into these pages somewhere. He pulled me through, contributing everything from big ideas to the smallest syntactical fixes. For Bob—after all we've been through together already and all that I forsee for the rest of our lives—I expect to feel gratitude for a long, long time.